Ethical Practice in Early Childhood

Education at SAGE

SAGE is a leading international publisher of journals, books, and electronic media for academic, educational, and professional markets.

Our education publishing includes:

- accessible and comprehensive texts for aspiring education professionals and practitioners looking to further their careers through continuing professional development

- inspirational advice and guidance for the classroom

- authoritative state of the art reference from the leading authors in the field

Find out more at: **www.sagepub.co.uk/education**

Ethical Practice in Early Childhood

Edited by
Ioanna Palaiologou

Los Angeles | London | New Delhi
Singapore | Washington DC

Los Angeles | London | New Delhi
Singapore | Washington DC

SAGE Publications Ltd
1 Oliver's Yard
55 City Road
London EC1Y 1SP

SAGE Publications Inc.
2455 Teller Road
Thousand Oaks, California 91320

SAGE Publications India Pvt Ltd
B 1/I 1 Mohan Cooperative Industrial Area
Mathura Road
New Delhi 110 044

SAGE Publications Asia-Pacific Pte Ltd
3 Church Street
#10-04 Samsung Hub
Singapore 049483

First published 2012

Commissioning editor: Jude Bowen
Editorial assistant: Miriam Davey
Project manager: Bill Antrobus
Assistant production editor: Thea Watson
Copyeditor: Peter Williams
Proofreader: Caroline Stock
Marketing manager: Lorna Patkai
Cover design: Wendy Scott
Typeset by Kestrel Data, Exeter, Devon
Printed by: Replika Press Pvt Ltd, India

Library of Congress Control Number: 2011943004

British Library Cataloguing in Publication data

A catalogue record for this book is available from
the British Library

ISBN 978-0-85702-852-5
ISBN 978-0-85702-853-2 (pbk)

Contents

Part 1 Ethical Issues in Research

Part 2 Ethical Issues in Policy and Practice

List of Figures and Tables

Figures

Tables

List of Abbreviations

AAC	augmentative and alternative communication
BERA	British Educational Research Association
BPS	British Psychological Society
BSS	British Sociological Society
CEMACH	Confidential Enquiry into Maternal and Child Health
CPR	child protection register
CRB	Criminal Records Bureau
CRC	Committee on the Rights of the Child
CYPSSP	Children and Young People's Services Scrutiny Panel
DCSF	Department for Children, Schools and Family
DENI	Department of Education Northern Ireland
DES	Department of Education and Science
DfE	Department for Education
DfEE	Department for Education and Employment
DfES	Department for Education and Skills
DHSS	Department of Health and Social Security
DHSSPS	Department of Health, Social Services and Public Safety
DOH	Department of Health
EBD	emotional and behavioural difficulties
ECM	Every Child Matters
ELG	Early Learning Goal
EYFS	Early Years Foundation Stage
EYPS	Early Years Professional Status
EYQCP	Early Years Questionnaire on Child Protection
GLA	Greater London Authority

ITT	Initial Teacher Training
MMR	measles, mumps and rubella
NCT	National Childbirth Trust
NI	Northern Ireland
NISRA	Northern Ireland Statistics and Research Agency
NPM	New Public Management
NSPCC	National Society for the Prevention of Cruelty to Children
OECD	Organisation for Economic Cooperation and Development
OFMDFM	Office of the First Minister and Deputy First Minister (Northern Ireland)
Ofsted	Office for Standards in Education, Children's Services and Skills
ONS	Office for National Statistics
PSED	personal, social and emotional development
PSNI	Police Service Northern Ireland
QCA	Qualifications and Curriculum Authority
QCA	Qualifications and Curriculum Authority
SCAA	School Curriculum and Assessment Authority
TDA	Training and Development Agency
UNCRC	United Nations Convention on the Rights of the Child
VI	visual impairment
YLT	Young Life and Times (Northern Ireland Survey)

About the Editor and Contributors

Editor

Ioanna Palaiologou is a chartered psychologist currently working as a lecturer and researcher in the Centre for Educational Studies in the University of Hull and is Chair of the British Education Studies Association for 2011–12. Her specialist interest and research is in the epistemic notion of pedagogy in the field of early childhood education and child development. She leads the Masters in Early Childhood Studies and is also Coordinator of Research Student Support in the University of Hull. Among her many publications she is the author of *Achieving EYPS: Childhood Observation* (Learning Matters, 2008) and the editor of *Early Years Foundation Stage: Theory and Practice* (Sage, 2010).

Contributors

Gary Beauchamp is Director of Research (Education) and Professor in Education at the University of Wales Institute Cardiff (UWIC). He began his career in education as a primary school classroom teacher and has also been Programme Director for Education Studies and Primary PGCE courses. In addition to being an external examiner for many teacher training courses, he also has experience as an Additional Inspector for Estyn (Her Majesty's Chief Inspectorate of Education and Training in Wales) in a range of educational settings. He has published widely in academic journals, curriculum publications and books.

Cheryl Ellis is a senior lecturer and programme director for the BA (Hons) Educational Studies course at the University of Wales Institute Cardiff (UWIC). She lectures on Additional Learning Needs modules and is also responsible for the coordination and delivery of postgraduate continuing professional development (CPD) programmes for educational practitioners. Prior to this she was a primary school teacher with 'Approved Teacher Status' for teaching individuals with dyslexia. Her research interests focus upon issues relating to inclusion and meeting the needs of pupils with a range of additional learning needs, in particular English as an additional language. This includes the exploration of methodologies that actively promote the involvement of children within the research process.

Colette Gray is a chartered developmental psychologist and currently a principal lecturer in Early Years Education at Stranmillis University College, The Queen's University of Belfast. Her research interests include inclusion and special needs, most particularly the inclusion of children with a visual impairment, the ethical implications for researchers of undertaking studies involving children and vulnerable groups, giving voice to the child with special needs, and research methodologies and factors that impact on children's academic success. She has an extensive publication profile and was recently appointed Visiting Professor of Child Development and Education at University College Plymouth St Mark & St John. Allied with her research interests, she is responsible for the coordination and delivery of a range of undergraduate (BA Early Years, Hons) and postgraduate MEd and MA (Early Years) courses.

Donna Green is currently an independent early years consultant working within Lancashire. Formerly she has been a university lecturer and programme leader for a number of early years BA (Hons) and foundation degree programmes. Her research interests are nurturing children's creativity in the early years and how the practitioner's understanding of creativity can impact upon practice. Donna has worked within a variety of settings across the early years sector during her career as an early years practitioner before becoming a lecturer and independent consultant.

Chantelle Haughton is a lecturer in Early Childhood Studies at the University of Wales Institute Cardiff (UWIC). Before this she worked within a variety of early years settings in different roles. She was a project coordinator for emotional literacy intervention and behaviour support, a parent inclusion coordinator, an additional learning needs tutor and a family support worker within many homes. Her research interests include inclusion in early years practice, most particularly the inclusion of children with emotional and behavioural difficulties and related issues around partnership with parents, culture, ethnicity and gender.

Sarah James has been a lecturer at the University of Hull since January 2004, having previously taught in an inner-city Hull primary school. Her principal roles at the university are for the Primary PGCE programme, as science and RE tutor and teaching practice supervisor, and as Programme Director for the BA (Hons) in Education and Learning (Top-up). Within CES Sarah also lectures for other undergraduate programmes and at Masters level, and also acts as a supervisor to both undergraduate and post-graduate research students. Sarah's interests are in the field of loss, bereavement and death and sustainable development and ecology. Her publications include L. J. Stern & S. James (2006) 'Every person matters: enabling spirituality education for nurses', *Journal of Clinical Nursing*, 15(7): 897–904.

Bronagh McKee is currently senior lecturer in the Department of Early Childhood Education, Stanmillis University College, The Queen's University of Belfast. She is an early years specialist with a background in social work. Bronagh teaches and coordinates undergraduate and postgraduate modules in the areas of multi-professional perspectives on the child, safeguarding and child protection, social work with children and families, critical perspectives in early years care and education, children's mental health and well-being, and improving outcomes for children. Her research interests include pre-service child protection training and safeguarding education, multi-agency collaboration in child protection and using arts-based education in learning and teaching activity. She coordinates a shared learning and teaching experience between early childhood and social work students, is a director on the Women's Aid Federation Management Board and sits on a Domestic Violence Research Special Interest Group. Bronagh oversees the child protection training requirements for all students and staff, chairs the Joint Consultative Child Protection Committee, is the editor of the *Child Protection and Safeguarding* newsletter, and serves as child protection coordinator for the college.

Trevor Male is a senior lecturer in education and Head of the Centre for Educational Studies at the University of Hull. His specialist interest and research is in the field of educational leadership. He joined the university in 2002, initially as a member of the International Educational Leadership Centre before transferring to the Centre for Educational Studies in August 2004. In previous careers he has been a teacher, an LEA officer and a tutor for the Open University. He has worked full-time in higher education since 1993, firstly at Brunel University, West London, where he was Director of the Centre for the Study of Leadership and Management in Education (CSMLE). He left in 1998 to join the team at the International Institute for Educational Leadership (IIEL) at the University of Lincoln, where he was Director of Headteacher Development and Director of Quality Assurance before moving to Hull. He is the author of the bestselling book *Being an Effective Headteacher* (Paul Chapman, 2006).

Barry Powell has worked in education for over ten years teaching across social science disciplines from GCSE through to undergraduate level. He currently teaches on a range of undergraduate courses at the University Centre at Blackburn College where he specialises in social policy and its management. Barry is also a member of Blackburn with Darwen's Community Safety Partnership and, in addition, teaches on an Open University pre-degree course aimed at widening participation.

Judi Williamson has over 30 years' experience of working with children, young people and adults in the education sector. She originally trained as a first school (4–8 years) teacher then later gained an additional qualification in the early years. Her work has taken her into infant classes, nurseries and on to teaching young people and adults through a variety of early years programmes in further and higher education. She completed her Masters degree and has held a variety of management roles in primary and further education. In recent years she has balanced working as an Associate Lecturer for the University of Hull teaching, supporting and assessing EYPS trainees with working in her local authority School Effectiveness Team on a variety of projects supporting the 14–19 curriculum reforms.

Acknowledgements

I would like to express my gratitude to a number of people without whom this book would have not been completed. A great 'thank you' to all the contributors who have given their ideas, views and propositions: Donna Green, Gary Beauchamp, Cherry Ellis, Collette Gray, Barry Powell, Sarah James, Chantelle Houghton, Bronagh McKee, Judi Williamson and Trevor Male.

I would also like to express my gratitude to my publisher at Sage, Jude Bowen, who believes in me and has supported me throughout. A great thank you also to Miriam Davey for all her help and patience.

Ioanna Palaiologou

Introduction: Towards an Understanding of Ethical Practice in Early Childhood

Ioanna Palaiologou

In recent years the field of early childhood studies has become increasingly concerned with applying ethical practices to educational environments and with creating a form of pedagogy for children. There is a growing concern to involve young children actively in every aspect of their lives and experiences. In the vast body of literature (Dahlberg & Moss, 2005; Edminston, 2008; Clark et al., 2005; Christensen & James, 2008; Harcourt et al., 2011) there is an ideological shift from the traditional constructions of childhood such as the polite, the innocent, the holy, the romantic, the developmental child or the child in need of protection (Benton, 1996; David, 1993; Dahlberg et al., 1999; Hendrick, 1997; Palaiologou, 2008) to the construction of the child as an active actor or socially active being.

It is now more than ever argued that children should be viewed as co-constructors of the knowledge and practices that influence their lives. Children should be recognised as a social group which shares with others a place in society; therefore, they should be perceived as socially constructed and embedded within a local context, recognised as being social actors, having agency, belonging to a unique culture and engaged in worthwhile, meaningful social relationships. In the light of this ideological shift children's participation and consequently children's voices have become the catalyst for engagement. Research and practice have been influenced to alter their methods and practices so as to place the child in the position of 'knower'.

Additionally, the ideological shift in research and practice is about creating autonomous learners and placing them in active control of their learning and experiences. Children are more often asked to be active and to participate 'on the basis of who they are, rather than who they will become' (Moss & Petrie, 2002: 6). In other words, they are considered social citizens in their own right, rather than future citizens in waiting.

The current ideological position regarding the simplicity of the developmental child who is viewed as a re-constructor of knowledge, values, cultures and identities is evolving into a complex construction of the child as an active citizen who is ready, can achieve and, hence, is able to participate in all activities involving him/her. Early childhood research and practice is now underpinned by an increasingly dominant view that children have the ability to take command of their own learning and to adopt shared responsibility for that learning. This shared responsibility involves all parents, children, teachers, practitioners and the local community. As a result the fundamental question that, before, dominated thinking on early childhood, concerning how practitioners can help children to learn how to learn, has now moderated to a consideration of how we can work with children so that they take responsibility for and ownership of their learning.

This has led to a situation where children's basic emotional and cognitive needs for autonomy, competence and participation in social circumstances has been extensively recognised. The focus is now on how the encouragement of autonomy and shared responsibility may be achieved.

However, there is a need to question further what is actually meant by the view of children as social actors. A social actor is someone who has the autonomy to act, who acts through a sense of reason and responsibility, and who lives within a system of law s/he respects and obeys. A person guided by reason, s/he desires to take account of the life and the good of individuals and the community; consequently, s/he lives in accordance with the laws and systems of the community. In such a context, the field of early childhood studies as a community should be developing a system of practices where children can become autonomous, responsible participants in their community. The discussion of what constitutes ethical practice in the field of early childhood learning has emerged from this context.

It is thus important to explain what is meant by the term 'ethical practice' before we embark on specifying what is intended by 'ethical practice' throughout this book.

The area of philosophy traditionally known as ethics aims to investigate human attempts to arrive at an understanding of the nature of human values, how humans ought to live their lives, what distinguishes right from wrong and what constitutes appropriate conduct (Mackie, 1977; Rawls, 1971; Peters, 1966, 1967; Borrow, 1972, 1975; Bradley, 1970; Ayers, 2004; Palmer, 2007; Stricke, 2007).

From a philosophical point of view, central questions to the study of ethics are: 'What traits of character make one a good person?' and by extension 'What is the right thing to do?' (Rachels, 1993). Research into these two questions has led philosophy in a number of different directions and theories. Theories about ethics are dominated by debates of rightness and obligation (Pincoff, 1986; Stocker, 1976); there are, however, other writers who object to this approach. They suggest that the discussions about obligation, rights and duty should be abandoned so that the central questions revolve around the concept of virtue (Anscombe, 1958). This section does not attempt to involve itself either in a philosophical debate of what ethics are, in a theoretical debate of different approaches to what ethics mean, or in a long discussion on what is a satisfactory theory of ethics. Instead, it holds the view that ethics are not concerned solely with the elucidation and justification of morality in the narrow sense.

On this basis, the term 'ethical practice' is concerned with how people around early childhood research and practice conduct their work through morally upright practices, and how different points of view are considered. Ethical practice considers questions about what could count as justifiable reasons for acting in one way rather than in another, and about what constitutes a good life for children.

Contemporary philosophers distinguish between 'substantive ethics' or normative ethics, and 'meta-ethics'. The fundamental difference between these is the emphasis on the questions each asks.

Substantive ethics is concerned with questions of what kinds of actions are good or right. In contrast, meta-ethics is concerned with issues of how to determine whether an action is good or right.

The second question above is more complex. It requires the development of ways of understanding through an analysis of the language used in the first question. Meta-ethics goes beyond the discovery of what is good or what is right; it extends into the search into what is intended when it is said of something that it is 'good' or 'right'. This idea of analysing further the language of 'good' and 'right', then trying to understand in depth the actions that make something good and right, seems highly appropriate in the field of early childhood. Early childhood could be said to deal with issues of actions and the complexities that have arisen from these actions. The message could be simplified: ethical practice is about good actions between adults and children. However, this view entails a major problem as 'good' and 'right' are subjective judgements as their meaning changes depending on the person's point of view, on culture, on religion and on different circumstances and contexts. Thus ethical practice should be concerned with the analysis of actions in the early years sector rather than what is good or right for children.

Nevertheless, in the name of research and practice for the 'good' of children, these actions are ignored. As professionals working in the field of early childhood we are, for example, involved in the balancing of the rightness of our practice through research from our point of view; we attempt to 'shield' children – but we do need to question whether we are actually doing these children a disservice. Do we really offer children the 'correct' perspective, or do we offer our own perspective? Do we act for the good of children? Or should we act with children for good?

If ethical practice is about dealing with issues of actions, the remaining question concerns *whose* actions. Ethical practice cannot be limited by the simplistic explanation that it is about 'good' actions. Complexities have arisen from these actions, for example complexities in research, in daily routine work with children, in dealing with parents, and in dealing with government agendas, inspections and regulations.

There are situations, such as in curriculum implementation and in assessment, where each context prescribes the actions between adults and children and these diverge; when two apparently contrary actions are initiated in the same subject area, a change must necessarily take place in one or both of them until any conflict is eliminated. This view of ethical practice contains a vast amount of tension and anxiety for the professionals, who are asked on the one hand to adhere to an ideological shift of actions 'with children' while on the other they are required by officialdom to measure children against models and a set of standards laid down in regulations. There is thus a mismatch between an ideological understanding of what is 'good' practice with children within the early years sector, and a number of practices that are laid down in the name of 'doing the best for children'. The dilemma here is that professionals try to act according to reason and hence attain ethical practice, yet external practices are imposed upon them in the name of the good of the children.

Therefore the concept of ethical practice may be extended to include the causality between adult actions through the essence of what these actions cause to children. Ethical practice requires logical sense and judgement or the assertion that the action is based on reason. Adults' actions are inseparable from the effect these have on children.

There is a necessity to be able to provide an environment and conditions for children that respects their nature and their dignity. Early childhood practice must allow all actions that fall within the scope of practice which are not contrary to children's nature. In that sense, ethical practice is not merely the necessity to 'do' good acts in the field of early childhood, but to questioning those actions. These actions must be related to the consideration of the causes in regard to the emotions, dignity, autonomy, protection from harm, and privacy of the child. An essential criterion for engagement and participation is for children to take pleasure in all they do, such as pleasure in the kind of knowledge that will be acquired through research or pleasure in whatever activity is involved.

Ethical practice should go beyond government agendas of what is 'good' and beyond the framing approach to children's good. The urgency experienced by governments to 'regulate' the upbringing and safeguarding of children goes beyond the children's control. The aspect of choice becomes an adult-oriented issue when the adult is imposing the choices and the children 'choose' what is to be chosen. This view, some might argue, is radical. However, a question remains: the notion of what is good for children, i.e. ethics, may be forced on children and is paradoxical in the sense that the discussion centres on children's participation and developing a sensitivity to listening to children – without actually taking account of children's views – in the name of the 'best interests of children'.

Addressing the complex issue of a balance between what is good for children and how we can act with children for their 'good' revolves around an examination of propositions by considering the fundamental question: *How do we know that we act* with *children?* It is proposed that ethical practices in the field of early childhood research and practice should be permissive only – permissive to individuals and their groups – rather than universal. Promoting the cultivation of an organised overarching ethical framework of good practice fails to address the emerging construction of children as social actors. In a framing environment with universal practices, autonomy becomes autocracy.

For example, although the rights of children are promoted throughout this book, at this point we will reflect on United Nations Convention on the Rights of the Child (UN, 1989). The UNCRC claims the universality of the rights of children; we need to question firstly whether these universal rights have passed the test of importance as shared ideals, and secondly whether these rights (i.e. social rights and participation) may be set against claims for the freedom of the human spirit or the right of the individual's cultural development.

This section has aimed to explain the notion of ethical practice in early childhood. It is suggested that this notion is complex and extends beyond the simplicity of discovering what is 'good' research, practice, interaction with children or terminology. Instead, ethical practice is concerned with the examination of concepts, with analysing concepts such as 'good' and' right', rather than actually using the concepts to talk about human conduct, and with the causality of the actions of adults and children.

About the Book

In the light of the above discussion this book makes no attempt to examine the philosophical debates of ethics in each relevant topic area discussed. Instead, it discusses ethical practice in terms of asking the fundamental questions of what is logical, reasonable and justified. It addresses whether, when researching or working with young children, we would like to foster and develop attributes and attitudes that support the children in facing challenges as they embark upon their journey towards lifelong learning and development. Development involves positive changes in a life, not merely the linear increase that determines learning.

The book does not wish to develop a moral vocabulary or step towards ethical practice. Instead, it aims to offer ideas of what is considered good practice, which incorporates the notion of rights as a valued part of human activity and goals. The scope of the discussion is to identify in early years research and practice problem areas that concern children.

It is therefore relevant to state that the book rejects the notion of providing a framework for ethical practice in early childhood work. Such an approach is in direct conflict with the actual search for good practice. The right *not* to have a specific kind of education, provision, practice or research with children is promoted and celebrated throughout the book. The notion of practice imposed upon children in the name of participation, protection or a belief only in 'what is best for children' is adult-oriented and contradicts the essence of children's autonomy.

However, rejecting the view that a framework of ethical practice is a cultivation of organised yet fragmented practices that actually highlight the 'deficits' of children instead of celebrating their diversity and participation, practices based on values, and judgements arising from sensitivity to individuals and society, this book claims to offer a pluralistic approach to ethical practice.

As has been stated, since the discussions offer propositions and address the right *not* to have a particular way of 'doing' things with children, it has been decided to interfere only minimally with the personal style of each author/s. This book does not claim to cover all debates and all issues around ethical practice with children, and certainly does not aim to become a predictable and uniform view of ethical practice. For the editor to 'control' the diversity and respective autonomy of the authors would have been paradoxical to the essence of the book.

The book is divided into two parts. Part 1 discusses issues around ethical practices and issues with regard to research. It consists of five chapters which explore and discuss key issues with regard to children's participation in research.

Chapter 1 provides a historical account of how children's participation as a topic was developed. The examination of the underpinning ideology of children's rights and the United Nations Convention on the Rights of the Child focuses on three rights vital when involving children in research: Article 2 – Non-discrimination; Article 3 – The Best Interests of the Child; and Article 12 – The Child's Opinion is to be Expressed and Considered.

Chapter 2 examines ethical practice when choosing research tools with young children. This chapter takes the stand that all research methods are appropriate when conducting research with young children if – and only if – these tools are underpinned by ethical practice and the central questions are examined under the lens of justified logical actions. A range of research methods must be considered so as best to inform the researchers' practice and to create methods suitable to the needs of children within their care.

Chapter 3 claims that the individual differences in children do not constitute a barrier to ethical concerns around young children. It states that the parents' permission is not enough when working with and researching young children; these children, too, have the right to be involved in ethical considerations in order to promote inclusion and participation at all levels. The chapter examines how to empower children through the use of relevant research tools (for example, using photographs to share thoughts through both verbal and non-verbal responses) to allow children a 'voice' within the research process. It considers the challenges of interpreting a wide range of responses reflecting the diversity of individual differences to gain informed consent and in the interpretation of data. This is set in the context of issues surrounding trust and any possible imbalance of power in relationships.

Chapter 4 extends the themes introduced in Chapter 3 and looks at ethical issues when working with and researching young children. Novice researchers who assume that new publications on research ethics merely follow a well-worn path may be surprised to note that the ethical implications of research involving children and vulnerable groups is a relatively new area of interest. The dearth of interest in this subject owes much to the fact that, for many years, researchers mistakenly believed that methodological integrity and ethical integrity were one and the same. The chapter begins with an overview of some of the research malpractices that led to calls for greater rigour in the care of research participants. The chapter continues by exploring the influences that led to a shift away from children being viewed as 'subjects' of research to children being accepted as 'participants' in research.

Chapter 5 deals with issues of researching other cultures. As early years settings are now becoming multicultural and multi-dimensional, it is important to address the fact that when working with children from cultural or ethnic backgrounds other than where they are attending centres, there is a need for effective communication as well as a need to accommodate the diversity of different cultures. This chapter discusses such issues in the light of the ethical implications when working with or carrying out research into children from other ethnic and cultural backgrounds.

Part 2 explores ethical practices around policy and practice. It is divided into seven chapters, the aim of which is not to provide a neat, unified account of ethical practice about the matters under discussion.

That would be too meagre an approach. Instead, these chapters aim to discuss ideas, practices, theories and arguments.

Chapter 6 identifies the recurring issues in implementing policy reform for those working with young children and assesses the effects of the fragmentation of social policy to analyse the importance of the role of practitioners in engaging with the issues and becoming activists. It is important for readers to understand the fragmentation of social policy that hinders child protection and development, and to gain awareness of their role as agents for ethical change. The chapter seeks to engage readers with the fragmentation of social policy over the last four decades and to do so as critical practitioners who can trace the historic substantive issues, outline why changes in the social fabric might see certain issues recurring and, finally, how they can think beyond their immediate roles and locate themselves in the landscape as actors for ethical change.

Chapter 7 discusses the ethical implications in an era of working in partnership. It examines ethical aspects of communication, team work, the sharing of information and practices. It examines the different ways of working in a 'joined-up' manner and attempts to address ethical challenges that professionals are facing in such environments.

Chapter 8 addresses the issues around loss and bereavement in early years. Professionals do not always know how to cope with and handle these situations; this chapter explores all these key issues with emphasis on the ethical implications when professionals are faced with such circumstances. It discusses children's emotional and social reactions in situations of loss and bereavement. It also explores issues of the role of the early years workforce when children are faced with loss and bereavement and explores ways how they can work in an ethical environment with children, families and other professionals.

Chapter 9 deals with issues of studying early childhood and the ethical challenges that students might face. This chapter discusses how students may be helped in implementing good ethical practices when they are in settings studying children. The chapter will also examine how students can plan an effective research project that allows a variety of voices (including children's, parents' and practitioners') to be heard. It will differ from earlier chapters in its focus on practical guidance for students on how to plan an ethical research project *prior* to undertaking research within an early years setting – the application of which has been covered in earlier chapters.

Chapter 10 extends the concepts of the previous chapter. It claims that key to improving the lives of children is the notion of a professional childcare workforce. During the course of early years study, developing professionals learn about definitions of childhood and how their practice, e.g. through curriculum delivery, relationships or interactions, affects the young child's identity and life-course options, as well as their quality of life. The chapter examines the theoretical underpinnings of professional development and training; in practice, it covers a number of ethical, rights-based issues with an impact on children's lives, including Northern Ireland as a society slowly emerging from conflict, poverty, disadvantage, mental ill-health, special educational needs, disability, children's well-being and quality of life.

Chapter 11 considers how the inspection and regulation of early years services conforms to ethical practice. The focus will be on the role of the Office for Standards in Education, Children's Services and Skills, known as Ofsted, which is identified as the independent body responsible for ensuring that early years settings meet the identified regulatory standards and educational framework of the Early Years Foundation Stage (EYFS) in England. The chapter aims to help students to develop an understanding of the role of Ofsted, to consider the implications of the role of inspection and regulation of early years settings, then critically to consider the relationship between inspection and quality processes leading to improvement.

Chapter 12 explores the challenges facing accountable leaders in education. Leadership is defined as a social construct with more attributes than the allocation of formal authority; it is one that requires the post-holder to demonstrate behaviours that not only modify the competencies and motivations of other adults, but also determine organisational purpose, aims and objectives. Formal leaders, it is argued, are faced with moral dilemmas with regard to the core purpose of their provision that should be resolved in concert with their local community as well as with their principal funding agency. Once confident of their organisational purpose and direction, the focus of attention switches to developing the capacity of their colleagues. In summary, the chapter provides prospective ethical leaders in early years settings with the means by which they can determine their core purpose and develop their staff to deliver that vision.

References

Anscombe, G.E.M. (1958) 'Modern moral philosophy', in *Philosophy*, 33 (reprinted in *Ethics, Religion, and Politics: The Collected Philosophical Papers of G.E.M. Anscombe*, Vol. III. Mineapolis, MN: University of Minnesota Press, 1981).

Ayers, W. (2004) *Teaching Toward Freedom: Moral Commitment and Ethical Action in the Classroom*. Boston: Beacon Press.

Benton, M. (1996) 'The image of childhood: representations of the child in painting and literature, 1700–1900', *Children's Literature in Education*, 27(1): 35–61.

Borrow, G. (1972) *Education and Politics*. London: Oxford University Press.

Borrow, G. (1975) *Moral Philosophy for Education*. London: Allen & Unwin.

Bradley, F.H. (1970) *Ethical Studies*. London: Oxford University Press.

Christensen, P. & James, A. (2008) *Research with Children: Perspectives and Practices* (2nd edn). London: Routledge.

Clark, A. & Moss, P. (2001) *Listening to Young Children: The Mosaic Approach*. London: National Children's Bureau.

Clark, A., Kjørholt, A.T. & Moss, P. (2005) *Beyond Listening: Children's Perspectives on Early Childhood Services*. Bristol: Policy Press.

Dahlberg, G. & Moss, P. (2005) *Ethics and Politics in Early Childhood Education*. London: RoutledgeFalmer.

Dahlberg, G., Moss, P. & Pence, A. (1999) *Beyond Quality in Early Childhood Education and Care: Postmodern Perspectives*. London: Falmer Press.

David, T. (1993) 'Educating children under 5 in the UK', in T. David (ed.), *Educational Provision for Our Youngest Children: European Perspectives*. London: Paul Chapman.

Edminston, B. (2008) *Forming Ethical Identities in Early Childhood Play*. London: Routledge.

Harcourt, D., Perry, B. & Waller, T. (2011) *Researching Young Children's Perspectives: Debating the Ethics and Dilemmas of Education Research with Children*. London: Routledge.

Hendrick, H. (1997) 'Construction and reconstruction of British childhood: an interpretive survey, 1800 to present', in A. James & A. Prout (eds), *Constructing and Reconstructing Childhood: Contemporary Issues in the Sociological Study of Childhood*, 2nd edn. London: Falmer Press, pp. 34–63.

Mackie, J.L. (1977) *Ethical: Inventing Right and Wrong*. Oxford: Oxford University Press.

Moss, P. & Petrie, P. (2002) *From Children's Services to Children's Spaces: Public Policy, Children and Childhood*. London: RoutledgeFalmer.

Palaiologou, I. (2008) *Achieving EYPS: Childhood Observation*. Exeter: Learning Matters.

Palmer, P. (2007) *The Courage to Teach: Exploring the Inner Landscape of Teacher's Life*. New York: John Wiley & Sons (originally published 1997).

Peters, R.S. (ed.) (1966) *The Concept of Education*. London: Routledge & Kegan Paul.

Peters, R.S. (1967) *Ethics in Education*. London: HMSO.

Pincoff, L. (1986) *Quandaries and Virtues: Against Reductivism in Ethics*. Lawrence, KS: University of Kansas Press.

Rawls, J. (1971) *A Theory of Justice*. London: Oxford University Press.

Rachels, J. (1993) *The Elements of Moral Philosophy* (2nd edn). New York: McGraw-Hill.

Stocker, M. (1976) 'The schizophrenia of modern ethical theories', *Journal of Philosophy*, 73: 453–66.

Stricke, K.A. (2007) *Ethical Leadership in Schools: Creating Community in an Environment of Accountability*. Thousand Oaks, CA: Corwin.

United Nations (1989) *The Convention on the Rights of the Child*. Geneva: Defense International and the United Nations Children's Fund.

Part 1

Ethical Issues in Research

1

Involving Young Children in Research

Donna Green

Chapter overview

The chapter discusses ethical practice when involving young children in research and it focuses on the crucial issue of 'participation' in the context of the rights of young children to be valued and respected. Although the issue of participation will be the main concern throughout the first part of the book, the chapter will attempt to illustrate the means by which young children are invited to participate in research as well as the importance of listening and tuning in to their early communications in order to gain their consent to research. Key policy and initiatives are evaluated critically to explore the emergence of a new wave in thinking in regard to children's rights and the wider impact these have upon research with children. Finally, the journey towards gaining ethical consent from young children and adults is defined through exploring the relative problems. The term 'children' is often used to refer to individuals across a variety of ages, in most cases to those under the age of 18 (UN, 1998); here, 'young children' includes those under the age of five. The chapter aims to examine the term 'participation' in the context of young children giving their consent; to evaluate the key policies and initiatives and their impact upon valuing young children in their own right, and: to evaluate the relative levels of informed consent and the ways in which it is elicited to gain the participation of young people/children in research.

A Right to 'Participation': When Does It Begin?

The term 'participation' means 'becoming actively involved' and 'the act or state of participating, or sharing in common with others' (Collins, 2001: 394). Given such meaning in the context of working directly with children, it could be said that we practitioners are all 'actively involved' in practice on a day-to-day basis and 'share in common' the best interests of all children with whom we engage. Taking participation a step further in the wider context we are ourselves 'participants' in the lives of certain children and their families. In real terms 'participation' may be seen as causing a ripple effect as individuals' actions touch others. Communication, both verbal and non-verbal, conveys meaning to others thus enabling connectivity through sharing common interests. Achieving inclusivity through being involved, irrespective of the level of engagement, is true 'participation'.

The infectious nature of what could be described as true participation unlocks the excitement and possibilities for children to become active meaning makers in their own lives. As such:

> [I]t could be argued that 'participation' in society begins from the moment a child enters the world and discovers the extent to which they are able to influence events by cries or movements, but it is worth bearing in mind that through these early negotiations, even in infancy, children discover the extent to which their own voices influence the course of events in their lives. (Hart, 1997: 4)

Babies communicate from their earliest weeks. Many months before their first recognisable words babies become adept at communicating, with a range of vocalisations through sound making, facial expressions and useful gestures such as pointing to direct attention and to share their current interests and dislikes (Lindon et al., 2001; Elfer et al., 2003; Keenan & Evans, 2009). Therefore, during such early stages babies are able effectively to participate in their environment, to communicate and ultimately to influence what happens to them. The importance and value of such participation should not be underestimated. Listening to children and acknowledging children's views has benefits for both children and the adults who are listening. Listening to children can impact positively upon their development of skills and understanding, raise their self-esteem and change their everyday experiences, whereas adults seeing and hearing children can gain unexpected insights into children's interests and capabilities, reveal different possibilities for engagement and share serious concerns (Clark, 2004: 2).

In terms of research, acknowledging that our youngest children are able effectively to participate, share their feelings and make a valuable contribution is essential, yet this acknowledgement in itself is not enough: the researcher has an immense responsibility to ensure that the best interests of the child are paramount and take priority over those of the research. Nevertheless, it may traditionally be seen that 'most research directly on children is devoted to measuring them, using the model of animal research to measure their growth, disease or behaviour'; 'this is usually to atomise and process them through the grid of adult-designed research' (Alderson, 1995: 40). This being the case, such non-child-centred research fails to uphold the best interests of child participants, nor does it respect the child as an individual; rather, it prioritises the interests of the outcome of the research and thus regards the child as a mere subject to be studied which informs current practice in the relative disciplines. It is here that the powerlessness and vulnerability of participants in relation to adult researchers is seen (Morrow & Richards, 1996; Valentine, 1999).

Some of the early pioneering work undertaken with young children has given invaluable insights into child development and still informs current practice. Although such work has contributed to the understanding of child development, the means by which such understanding was achieved could only be described today as unethical. The following cases serve as an example of practice where young children, and in some cases their carers, were powerless and vulnerable within research.

 Case study 1

Dennis & Dennis (1941): Infant Development Under Conditions of Restricted and Minimum Social Stimulation

The aim of the study was to create a situation in which young children were deprived of stimulation in a controlled environment. Dennis and his wife cared for two female fraternal twins from the age of one to 14 months. However, the term 'care' in this situation is used to describe the existence of the twins within the home of the researcher, in a heated room with no pictures or toys and minimal furniture, being fed and changed regularly, with very limited social interaction.

▶

During the first seven months of the research it appeared that the twins remained within normal developmental limits for their age, although slightly below average. However, in the second part of the experiment, from ages seven to fourteen months, development became more seriously impaired and at 14 months the twins were classified as seriously retarded (Jarvis & Chandler, 2001: 181).

 Case study 2

Watson & Rayner (1920): Little Albert (Classical Conditioning)

Watson and Rayner trained Albert, a nine-month-old baby, to fear a neutral stimulus (a white rat) after presenting it several times in the company of a loud sound (clanging an iron bar behind the infant's head). While initially Albert reached out to touch the rat, he soon learned to fear it, 'crying and turning his head away from sight of the animal' (Harris, 1979; Keenan & Evans, 2009). Baby Albert in this case was subjected to a stressful situation where his communicated distaste and fear for the situation were subsequently ignored. Watson and Rayner had exercised their power status over baby Albert.

 Case study 3

Gessell (1932): The Developmental Morphology of Infant Behaviour Patterns

Arnold Gessell's pioneering work on capturing developmental milestones in child development further depicts children as research subjects rather than as participants: 'our subjects are normal infants selected as to race, gestation period, health, parentage and socio-economic factors' (Gessell, 1932: 140). The way in which he conducted his research was by no means as damaging to children as in the two cases previously mentioned; however, they were non-naturalistic in the sense of the environment in which they took place. Young children were placed in what Gessell referred to as the 'observation dome'. The operator, observers and parent are stationed outside; the infant is in the crib in the universal focal area of the cameras. The surrounding laboratory is darkened, effectively concealing the observers from the infant – who himself is clearly perceived as he displays his repertoire of behaviour in his crib (Gessell, 1932: 40).

> The children who took part in Gessell's research were observed in a scientific environment, viewed as objects similar to animals in a zoo. The mere fact that children were placed in such non-naturalistic surroundings and unable to see their parents would have been stressful for them. Given what is known today about 'attachment theory', the participant-children had, in the absence of their parents, no safe base from which to explore, and no source of comfort, encouragement or guidance (Crawford, 2006: 43).

The building of relationships between practitioners and young children, as well as those adults responsible for their care, is essential to ensure equality in power and status when undertaking research. However, the building of relationships has inherent possible difficulties, such as children feeling let down when a research project ends, difficulties in establishing rapport with young children, their parents and other key people involved in their care, and environmental barriers beyond the researcher's control. Hart (1997) argues that some of the inclusive practices to involve children in research are actually limited and he adopts the term 'tokenism'. Tokenism in that context is a false appearance of inclusive participation of children in research. It is also a difficult issue because it is often unintentionally applied by adults who wish to give children a voice, but have not considered it carefully or critically; this results in children having little or no choice about the subject or the style of communicating it, or the time to formulate their own opportunities (Hart, 1997: 41). Lansdown (2005) proposed the ethical approach to prevent adult manipulation or control. Creating meaningful participation provides a useful tool for good practice in this regard. The process has to be transparent and honest; staff should have a shared understanding and commitment and shared principles of behaviour towards each other; children must have appropriate information; the barriers children might face should be considered; and staff should work towards creating a space in which children are able to develop their own ideas (Lansdown, 2005: 29).

It is evident that researchers today have a huge amount of responsibility when embarking upon research involving the participation of young children. Given what is now known about the capabilities of young children, current practitioners are readily able to pass judgement on the work of our research forbears. It is therefore essential that an appreciation exists of the emergence of a new wave in thinking in regard to valuing the participation of young children.

Before the chapter moves on to discuss the developments of the new wave of thinking about research involving young children it must at this point be emphasised that a key element in children's participation in research is simplicity. When young children are involved in research it is essential for researchers to create an environment where it allows time for all (children and adults/researchers) to reflect; time for children to express themselves free from pressure; time to ensure the environment is suitable for purpose and does not constitute a barrier; time to listen and observe responses; and time to build relationships between researcher and children. In addition, physical space holds an equally central place in achieving simplicity in space: for children to be able to express themselves and for key people to meet and discuss issues around the research. Finally, the key issue in achieving simplicity is mutual respect among all concerned, shared understanding and commitment, alongside engagement with young children and the key people in their lives. The researcher needs to acknowledge these issues in order to be able to create the conditions to achieve participation of children. Such simplicity is also important in the choice of ethical child-centred research methods that ensure children are active participants rather than mere 'research subjects'.

The Emergence of a New Wave of Thinking

There is today an acknowledgement that children have a right to a voice and to be heard, and are therefore entitled to be:

> participants in their own lives, to influence what happens to them, to be involved in creating their own environments, to exercise choices and to have their views respected and valued. (Lansdown, 2005)

However, the emergence of such thinking has developed slowly over a period of time.

The Plowden Report (1967) *Children and Their Primary Schools* has been influential in bringing together a range of theories of learning, which encouraged and endorsed 'child-centred' practice. Plowden maintained that:

> at the heart of the educational process lies the child. No advances in policy or acquisition of new equipment will have their desired effect unless they are in harmony with the nature of the child and they are fundamentally acceptable to him. (DES, 1967: para. 9)

At this point in time the importance of listening to and responding to the needs of children to ensure child-centred practice had emerged. The late twentieth century saw the real beginnings of the move to recognise the rights of children in a significant way. The Children Act 1989 became a catalyst for policy change in the UK, as did the United Nations Convention on the Rights of the Child (UNCRC) at an international level (Christenson & James, 2008: 12). These ideals placed the child in high regard, requiring all children to be respected in their own right.

Conversely, the ideal in the context of ensuring that even our youngest children have a right to be respected within the UNCRC could be construed as being piecemeal in approach. Article 12 of the UNCRC reiterates the importance of children being active participants in their lives, firmly maintaining that:

> States Parties shall assure to the child who is capable of forming his or her own views the right to express those views freely in all matters affecting the child, the views of the child being given due weight in accordance with the age and maturity of the child. (DOH, 1999: 46)

This could on closer inspection be viewed as inadvertently omitting the views, thus devaluing the participation, of those children under the age of five years. In direct contrast, Article 13 states that

> [T]he child shall have the right to freedom of expression; this right shall include freedom to seek, receive and impart information and ideas of all kinds, regardless of frontiers, either orally, in writing or in print, in the form of art, or through any other media of the child's choice. (DOH, 1999: 46)

In essence, Article 12 pertains to the maturity of the child as an indicator of participation, whereas Article 13 may be perceived as valuing a child's participation in any shape or form relative to the individual. Others who perceive the participation of very young children not to be of worth simply because of their age are through Article 12 provided with a tool to reinforce such a belief, an attitude that could be detrimental to a young individual.

The late twentieth century also saw the introduction of the National Curriculum in 1989. With its highly diverse knowledge content, this failed to acknowledge in any shape or form the educational rights of young children until the revised National Curriculum changes were introduced between 1995 and 2000. From then the beginnings of positive change for children within their earliest years can be documented. The Early Learning Goals were developed, initially by the School Curriculum and Assessment Authority (SCAA) as 'Desirable Learning Outcomes' and later completed as Early Learning Goals (ELGs) by the Qualifications and Curriculum Authority (QCA) in the late 1990s. These included a major area of experience for under-fives as being 'creative development', to 'focus on the development of children's imagination and their ability to communicate and to express ideas and feelings in creative ways', thereby fully recognising young children's right to express themselves in accordance with UNCRC Article 13 and to be heard (DFEE & SCAA, 1996: 4). The introduction of the Foundation Stage in 2000 for children aged three to five years further emphasised early years education as distinct from that of the National Curriculum.

The drive to focus on early years education as a discrete and important phase did not end with the introduction of the Foundation Stage. This was just the start of change for children from their earliest years. In 2001 the Department for Education and Skills (DfES) published guidance from the Children and Young Persons Unit entitled *Learning to Listen: Core Principles for the Involvement of Children and Young People*, providing an official common framework for departments to develop tailored policies, action plans and effective practice for involving children and young people in the design, provision and evaluation of those services that affect them (Greig et al., 2007: 158). The framework makes clear that even the youngest children have an entitlement to participation: 'Children and young people are not discriminated against or prevented from participating effectively on grounds of race, religion, culture, disability, age, ethnic origin, language or the area in which they live' (DfES, 2001: 11). The links to UNCRC, Article 13, are evident here; the framework goes further to provide examples of how it will support children under the age of five to participate. The Save the Children Fund and the Children's Society undertook some consultation work with children aged 2–4 years for the Greater London Authority (GLA). The children were to give their views and perceptions of London and to do this they were taken on a 'sensory walk'. The children were encouraged to talk about what they saw, smelt, touched, tasted and heard as they walked along. Some of the children took photographs and drew pictures that showed how things look from their perspective. The children's views are being fed into the GLA strategy (DfES, 2001: 11). Here it can be seen within the 'Learning to Listen' framework how children under the age of five years are empowered to participate, express their views in ways relevant to them and be valued irrespective of their age.

The introduction of the Birth to Three Matters Framework in 2002 provided a framework within which to 'provide support, information, guidance and challenge for all those with the responsibility for the care and education of babies and children from birth to three years', fully celebrating the uniqueness and potential abilities of children under the age of three years (DfES, 2002: 4). Furthermore, the introduction of Every Child Matters and the Children Act 2004 clearly outlines the right of every child through the five key outcomes of being healthy, staying safe, enjoying and achieving, making a positive contribution and achieving economic well-being (Bruce, 2009: 271). The Childcare Act 2006, a pioneering piece of legislation, is the first ever to be concerned with early years and childcare services, aiming to reduce child poverty and inequality, and to improve the well-being of young children by focusing on the five Every Child Matters outcomes (DfES, 2007a).

> Sections 39–48 introduced the *Early Years Foundation Stage 2008* (EYFS) which has built upon and brought together the existing Birth to Three Matters, Foundation Stage and National Standards for day care and child minding. This framework supports providers in delivering quality integrated early education and care for children from birth to age five. (DfES, 2007a)

There has been a remarkable move towards giving our youngest children status and value in their own right. Since the introduction of the Children Act 1989 and the UNCRC (UN 1989), there has been an array of policies providing a vehicle with which to drive a growing acknowledgement for the need of an integrated approach to care and education culminating in the development of the EYFS (2008). Given the growth of such recognition it is worth questioning why there has also been an assortment of government publications during this time, which have undermined and devalued such progress by failing even to acknowledge our youngest children.

The DfES publication *Working Together Giving Children and Young People a Say* (2004) fully supports the UNCRC, Article 12, by giving children and young people the right to put forward their views and ensure that those views are taken seriously (DfES, 2004). However, it is the views of 'children', particularly those children over the age of five, to which the document pertains, those children of school age, thus reiterating the problematic wording of UNCRC Article 12 in relation to 'due weight in accordance to the age and maturity' at which children can fully participate. The Children's Plan (2008), produced by the Department of Children, Schools and Families (DCSF), further demonstrates this point. This is rather discouraging, as a document that prides itself on a future vision for services for children and young people, planned to meet the needs of children and young people, failed to consult with or take account of our youngest children. 'Consultation' consisted of: main consultation events with young people aged 16 and over; focus groups held with small groups of children and young people aged between eight and 15; deliberative events held with 30 parents of children and young people; balanced representation from parents of children aged 0–7, 8–13, and 14–19; the views of 30 young people aged 16–19, and 40 practitioners and policy experts working with children of all ages (DCSF, 2008: 155). It could be argued that our youngest children were represented by their parents and caregivers, alongside those experienced in the field of working with very young children. However, the question remains as to how young children were truly active participants in the consultation process.

The *Working Together: Listening to the Voices of Children and Young People* (DCSF, 2009) guidance promotes the participation of children and young people in decision-making in school, local authority and related settings; it provides advice on the principles and practice that support such involvement. Again, while on the surface it regards the participation of children as positive, it is rather contradictory in stating: 'As we set out in the Children's Plan, our aim is for all young people to want and be able to participate and take responsible action', then claiming that 'giving children and young people a say in decisions that affect them can improve engagement in learning, help develop a more inclusive school environment and improve behaviour and attendance' (DCSF, 2009: 1). The switch in emphasis from young people to children and young people either reinforces the recurring notion that the participation of young people is more beneficial in meeting policy requirements or that the participation of children is held in less regard. Finally, the document relates only to those children above the age of five. Very slow progress has been made giving the early years of young children's lives the importance they deserve or their being seen as a distinct phase. There is still much more work to be done to eliminate the contradictions in policy often caused by the lack of thought in regard to the terminology used when describing the very children who constitute the theme of a policy.

The Ongoing Journey to Consent

'A great deal of thought and attention has to be given to ethics of all research studies and this should not be any less rigorous just because it is children who are carrying out the research' (Kellett, 2005: 31). Gaining children's views without exploitation or causing distress and the building of relationships to facilitate child-centred methods is of paramount concern. Having a genuine respect for a child's position and interest in them, as individuals, may help to guard against exploitation and distress (Coad and Lewis, 2004: 18).

With regard to gaining ethical permission from children, as well as from their parents and carers or other key people in their lives, it can be seen that there is an ongoing journey which in part includes building relationships, listening and ensuring positive participation without tokenism before young children can truly be involved and actively give their own ethical permission. However, it is worth noting that such an ongoing journey cannot be undertaken lightly and it will never end where holding meaningful ethical consent is concerned. Before such a journey can be embarked upon it is imperative that consent in the context of researching with young children is understood to uphold ethical regard for all involved. The issue of informed consent when considering the participation of young children is complex because of their 'minority status'. Therefore informed consent is required from those who have legal care and control, such as a parent, guardian or local authority figure. Informed consent also relates to ongoing consent in that participants may withdraw their consent at any time and for any reason (Kellett, 2005). This is where the distinction between the three terms 'informed consent', 'assent' and 'dissent' needs to be understood in the context of research involving young children.

- informed consent – consent given by the adult for the child

- assent – permission given by the child

- dissent – child withdrawing permission.

Even though informed consent may have been given on behalf of a young child by an adult, it is desirable as far as possible for all children to be approached about giving their consent (Kellet, 2005). The researcher has a responsibility to establish that ongoing consent from the participants has indeed been given, and not merely feel safe in trusting that informed consent has been given by an adult. Mary Ainsworth's Strange Situation test (see Ainsworth, 1967, 1979; Ainsworth & Bowlby, 1965; Ainsworth et al., 1978) has been criticised on ethical grounds for placing young children aged 12 to 18 months old in a continuing stressful situation. Over a period of time and with parental informed consent, the children were subjected to a series of events in unfamiliar environments and their reactions were observed. The observed reactions from the participants at each stage clearly communicated their assent and dissent during the test.

The strange situation series of events

Parent and child alone. The child is observed happily exploring the environment with the added comfort of a parent, therefore assenting to the situation.

Stranger joins parent and child. The stranger begins to interact with parent and child. Child is observed to be reluctant and to seek reassurance from parent. Although reluctant the child appears to assent to the change in the situation as the parent is still present.

Parent leaves child and stranger alone. The child attempts to follow the parent, cries and shows definite signs of distress. At this point the child is giving a very clear indication of dissent: they are not happy with the situation, at which point the experiment should have ceased.

Parent returns and stranger leaves. The child is still distressed, requiring comfort from parent and giving further indications of dissent.

Parent leaves and the child is left completely alone. The child is extremely distressed, giving further dissent signals.

Stranger returns and tries to comfort the child. The child is still distressed and communicating dissent.

Parent returns and stranger leaves. The child's distress is eventually relieved by the parent's return.

(Ainsworth, 1967, 1979)

At each stage of the observation the child was placed in distress for the sake of research. Clear communication of assent and dissent can be detected through the participants' reactions to the strange situation, yet the experiment (unethically) continued because informed consent had been given by the parent. Thus both researcher and parents were guilty of unethically devaluing the young children's capabilities to say 'no'.

It is clearly evident that young children are experts in their own lives, skilful communicators, active agents influencing and changing the world around them, and meaning makers constructing and interpreting meaning in their lives (Clark & Moss, 2001, cited in Lansdown, 2005: 1). It is, furthermore, possible that young children are able to offer ethical consent in a variety of ways from a very early age. It is the 'adults with expertise who respectfully watch children engaged in their process of living, learning, loving and being who are in a better position to understand what it is these youngest citizens are trying to say and to find ways of helping them to say it' (Nutbrown, 1996: 55). This being so, it is evident that researchers must build relationships with the key people in young children's lives to ensure that the children are offered opportunities to express themselves in ways that are meaningful to themselves. Researchers can gain valuable insights into young children's capabilities, ultimately providing a tool to enable positive practice in the context of gaining ethical consent.

☐ Conclusions and summary

In conclusion, it is evident and rather encouraging that there are neither definitive methods nor stringent guidelines on 'how to' gain consent from young children as each is an individual in her/his own right. The emphasis here is that what is appropriate for one young child may not be so for another. The key to ensuring informed consent from both adults and young children while ensuring young children's communication of ongoing assent and dissent is to acknowledge simplicity: simplicity in terms of simply standing back, taking time to think and reflecting before taking any action. It is when this takes place that the real issues of the environment in which research takes place and communication with regard to ensuring child-centred ongoing consent emerges.

Key points to remember

At the start of a research project, in order to handle the deception issue, have you ensured the following?

• Children's participation

• Parents' permission

- Early Years settings management permission

- Voluntary informed participants

- Right to withdraw (the basic right of participants in a research project to end their involvement at any point)

- Debriefing

- Provision of information about the research

- Attempts to reduce any distress that may have been caused by the research

- Confidentiality

- Protection from harm

- Consent

- Privacy

- Knowledge of results

- Beneficial treatment.

When involving young children in research, it is essential to ask the following questions:

Have the participants given their consent?

- Have the participants been informed about the true nature of the study? If no, then ask: is this justifiable?

- Have you explained that all details about the participants will remain confidential?

- Will all of the participants have the right to withdraw from the study at any time, without having to justify their actions?

- Have the participants been informed that they will be debriefed at the end of the study, their role fully explained and an opportunity given to see the completed study?

- Have the participants been protected from any psychological, emotional, social and physical distress?

Points for discussion and reflection

1. How do you evaluate the participation of children with regard to key policies and initiatives that have an impact upon their lives?
2. The importance of listening to young children has been emphasised throughout this chapter. How can you ensure that children have a voice when gaining ethical permission for research?
3. The UNCRC (UN, 1998) has changed our perspectives on children's voices. How do you rate children's involvement in the UNCRC?

Further reading

Farrell, A. (2005) *Ethical Research with Children*. Maidenhead: Open University Press.
Harcourt, D., Perry, B. & Waller, T. (2011) *Researching Young Children's Perspectives: Debating the Ethics and Dilemmas of Educational Research with Children*. London: Sage.
Kellet, M. (2010) *Rethinking Children and Research: Attitudes in Contemporary Society*. London: Continuum.

Useful websites

British Education Research Association ethics code: http://www.bera.ac.uk/system/files/3/BERA-Ethical-Guidelines-2011.pdf
British Psychological Society ethics code: http://www.bps.org.uk/what-we-do/ethics-standards/ethics-standards
United Nations Convention on the Rights of the Child: http://www.unicef.org/crc/

References

Ainsworth, M. (1967) *Infancy in Uganda*. Baltimore, MD: Johns Hopkins.
Ainsworth, M. (1979) 'Infant–mother attachment', *American Psychologist*, 34(10): 932–7.
Ainsworth, M. & Bowlby, J. (1965) *Child Care and the Growth of Love*. London: Penguin Books.
Ainsworth, M., Blehar, M., Waters, E. & Wall, S. (1978) *Patterns of Attachment*. Hillsdale, NJ: Erlbaum.
Alderson, P. (1995) *Listening to Children: Children Ethics and Social Research*. Barkingside: Barnardos.
Bruce, T. (2009) *Early Childhood* (2nd edn). London: Sage.
Christenson, P. & James, A. (2008) *Research with Children: Perspectives and Practices* (2nd edn). London: Routledge.
Clark, A. (2004) *Listening as a Way of Life*. London: National Children's Bureau.

Clark, A. & Moss, P. (2001) *Listening to Children: The Mosaic Approach*. London: National Children's Bureau, cited in Lansdown, G. (2005) *Can You Hear Me? The Right of Young Children to Participate in Decisions Affecting Them*, Working Paper 36, in Early Childhood Development. The Hague: Bernard Van Leer Foundation.

Coad, J. and Lewis, A. (2004) *Engaging Children and Young People in Research*. Literature review for the National Evaluation of the Children's Fund (NECF), London.

Collins Gem (2001) *English Dictionary* (10th edn). London: HarperCollins.

Crawford, K. (2006) *Social Work and Human Development*. Exeter: Learning Matters.

Dennis, W. & Dennis, M.G. (1941) *Infant Development Under Conditions of Restricted Practice and of Minimum Social Stimulation*, Genetic Psychology Monographs Vol. 23.

Department for Children Schools and Families (DCSF) (2007) *The Children's Plan: Building Brighter Futures*. Norwich: TSO.

Department for Children Schools and Families (DCSF) (2009) *Working Together: Listening to the Voices of Children and Young People*. Teacher net downloadable publications at: http://www.teachernet.gov.uk/publications.

Department for Education and Employment & Schools Curriculum and Assessment Authority (DfEE & SCAA) (1996) *Desirable Outcomes for Children's Learning on Entering Compulsory Education*. London: DfEE & SCAA.

Department for Education and Skills (DfES) (2001) *Learning to Listen: Core Principles for the Involvement of Children and Young People*. Nottingham: DfES.

Department for Education and Skills (DfES) (2002) *Birth to Three Matters: A Framework to Support Children in Their Earliest Years*. London: DfES.

Department for Education and Skills (DfES) (2004) *Working Together Giving Children and Young People Say*. London: HMSO.

Department for Education and Skills (DfES) (2007a) *Every Child Matters: Change for Children*. London: HMSO.

Department for Education and Skills (DfES) (2007b) *Statutory Framework for the Early Years Foundation Stage: Setting the Standards for Learning, Development and Care for Children from Birth to Five*. Nottingham: DfES.

Department of Education and Science (DES) (1967) *Children and Their Primary Schools: A Report of the Central Advisory Council for Education (England)*, Vol. 1. London: HMSO.

Department of Health (DoH) (1999) *Convention on the Rights of the Child*, Second Report to the UN Committee on the Rights of the Child by the United Kingdom Executive Summary. London: TSO.

Elfer, P., Goldschmied, H. & Selleck, D. (2003) *Key Person in the Nursery: Building Relationships for Quality Provision*. London: David Fulton.

Gessell, A. (1932) 'The developmental morphology of infant behaviour patterns', *Proceedings of the National Academy of Sciences*, 18(2) 139–43.

Greig, A., Taylor, J. & Mackay, T. (2007) *Doing Research with Children*, 2nd edn. London: Sage.

Harris, B. (1979) 'Whatever happened to Little Albert?', *American Psychologist*, 34(2): 151–60.

Hart, R.A. (1997) *Children's Participation. The Theory and Practice of Involving Young Citizens in Community Development and Environmental Care*. London: Earthscan.

Jarvis, M. & Chandler, E. (2001) *Angles on Psychology*. Cheltenham: Nelson Thornes.

Keenan, T. & Evans, S. (2009) *An Introduction to Child Development* (2nd edn). London: Sage.

Kellett, M. (2005) *How to Develop Children as Researchers*. London: Sage.

Lansdown, G. (2005) *Can You Hear Me? The Right of Young Children to Participate in Decisions Affecting Them*, Working Paper 36, in Early Childhood Development. The Hague: Bernard Van Leer Foundation.

Lindon, J., Kelman, K. & Sharp, A. (2001) *Play and Learning for the Under 3's*. London: TSL Education.

Morrow, V. & Richards, M. (1996) 'The ethics of social research with children: an overview', *Children and Society*, 10: 90–105.

Nutbrown, C. (1996) *Respectful Educators Capable Learners: Children's Rights and Early Education*. London: Paul Chapman.

United Nations (1989) *The Convention on the Rights of the Child*. Geneva: Defense International and the United Nations Children's Fund.

Valentine, G. (1999) 'Being seen and heard? The ethical complexities of working with children and young people at home and at school', *Ethics in Place and Environment*, 2(2): 141–55.

Watson, J.B. & Rayner, R. (1920) 'Conditioned emotional relations', *Journal of Experimental Psychology*, 3(1): 1–14.

2

Ethical Praxis When Choosing Research Tools for Use with Children Under Five

Ioanna Palaiologou

Chapter overview

This chapter explores the ethical challenges faced by researchers when choosing research tools applied with young children. The ethical practice or praxis, as it will be referred in this chapter, of conducting research with young children will be discussed in order to shed light on the research tools that may be used with children under the age of five. The chapter is based on the belief that children, just as adults, are individuals with their own views and perspectives; they have competencies and they are able to speak for themselves if the appropriate method(s) is/are used. It also discusses the ethical challenges faced by the researcher in being able to separate what is based on experience from what is based on assumptions, both without dismissing or interpreting erroneously what the child is saying.

Introduction

Chapter 1 focused on key areas of child participation in research; it also discussed the historical developments in terms of children's participation. It is evident from the vast body of literature, policy and implementation of practice, as will be explored in the second part of this book, that recent discussions on children's views and voices have increased. In the current literature (Alderson, 2000, 2004; Clark, 2005a, 2005b; Dockett & Perry, 2003, 2005; Farrell, 2005; Christensen & James, 2008; Harcourt et al., 2011) much work has been conducted into children's participation and issues of power with regard to the children's voice in participation in research.

As mentioned in Chapter 1, the United Nations Convention on the Rights of the Child (UNCRC) and, in particular, Article 12 of the Convention states that all state parties should ensure that a child who is capable of forming his/her own view should have the right to express these views freely on all matters affecting the child and those views should be given weight in accordance with age and maturity (UN, 1989). The publication of the UNCRC in 1989 caused a number of countries that ratified the convention to re-examine their policies and practices on key provisions for children. While it recognises that the family is the best or natural environment for a child to grow up in and places responsibilities on parents to provide a loving, nurturing environment, it also places a primary obligation on the state to protect children from all forms of abuse, neglect and exploitation and to actively promote these provisions. These key provisions are related to survival or subsistence rights such as clean water and food, developmental rights such as health, rights to protection from harm and child labour and, finally, participation rights so that children are themselves to have a voice in decisions involving them. There is a criticism of the UNCRC about children's participation in the writing of the rights, such as the fact that the language used is inaccessible to young children, it imposes Western views and it takes little account of other cultures or religion beyond the Western thinking of childhood (Raman, 2000; Willow, 2002; Alderson, 2008). Nevertheless, it is important to emphasise that:

> Participation is the keystone of the arch that is the UNCRC. Without the active participation of children and young people in the promotion of their rights to a good childhood, none will be achieved effectively. (Badham, quoted in Willow, 2002: vi)

In an era where children's participation in all aspects of their lives is considered, a number of researchers (see Evans & Fuller, 1996; Clark & Moss, 2001; Einarsdottir, 2003, 2005) have changed the way children are viewed in research. These studies attempt to incorporate the participation of children into research, and have examined a number of innovative ways in which children can be involved in research.

They have concluded that children should not be viewed as objects (research on children); rather, that children should be viewed as subjects (participatory-research with children). From developments at the policy level and findings from current research a new construction of childhood has emerged. Children are now viewed as social actors in their cultural, religious and ethnic groups, with the capacity to think, reason and actively construct knowledge through their own actions and explorations (Clark & Moss, 2001; Christensen & James, 2008).

Consequently there is a methodological shift in choosing research methods when children are involved in the research. The emphasis now is on 'commitment to conducting research with children, rather than on children or without them or about them' (O'Kane, 2008: 125). Consideration and emphasis should be given to ethical practice when the research participants are children. A number of methods used widely within research were designed *by* adults *for* adult participants. Therefore, when choosing methods for research with children, it is important that these methods may be relayed at the level of communication appropriate for children. As Thomas & O'Kane (1998a, 1998b) stress in the context of conducting research with children there are a number of challenges and ethical implications because of differences in children's experiences, as well as the ways in which children communicate and understand the world. One of the key challenges for any researcher is to consider and take account of children's views on the one hand and the requirements of the rigour of the research on the other.

Thus this chapter will discuss the ethical practice (praxis) of choosing research tools with children under five; it will then explore the methods widely used when children are participating in research.

Ethical Praxis When Choosing Research Tools with Young Children

There is a wide range of research tools to use when researching young children (Coady, 2001; Clark & Moss, 2001; Clark, 2005a, 2005b; Thomson, 2008; Farrell, 2005). The focus of this chapter is on the ethical issues and practice underpinning the research project. It is important to state that ethics praxis is not meant to become a framework for choosing research methods with children under five. Framing research methods with young children is fragmented; it does not necessarily combine effectively the causality of the research enquiry and methods, the collection of data and the findings. Instead, what is proposed here is an attempt to address the ethical issues of a particular set of problems around research methods with the under fives.

It is suggested that ethical praxis in research is concerned with the scope of responsible judgement on the part of the researcher to reflect on deeper questions concerning the nature of the research. In that sense, all methods become relevant and ethical with regard to research with children – there are no 'good' or 'right' methods. Ethical practice in research then is not about the methods but about when the nature of the research not only is concerned with the benefits (to the individuals and society at large), but also addresses how the methods that are employed are clarified and purified and also how knowledge and deeper understanding of children's lives, development and pedagogy are acquired. These issues are not external matters: they are intrinsic to any research method chosen.

On this basis, ethical praxis is concerned with the exercise of logic, moral judgement and sensitivity to the contexts of children's lives, involving the latter's culture, religion, social values and economic and political situation. Thus the researcher should firstly develop a full understanding of the nature of the projects and methods under the lens of a set of principles orienting the ethical praxis.

At the outset, researchers should consider the principle of *indivisibility*. This is because in the nature of the construction of knowledge, indivisibility is concerned not only with the nature of knowledge and understanding that is about to be acquired from the research, but also whether the process of acquiring this new knowledge or understanding may violate children's dignity, rights and privacy.

Chapter 1 contained an example in which the study of attachment by Mary Ainsworth was discussed. As mentioned, the experiments on attachment led to children crying when their mother left the room and were thus in a stressful situation also connected with their fear of a stranger. There is no doubt that Ainsworth's experiments into attachment have furthered our understanding and knowledge in terms of the bonding of children with their carers, despite the questionable ethics of the practices employed.

In 2000 BBC launched the series *Children of Our Time*, part of a longitudinal study of children's lives. In this series a number of issues around children's development were examined. The second episode of the series made an attempt to examine the nature and quality of attachment between mothers and their children. The producers of the programme used Ainsworth's experimentation into attachment; as can be seen in this series, the children are obviously distressed under the conditions of the experiment. One needs to question exactly what the reconstruction of the experiment has added to the body of knowledge, and how certain rights of children such as privacy and dignity were violated. It could be claimed that the parents gave their ethical consent; however, when watching this episode, the children's willingness to participate in the process is not made obvious.

The fact that the experiment has added no new knowledge to what is already known about attachment nor has it furthered our understanding of this phenomenon calls the ethics of the experiment into question. The children were put under conditions that caused them distress. At this moment the exercise of logical, reasonable judgement was sacrificed only to create a television series that violated these children's dignity and privacy.

Secondly, the necessity for the research, the purposes of the research, the sensitivity to contexts and how the resulting information is shared need to be considered. Enquiry that involves children should establish a sustained practice of asking questions about a set of problems or practice with progressively refined methods of approach. In forms of enquiry central to early childhood research it is necessary to incorporate questions about development pedagogy, to question the nature of the benefits to be achieved by the research project – and also to examine decent methods on which to base the enquiry. In other words, the acquisition of knowledge through rigorous research forms the internal element of the tools applied in the research.

Moreover, the prerequisite underpinning of the achievement of objectivity in the choice of research methods can be secured only by admitting the limitations of objectivity. The term 'objectivity' is a myth and is profoundly misleading to the researcher. '[O]bjectivity that characterises academic study resides precisely in the responsible exercise of judgement' (Standish, 2008: 168).

For example, to claim that participant observation is the only tool with which to research young children under five can be the product only of adult-oriented judgement. The data collected will require interpretation against what has been recorded. Part of ethical practice in that sense is the exercise of good judgement, which seeks trustworthiness within communities of practice that characterise the subject of an enquiry. It is in such a context that objectivity is relative; the researcher should seek reasoning rather than objectivity. Reasoning is not achieved in isolation as it cannot be divorced from the context. The search for reasoning is internal to the community in which the enquiry is researching and also how it is researched, i.e. the methods applied.

Inevitably, the necessity for research should be underpinned by an enquiry with a clear understanding, reflection and the development of practical reasoning. The Aristotelian term *phronesis*, the virtue of practical thought, may become the second principle of ethical praxis. In research with children under five, it is suggested that there are three key elements to achieving phronesis: the necessity for research, the exercise of decent judgement and respect for the communities of practice, which should be based on dialogue among participants within the subject of the enquiry.

The third principle suggested here is *parsimony*. When conducting research with young children researchers should always seek the simplest methods, research tools and explanations when the data are analysed. This is a way of ensuring that children are involved actively in the process of the research and that they understand both the nature of the enquiry and its methods. Parsimony goes beyond the traditional means of consent since it is a practical way of consulting children in the research and also of reconfirming the subject children's participation in the research.

Throughout this book the concept of children's participation will be explored from a number of different perspectives. What is claimed here is that central to listening to children's voices should be the constant attempt actually to listen to what children say, not listening from an adult-oriented, possibly biased approach. Seeking and applying simplified methods, research tools and explanations of data constitute a way in which children may become involved and the resulting data may be shared with children. There are, therefore, elements towards achieving parsimony in research: firstly, sharing information at the appropriate level and where the children's age permits; secondly, understanding that children might prefer different methods from the ones on offer; and thirdly, that achieving problem-solving and deciding the choice of methods with the children will lead to the evolution of a new, common understanding.

This leads us to the fourth key principle in choosing research tools for research with young children under five: *equilibrium*. Achieving balance among research tools, evidence-based research and children's participation is a challenging and complex process. On the one hand, in terms of collecting data, as well as in terms of the findings, the research needs to be valid, reliable and trustworthy; on the other hand, the researcher has an ethical obligation to ensure that children are actively involved throughout the process. Research with very young children, especially babies and toddlers who as yet lack the development of language, makes it difficult or almost impossible for children to evaluate for themselves what participation in the research will mean for them. For those reasons it is essential for the researcher to look at other aspects such as the children's emotional reactions and should seek the opinions of carers or parents who know their children and their reactions very well. It is central to any research with children to explain the research in language appropriate to their level of understanding; where this is lacking or limited, the emotional reactions of children when certain methods are used must be considered. It is therefore essential to decide from the beginning of the research the level of input from the children and their parents or carers. Secondly, researchers should reason from the perspective of the key elements of the children's emotions and actions, especially when conducting research with very young children (under three years of age) and babies.

Chapter 1 discussed the research of Watson & Rayner (1920) on Little Albert (classical conditioning). In the original paper Watson & Rayner stated:

> During the course of these experiments, especially in the final test, it was noticed that whenever Albert was on the verge of tears or emotionally upset he would continually thrust his thumb into his mouth. The moment the hand reached the mouth he became impervious to the stimuli producing fear. Again and again while the motion pictures were being made at the end of the thirty-day rest period, we had to remove the thumb from his mouth before the conditioning response could be obtained. (1920: 13)

In their study Watson & Rayner found that every time Little Albert was anxious he sucked his thumb in response to disturbing stimuli. Their study has furthered our understanding of anxiety and other mental health conditions (Carey, 2011). Although this experiment has contributed greatly to the understanding of children's anxieties, throughout this experimentation Little Albert became distressed and anxious; it was obvious that his crying was the behaviour of non-participation. It is therefore argued that, in this experiment, neither the ethical principles of the development of practical reason and exercise of responsible judgement justified by actions (phronesis), nor reasoning from this child's emotional reactions (equilibrium), were taken into account.

Finally, the researcher needs to consider the *power of the relationship and interactions* between participants and researchers (Coyne, 1998; Balen et al., 2001; Flewitt, 2005). Children are likely to see adults as the authority figures because they are the ones who create their environment, set the rules, organise their daily programme and are responsible for the children. There is always a risk of potential conflict between the adults' duty of care and protection and the children's participation. In some cases what children want is not necessarily in the best interests of the children in terms of protection. Thus there is always a dilemma in children's participation given the children's view of adults: that adults are always the ones with the power. It cannot be ignored, either, that children might through their responses or interactions try to please adults. It is important to consider the cultural differences, as some children from certain cultural backgrounds are not used to being asked for their participation (for more on this, see Chapter 5).

To conclude: a researcher must not become lost in the abstract and complex argumentation that accompanies children's rights and voices. This chapter suggests there should be a shift from the discussion of what constitutes the best methods and instead focuses on the ethical aspects of research with young children. The methods are relevant to the purpose of the research only if they meet the principles of ethical practice. In this chapter, the use of the principles of ethical praxis as the sole framework for research is not suggested. The notion of a conceptual framing of research with young children limits, as mentioned above, the creativity and innovation of methods to be used with young children. Instead, ethical praxis when choosing research methods with young children introduces into research a set of necessary connections, whereas the methods are solely concerned with providing factual data. At the same time, children's actions, emotions, dignity, privacy, autonomy and freedom to have opinions on all matters affecting them should be respected and be given due weight. The choice of research tools with young children should be interrelated by causality among the research enquiry, methods, collection of data and analysis of the findings.

Research Tools to Use with Children Under Five

There is a wealth of research tools that researchers may apply in conducting research with children in order to gain an understanding of children's lives, views, development and education. Research with children, especially the very young, should be creative in terms of the methods used and in ways appropriate to children's age and context. A variety of methods, rather than one method, usually offers rich data and information about children's lives and views. It should also be recognised that if the researcher wants children actively to participate in research, children (like adults) have different ways of communicating; therefore, it might be preferable to use a range of methods that extend beyond observable data. Jipson & Jipson (2005), Kjørholt (2005) and Kjørholt et al. (2005) have demonstrated that a key element of children's participation is the critical examination of the social conditions created for children by adults. For example, a child in an interview context might say that s/he does or does not prefer a certain activity, yet observations might show the opposite. It is important to recognise that children's perspectives, feelings and views can change over the interview time depending on the environment, on changes in their feelings and on their social contexts, such as peer interaction, at the time the method is used. The methods used with children should be suitable and comply with ethical practice.

Narrative Methods

To begin with the narrative methods, these may be observations (unstructured, or self-observations with the use of media), interviews (individual or group interviews), children's stories, drawings, role-play and digital media. The researcher may interview the children or the children may interview other children, create stories, make drawings, take photos or use cameras then talk about these, depending on their age. It is important to recognise and emphasise that when children are placed in a position to use these methods, the researcher does not seek to analyse the product of their data collection, for example the story or the drawing; the researcher needs only to listen to the children when they use these methods and give their interpretations of their stories, their drawings or their photographs. What children 'tell' during their participation has greater significance than the researcher's attempt to interpret a child's actions.

In such situations authentic participation is when children decide the subject and what they wish to tell. That implies children who indeed have a use of language, whereas with babies and toddlers in whom language is not yet sufficiently developed the emotions and the researcher's sensitivity towards them must be taken into account. However, research with children requires a firm foundation of reflection on theory and practice; it also requires an openness to change – and to surprises. The (adult-oriented) assumption that children express their voices and participate by being asked to use certain methods such as role-play, painting, observations or storytelling is based on the view that these are activities in which children engage, enjoy and are able to deliver. However, certain children prefer to engage through other types of activities or methods (Dockett et al., 2011). There is also an assumption that children use language at a level at which they mean what they say. Thus narrative methods have hidden pitfalls because of the particular uses of language and this requires adults and children to communicate with clarity and describe the forms of their actions.

Quantifying Methods

Although not a commonly used approach with young children, quantifying is an assumption that excludes children from active participation; nevertheless, quantifying is a valid tool as it offers rich data and may be used with children in the form of a game. It is an important tool when used in combination with narrative methods. The methods involve structured observations, such as event sampling, time sampling, questionnaires or even surveys, all in the form of a game. The methods offer an in-depth understanding of children's preferences at that given time and help the collection of data on frequencies.

 Case study

How Young Children Construct the Concept of Danger: The Use of a Pictographic Questionnaire

In this project the aim was to gain an understanding of how young children in the age group between two and four years old construct the concept of danger. The initial investigation was to gain an understanding of which areas children consider as a danger to them; the next stage was to investigate children's understanding of the level of danger of each area. In an attempt to involve children in this questionnaire, Table 2.1 was designed in the form of a pictographic representation, i.e. a semiotic system was employed. Different age groups were asked to respond as shown in the table.

Table 2.1 Sample of a pictographic questionnaire

Area			Level	Response
🍽	Meal time	☺ 😐 ☹ ⛑	None Sometimes Hurts Needs nurse	
✂	Playing with scissors	☺ 😐 ☹ ⛑	None Sometimes Hurts Needs nurse	
🔌	Electricity	☺ 😐 ☹ ⛑	None Sometimes Hurts Needs nurse	
⛺	Outdoors	☺ 😐 ☹ ⛑	None Sometimes Hurts Needs nurse	
🚓	Cars	☺ 😐 ☹ ⛑	None Sometimes Hurts Needs nurse	
🐕	Animals	☺ 😐 ☹ ⛑	None Sometimes Hurts Needs nurse	
🔧	Tools	☺ 😐 ☹ ⛑	None Sometimes Hurts Needs nurse	

By actively completing this pictographic questionnaire the children were using a method of data-gathering. The younger group (aged 2–3) completed the questionnaire with the help of the researcher, while the older group (aged 3–4) discussed it among themselves and completed it on their own.

The pictographic questionnaire was not used outside of the children's daily routine: the data were collected during the children's daily activities.

Conclusions and summary

A vast body of literature (Clark, 2004; Clark & Moss, 2001, 2005; Thompson, 2008; Farrell, 2005) discusses methods to be used with young children in research. In the light of the UNCRC (1989) and in an attempt to meet the key provisions of the UNCRC in terms of developmental rights, survival rights, protection rights and participation rights, there is a methodological shift in the research in terms of children's protection and participation in research. A number of researchers mentioned throughout the chapter have offered creative and innovative research tools that enable young children to participate in research. This chapter was developed around the principle that all tools are relevant in research with young children if these tools are underpinned by ethical practice. It has been claimed that ethical praxis is the exercise of logic, clear judgement and sensitivity to children's social, cultural, religious, economic and political contexts. In order to achieve the full participation of children in research, ethical practices are internal rather than external processes into researching the tools chosen. Thus all methods become appropriate if the nature of the research enquiry has been viewed as a series of problems for which resolutions have been found.

Key points to remember

• All methods become relevant to research with children and are appropriate when ethical practice characterises the nature of the project.

• Ethical praxis revolves around the key principles of indivisibility, phronesis, parsimony, equilibrium and, finally, the power of relationships and interaction between children and adults.

- Methods to be used with young children should be determined by the children's age, context and feelings. More than one method should be employed to collect data, as different children have different ways and prefer different methods of communicating.

Points for discussion and reflection

1. Ask yourself what is more important, the rights of the individual participant or the benefits that research may bring to the majority?
2. The human participants – and particularly children – are in a rather vulnerable and potentially exploitative situation. How can you make sure that children are protected at all times during your research project?
3. Ethical problems may occur while participants are actually taking part in research, so how are you going to use data in a way that is ethical?

Further reading

Christensen, P. & James, A. (2008) *Research with Children: Perspectives and Practices* (2nd edn). London: Routledge.

Harcourt, D., Perry, B. & Waller, T. (2011) *Researching Young Children's Perspectives: Debating the Ethics and Dilemmas of Education Research with Children*. London: Routledge.

Kellet, M. (2010) *Rethinking Children and Research: Attitudes in Contemporary Society*. London: Continuum.

References

Alderson, P. (2000) 'Children as researchers: the effect of participation rights on research methodology', in P. Christensen & A. James (eds), *Research with Children*. New York: Falmer Press.

Alderson, P. (2004) 'Ethics', in S. Fraser, V. Lewis, S. Ding, M. Kellet and C. Robinson (eds), *Doing Research with Children and Young People*. London: Sage.

Alderson, P. (2008) *Young Children's Rights Exploring Beliefs, Principles and Practice*. London: Jessica Kingsley.

Balen , R., Hlroyd, C., Mountain, G. & Wood, B. (2001) 'Giving children a voice: methodological and practical implications of research involving children', *Pediatric Nursing*, 12(10): 24–9.

Carey, T. (2011) 'Little Albert – were we all duped?', *The Psychologists*, 24(10): 712.

Christensen, P. & James, A. (2008) *Research with Children: Perspectives and Practices* (2nd edn). London: Routledge.

Clark, A. (2004) *Listening as a Way of Life*. London: National Children's Bureau.

Clark, A. (2005a) 'Listening to and involving young children: a review of research in practice', in A. Clark, A.T. Kjørholt & P. Moss (eds), *Beyond Listening to Children on Early Childhood Services*. Bristol: Policy Press.

Clark, A. (2005b) 'Listening to and involving young children: a review of research and practice', *Early Child Development and Care*, 175(6): 489–505.

Clark, A. & Moss, P. (2001) *Listening to Young Children: The Mosaic Approach*. London: National Children's Bureau.

Clark, A. & Moss, P. (2005) *Spaces to Play: More Listening to Young Children Using the Mosaic Approach*. London: National Children's Bureau.

Clark, A., Kjørholt, A.T. & Moss, P. (eds) (2005) *Beyond Listening to Children on Early Childhood Services*. Bristol: Policy Press.

Coady, M.M. (2001) 'Ethics in early childhood research', in G.M. Naughton, S.A. Rolfe & I. Siraj-Blatchford (eds), *Doing Early Childhood Research: International Perspectives on Theory and Practice*. Buckingham: Open University Press.

Coyne, I.T. (1998) 'Researching children: some methodological and ethical considerations', *Journal of Clinical Nursing*, 7: 409–16.

Dockett, S. & Perry, B. (2003) *Children's Voices in Research on Starting School*. Paper presented at the Annual Conference of the European Early Childhood Education Research Association, Glasgow, September.

Dockett, S. & Perry, B. (2005) 'Researching with children: insight from the starting school research project', *Early Child Development and Care*, 175(6): 507–22.

Dockett, S., Einarsdottir, J. & Perry, B. (2011) 'Balancing methodologies and methods in researching with young children', in D. Harcourt, B. Perry & T. Waller (eds), *Researching Young Children's Perspectives: Debating the Ethics and Dilemmas of Education Research with Children*. London: Routledge.

Einarsdottir, J. (2003) 'When the bell rings we have to go inside: preschool children's views on the primary school', *European Early Childhood Educational Research Journal: Transitions*, Themed Monograph Series 1, pp. 35–50.

Einarsdottir, J. (2005) 'Play school in pictures: children's photographs as a research method', *Early Childhood Development and Care*, 175(6): 523–41.

Einarsdottir, J. (2007) 'Research with children: methodological and ethical challenges', *European Early Childhood Research Journal*, 15(2): 197–211.

Evans, P. & Fuller, M. (1996) 'Hello. Who am I speaking to? Communicating with pre-school children in educational research settings', *Early Years*, 17(1): 17–20.

Farrell, A. (ed.) (2005) *Ethical Research with Children*. Maidenhead: Open University Press.

Flewitt, R. (2005) 'Conducting research with young children: some ethical considerations', *Early Child Development and Care*, 175(6): 553–66.

Harcourt, D., Perry, B. & Waller, T. (2011) *Researching Young Children's Perspectives: Debating the Ethics and Dilemmas of Education Research with Children*. London: Routledge.

Jipson, J. & Jipson, J. (2005) 'Confidence intervals: doing research with young children', in L.D. Soto & B.B. Swander (eds), *Power and Voice in Research with Children*. New York: Peter Lang.

Kellet, M. (2010) *Rethinking Children and Research: Attitudes in Contemporary Society*. London: Continuum.

Kjøholt, A.T. (2005) 'The competent child and the right to be oneself: reflections on children as fellow citizens in an early childhood centre', in A. Clark, A.T. Kjørholt & P. Moss (eds), *Beyond Listening to Children on Early Childhood Services*. Bristol: Policy Press.

Kjørholt, A.T., Moss, P. & Clark, A. (2005) 'Beyond listening: future perspectives', in A. Clark, A.T. Kjørholt & P. Moss (eds), *Beyond Listening to Children on Early Childhood Services*. Bristol: Policy Press.

O'Kane, C. (2008) 'The development of participatory techniques: facilitating children's views about decisions which affect them', in P. Christensen & A. James (eds), *Research with Children: Perspectives and Practices* (2nd edn). London: Routledge.

Raman, V. (2000) 'Politics of childhood: perspectives from the South', *Economic and Political Weekly*, 11 November, pp. 4055–64.

Standish, P. (2007) 'Rival conceptions of the philosophy of education', *Ethics and Education*, 2(2): 159–71.

Thomas, N. & O'Kane, C. (1998a) *Children and Decision-Making: A Summary Report*. International Centre for Childhood Studies, University of Wales, Swansea.

Thomas, N. & O'Kane, C. (1998b) 'The ethics of participatory research in middle childhood: the example of children "looked after" by local authorities', *Childhood*, 6(3): 369–87.

Thomson, P. (2008) *Doing Visual Research with Children and Young People*. Oxford: Routledge.

United Nations (1989) *The Convention on the Rights of the Child*. Geneva: Defense International and the United Nations Children's Fund.

Watson, J.B. & Rayner, R. (1920) 'Conditioned emotional relations', *Journal of Experimental Psychology*, 3(1): 1–14.

Willow, C. (2002) *Participation in Practice: Children and Young People as Partners in Change*. London: Save the Children.

3

Ethics in Researching Children with Special Educational Needs

Cheryl Ellis and Gary Beauchamp

Chapter overview

This chapter will explore how undertaking research with young children with special educational needs (SEN) can create challenges requiring creative responses sensitive to the needs of the participants within a specific research context. It will argue that gaining consent is a complex issue; in order to promote inclusion and participation at all levels, the right of the child to be a partner in the process is the central consideration.

This chapter will examine how to empower children with SEN through the use of relevant research tools (for example, using photographs to share thoughts through both verbal and non-verbal responses) that allow children a 'voice' within the research process. It will consider the challenges of interpreting a wide range of responses, both verbal and non-verbal, which reflect the diversity of individual differences for children with SEN. In particular, the issues surrounding the collection and interpretation of data will be examined. The discussion is set within the context of a consideration of power relationships in which the need to gain the trust of children and their carers, and to develop a detailed awareness of their unique circumstances, is balanced against the need to remain objective as a researcher.

Introduction

The key principle of this chapter is that all young children, regardless of their perceived stage of development or 'ability', should be a 'participant' in, rather than a 'subject of', research. While working with young children who have cognitive, physical, communicative or emotional difficulties can make the research process more challenging, the same rights and responsibilities between the participant and the researcher should apply as those pertaining to any other research project involving children. Each participant should therefore take an active, willing and engaging role in the research process (Doyle, 2007). As the Department of Health (1991: 14) states: 'Even children with severe learning disabilities or very limited expressive language can communicate preference if they are asked in the right way by people who understand their needs and have the relevant skills to listen.' The fundamental issues when carrying out research with young children with SEN focus upon: how well the child understands what is being communicated, how able s/he is to process this information and how well s/he can express her or his own views. A further compounding factor is how well the researcher can understand (or interpret) what the child is communicating. There is a danger that attempts by the participant to communicate may not be recognised or may be misinterpreted by the researcher. It is very important, therefore, to understand the capabilities of each individual for communication and to provide the relevant mechanisms to enable effective communication to take place. A key element of the research process with young children with SEN is that time will need to be spent to get to know the individual and how s/he communicates her/his thoughts, feelings and opinions. Research into young children with more severe forms of SEN has been a somewhat neglected area, possibly due to the challenges presented within the research process. Nevertheless, young children with SEN are 'experts on their own lives'; there thus remains a duty for researchers to 'give voice to the voiceless' (Visweswaren, 1994, cited in Thomson, 2008: 3) so that the thoughts, feelings and opinions of this vulnerable population can be heard.

Before exploring this process in greater detail, it is necessary briefly to examine definitions of SEN and how these may affect children's ability to participate in the research process.

Definitions of SEN

The Special Educational Needs Code of Practice (DfES, 2001: 6) provides a definition of SEN and key terms that form the basis of discussion in the remainder of this chapter. The list is reproduced in full (below) due to its centrality to the rest of the chapter. The special position of very young children in this should be noted:

> Children have special educational needs if they have a learning difficulty that calls for special educational provision to be made for them.
>
> Children have a learning difficulty if they:
>
> a. Have a significantly greater difficulty in learning than the majority of children of the same age;
>
> b. Have a disability which prevents or hinders them from making use of educational facilities of a kind generally provided for children of the same age in schools within the area of the local education authority;
>
> c. Are under compulsory school age and fall within the definition at (a) or (b) above or would so do if special educational provision were not made for them;
>
> Children must not be regarded as having a learning difficulty solely because the language or form of language of their home is different from the language in which they will be taught.
>
> Special educational provision means:
>
> a. For children aged two or over, educational provision which is additional to, or otherwise different from, the educational provision made generally for children of their age in schools maintained by the LEA, other than special schools, in the area;
>
> b. For children under two, educational provision of any kind.
>
> (See Section 312, Education Act 1996)

Definitions in the Children Act 1989 and the Disability Discrimination Act 1995

A child is disabled if he is blind, deaf or dumb or suffers from a mental disorder of any kind or is substantially and permanently handicapped by illness, injury or congenital deformity or such other disability as may be prescribed. (Section 17 (11), Children Act 1989)

A person has a disability for the purposes of this Act if he has a physical or mental impairment which has a substantial and long-term adverse effect on his ability to carry out normal day-to day activities. (Section 1 (1), Disability Discrimination Act 1995)

It is important to note that these categories are not mutually exclusive and that a young child may fall into more than one, depending on the complexity of their respective needs. In addition, the level and type of severity should be considered. Broad categories of learning difficulties include:

1. Specific

2. Moderate

3. Severe

4. Profound

5. Multiple.

Given the complex nature of SENs within these categories, it may be helpful when planning research to attempt to group such needs in order to assess the different ethical dilemmas with each. One example is that provided by the Department of Education Northern Ireland (DENI) (1998):

• Learning difficulties

• Specific learning difficulties (for example, dyslexia)

• Emotional and behavioural difficulties (EBD)

• Physical disabilities

• Sensory impairments: hearing difficulties

• Sensory impairments: visual difficulties

• Speech and language difficulties

• Medical conditions.

The particular needs of each group will vary, yet with young children in all of these groups there will be a need to involve others close to them in the research process. The remainder of this chapter will consider how young children with SENs, and those close to them, can be involved in gaining consent, gathering data and then interpreting and reporting these data.

Informed Consent

The challenges surrounding the gaining of fully informed consent (British Educational Research Association (BERA), 2004) from young children for them to be involved in research activities needs further consideration of the context concerning young children with SENs. An already complex process is further complicated when working with young children who have cognitive, physical, communicative or emotional difficulties as these difficulties may affect the ability of young children to understand what the research is about and their role within the research process. Unless the researcher is totally committed to involving the child in this process, whatever the latter's particular needs, there is a danger that only 'lip service' will be paid to the process of gaining informed consent from them. As Morrow (n.d.: 11) asserts, researchers need to respect children's competencies and 'respect needs to become a methodological technique in itself'. This is particularly true when researching in conjunction with young children with SENs.

With such respect in place, the ultimate aim would be to gain the explicit informed *consent* of each young child, who states that wherever possible s/he agrees to participate; this is in addition to the consent given by their parents or carers. If this is not possible, perhaps due to severe communication difficulties, it is necessary to gain the informed *assent* of the children involved. In this context Murray (2011) defines 'assent' as proactive affirmative agreement from the participant(s) and in that case from the child, and 'informed consent' as the approval of the competent child or of the legal representative of the child. The decision-making process regarding how a child may be judged 'competent' is central to this discussion. Although at one level there may appear to be little difference between consent and assent, as both are indicating agreement to participate, Murray (2011: 96) suggests that 'denying the child what is the adult's [right] denies the child full participation.' The sequence in which consent and assent happen should be considered carefully. In most cases it would be appropriate for assent to be a process parallel to that of consent; however, with young children with SENs, it may be better to ensure that parents or carers have been involved at an earlier stage to help in communication, as is discussed below.

In order to allow children, both with and without SEN, to make informed decisions, information concerning the aims of the project and the role of the individual will need to be communicated in an appropriate way. This may be by word of mouth, by the use of sign language and/or Braille, and by using visual images such as photographs; simple, clear vocabulary and grammar may aid this process. Some young children may find it difficult to express their consent; therefore, appropriate ways to do this should be sought. For example, a handprint in paint may represent a record of agreement to participate – although some would challenge this in itself, as there is no proof that the child understood the implications of making the handprint. In seeking to fulfil this duty, however, it must be acknowledged that in reality the type and level of severity of impairment will influence a child's ability to give informed consent and affect their ability to participate fully in the process unaided.

The gaining of informed consent must not be seen as a one-off process; instead, it should be viewed as an ongoing, two-way process using a method or methods of communication understood by the researcher, the child and any other parties involved. This will enable the participant to withdraw from the research process at any point in time if they so wish. Children with SEN may be reluctant to tell the researcher that they do not wish to answer a question or that they no longer wish to participate. Knight et al. (2006) suggest using a 'traffic light' system whereby the child will give the researcher a yellow card if s/he does not wish to answer a specific question and a red card if s/he wishes to end the session altogether – although Knight et al. stress that this should be practised before the session begins so that the child fully understands how the system will work. This type of approach can obviously be adapted to suit the age and needs of the child, while the main concern remains the need for an agreed 'signal'. The researcher also needs to be aware of any changes in body language and non-verbal cues possibly indicating that the child no longer wishes to continue. Therefore, the importance of gaining knowledge and competence in the young child's preferred ways of communicating cannot be underestimated.

In this context it is impossible to prescribe a 'correct' ethical approach to gaining consent and then collecting, interpreting and reporting data when working with young children with special educational needs. What can be suggested is a range of 'tools' that may be used (see below). However, throughout the research process, it is essential to triangulate the responses of the individual children with those persons who know them best (in educational or family settings). Parents and carers can be a valuable asset to the research process as they can 'translate' reactions, which is essential to ensuring that 'authentic responses' (BERA, 2004: 4) are obtained. If such responses are gained, they may provide a unique and specific insight into the daily lives of children with SEN, the challenges they may face and their hopes for the future.

The need for creative approaches to gaining informed consent and the role of parents and carers is evidenced by both the British and the Scottish Educational Research Associations in their Guidelines for Educational Research (BERA, 2004; SERA, 2005). Both organisations share a common statement that:

> In the case of participants whose age, intellectual capability or other vulnerable circumstances may limit the extent to which they can be expected to understand or agree voluntarily to undertake their role, researchers must fully explore alternative ways in which [these participants] can be enabled to make authentic responses. In such circumstances, researchers must also seek the collaboration and approval of those who act in guardianship (e.g. parents) or as 'responsible others' (i.e. those who have responsibility for the welfare and well-being of the participants, e.g. social workers). (BERA, 2004: 6; SERA, 2005: 6)

The British Psychological Society (BPS) guidance also requires that children be 'given ample opportunity to understand the nature, purpose, and anticipated consequences of any professional services or research participation, so that they may give informed consent to the extent that their capabilities allow' (BPS, 2009: 12). A key element for research with young children with special educational needs, as with any ethical research, is that the findings should be of direct or indirect benefit to the participants or to others in similar circumstances (Knight et al., 2006). The present chapter focuses on a variety of techniques allowing young children with SEN to use their capabilities to become active participants in ethically sound research. In order to do so, however, it is necessary to consider briefly the range of special educational needs and how these affect a young child's ability to take an active part in the process.

Gathering Data

Interpretation and Validation: The Role of Parents and Significant Others

As stated earlier, it is important to use all available means to validate and triangulate the responses of children with SENs. Given the respective nature of their difficulties, some young children are able to respond only in ways that will not be understood by someone who is not in regular contact with them, someone who understands their needs. Depending on the needs of the child, it may be that there is only one person capable of understanding and then explaining the responses a child with special needs may give. In such a scenario, these other agencies can act as 'interpreters' between the researcher and the child. This can apply in both a literal sense in terms of language (verbal and non-verbal), and also in dealing with any cultural or other considerations (such as family issues) that may affect the research process.

Perhaps the most obvious interpreter is a parent. The SEN Code of Practice (DfES, 2001: 16) is clear that 'parents hold key information and have a critical role to play in their children's education. They have unique strengths, knowledge and experience to contribute to the shared view of a child's needs and the best ways of supporting them.' Part of this unique strength will be the parents' ability to interpret the responses and level of understanding of their child. Other individuals who may offer additional valuable access and insights include carers, teachers or other professionals working for a variety of agencies, as well as others with specialist knowledge about the condition affecting the child. It is important, however, that these sources remain as unbiased as possible. There is always a danger that because of their closeness to the child, they will try and interpret responses to present the responder in the best light. In addition, as examined elsewhere in this book, they may also be working from a 'deficit model'. In such a model, the person interpreting the response of the child may make the assumption that the child is not capable of either understanding or answering a question and thus answer as they deem appropriate. This is because they see more of the child and are more familiar with the way he or she responds and they are also acting in what they perceive to be the best interests of the child. As a researcher, however, it important to consider whether you need to challenge the viewpoint of the 'interpreter' if you feel the child is capable of both understanding and responding to the research. In order to ensure that such a situation is avoided, it is important that all participants fully understand the aims of the research. In fact, involving those closest to the child in the initial design of the research can be very beneficial both in briefing them of your aims, and in seeking their views on how to explain what is required to the child and what would be a suitable response. Furthermore, it is not only good practice to seek such involvement at the beginning of the project; it is vital to the validity of the project that those close to the child remain involved throughout it.

Communication Difficulties

As well as the more obvious issues, such as speech and language difficulties, many other groups with special needs can be affected by communication difficulties. This does not mean, however, that young children with SEN cannot communicate, provided researchers are aware of some general points to avoid. Although not specifically about early years children, Morris (2002: 7–8) outlines some aspects that young people with communication impairments said 'really annoy them' about other people's ability to communicate with them:

- 'They don't wait for me to finish what I've got to say – it takes longer for me to use my communication book than if I was using speech.'

- 'They pretend they understand what I've said.'

- 'They finish my sentences for me without asking me whether that's OK – sometimes it's OK sometimes it's not but they should ask me.'

- 'They talk to the person who is with me and not to me.'

- 'They ask me more than one question at a time.'

- 'They act as if I'm six months old.'

It is therefore imperative that the researcher be aware of these possible pitfalls when interacting with children with communication difficulties.

Morris (2002: 3) continues to point out that besides language, 'there are also a large number of other ways of communicating, apart from language. These include tone of voice, sounds (crying, laughing, etc.), facial expression, using parts of the body (like pointing, turning away, etc.).' Such methods of communicating are called augmentative and alternative communication (AAC). This refers to

> [A]ny means by which an individual can **supplement** or **replace** spoken communication. Communication may range from any movement or behaviour that is observed and interpreted by another person as meaningful, to the use of a code agreed upon between people where items have specific meanings, i.e. a language. We all use some form of augmentative communication in our daily life, for example, gesture (waving goodbye) and graphic symbols (washing label symbols, road signs). (Chinner et al., 2002: 1)

AAC can be divided into aided (requiring equipment such as objects, photographs, keyboards or use of a pointer control system such as a joystick or trackerball) or unaided (such as body language, eye pointing, sign language or signed vocabulary), which employs only the user's body. It is clear that choosing a suitable means of communication is complex yet central to involving young children with SEN in the research process.

Although this may seem a daunting task, Morris advises:

> [A]lways start from the assumption that a young person is at least capable of expressing a preference . . . It is always a good idea to find out if the young person has a way of expressing 'yes' and 'no' (and ideally 'maybe' and 'don't know'). If they do then there are huge opportunities for communication. (2002: 10)

Again, the role of parents and carers is central in helping to select a suitable method of communication between the researcher and the child. One simple step is to spend time with the children and their carers. This will not only put the children more at ease; it will also help you to understand at first hand how a child communicates. A possible difficulty with this, as with ethnographic research in general, is the tendency to 'go native' (that is, to lose a level of detachment from the setting) and become immersed within the setting. There is a danger that the researcher's level of objectivity may as a result become impaired.

Research Tools

Having established a means of communication it is now necessary to consider a range of tools that can be used to help researchers listen to and observe children and to collect 'physical traces' of their lives (Graue & Walsh, 1998). Research tools should be tailored to the communication strengths of the individual child; also, the research process should be a non-threatening and positive experience.

In carrying out research, the researcher should be aware of the inequalities and power relations between him/herself and the children with SEN. One way to help minimise this imbalance is to encourage the children to have 'ownership' of the research process. It may be achieved by involving them as much as possible in the design of the study and also by encouraging them to be partners in the research process. The key shift here is away from the child as subject of enquiry, where research is something that is 'done' to them, towards the situation where the child is encouraged to take a more active part – perhaps by creating or identifying images for themselves – enabling him/her to have greater control within the research process. (See Table 3.1 for the distinction between child as subject and child as partner within the research process.)

Table 3.1   Child as subject or partner in research

Child as the **subject** of inquiry: the adult is in control of the process and provides the stimulus and tools for response	
Adults use images to elicit views of young people	Children's drawings based on a given focus, e.g. draw pictures of things you would like to change
	Collage based on a given focus, e.g. of places where child is happy or activities they enjoy
	Photographs or video footage provided by the researcher as 'stimulus' for conversations
	Websites where children can add own thoughts and opinions which are then interpreted by the researcher
	Use of toys and puppets to stimulate a narrative based on questions or prompts from the researcher
Child as **partner** in research: the child has some control and choice in stimulus and tools for response	
Adults analysing images created or identified by children	Analysis of children's mark making – children are encouraged to explain as appropriate
	Analysis of children's impromptu 'free' drawings – children are encouraged to explain as appropriate
	Photographs or video footage (children's choice of what to record) – children are encouraged to explain as appropriate
	Video diaries (children's choice of what to record) – children are encouraged to explain as appropriate
	Cartoons (children's free choice) – children are encouraged to explain as appropriate
	Artwork/scrapbooks (children's free choice) – children are encouraged to explain as appropriate

A range of methods that may be used with young children in general can also be used with young children with SEN depending on their 'fitness for purpose' (Denscombe, 1998). Perhaps the main difference will be in how the information will be communicated. For example, informal interviews or 'conversations' may be carried out via the spoken word or by signing. More creative and flexible approaches may also be required, for example the use of sorting boxes – a brightly coloured box with a smiley face for 'happy' and a dull coloured box with a sad face for 'sad' – to indicate feelings. The use of third-person questioning may also be appropriate, as some young children may prefer to talk about the thoughts and feelings of someone else rather than their own. A puppet may act as a useful prop in this instance, enabling questions such as 'What would . . . do if . . . ? How would . . . feel if . . . ?'

Another suitable approach, originally developed with young children under five years of age, but also used with children with SENs, is the Mosaic approach. The basis for the development of this approach was to 'find methodologies which played to young children's strengths rather than weaknesses' (Clark, 2004: 144). A variety of visual and verbal methods are used to enable children to express their own views on their lives. These methods include the use of photographs taken by children (or indeed their helpers on the children's advice if the children are unable to use a camera), map making and a child-led tour of the setting. This latter approach could be used in its own right to enable children to take you to their favourite places (indoors and out) or show you particular equipment that makes their lives easier or more fun.

It is suggested that image-based research, or visual elicitation, may provide children who have difficulty communicating with words with an alternative means of expression or communication (Moss, 2008). This could include using existing pictures to help children sort things they like into groups, or to answer questions by pointing or signalling their choice in some other way. Such an approach still places the onus on the researcher to ensure that a child's response is interpreted appropriately – a child's interpretation may differ from an adult's interpretation. In addition, Thomson (2008: 10) warns that 'visual analysis requires the use of specific and explicit approaches which must be systematic, thorough and open to scrutiny'.

One final consideration is when and where the research takes place. For many children with SEN, any disruption to a routine or a change in surroundings may cause them to feel upset. It would therefore seem appropriate to undertake research in a setting that the child, and/or their carers, feel is appropriate and at a time that suits them. It should also be remembered that some children may be taking some form of medication and that it may affect their ability to participate at certain times, so the researcher must always check with those who are familiar with the child and his/her needs. The researcher may be inconvenienced yet the guiding factor must remain the welfare of the young child.

Interpreting Data

Validity of Responses

Having gathered data it is necessary to consider how these are to be interpreted to ensure the 'authentic voice' of the child is heard. Given the complexities of the process, it may be necessary to seek the views of those who know the child well. At the same time, the researcher must stay aware of the concerns raised above: that there is a possibility parents/carers may 'interpret' any response in the best interests of the child – or, indeed, of themselves.

Although the actual data will vary considerably, there remain certain key issues to consider when trying to correlate and apply them. It is perhaps easiest to pose some questions that need to be asked in this process, as follows.

Did the child feel under pressure to answer?

It is important to recognise that, however hard researchers try to reassure young children with SENs, researchers need to remain aware of inequalities and the perceived power in such a relationship. Some children may feel intimidated by an unknown adult researcher, thus are reluctant to say anything they perceive may displease the interviewer; children may feel the need to say what they think is expected of them (that is, what the researcher wants to hear and not what they really think/feel). Children with SEN may not be familiar with adults asking for their views. As they 'may not think their views are important . . . [they] may have a tendency to acquiesce to the suggestion of others, because they are so used to being controlled by others' (Knight et al., 2006: 7). However, it is not just the researchers who may have an impact. Although perhaps less likely, when parents/carers are present the child may feel inhibited by their presence or feel pressurised into giving certain answers perhaps due to familiarity or fear of disappointing the caring adults.

Did the child tell you what you want to hear?

Children with SEN are susceptible to socially desirable responding – telling the researcher what they want to hear. Although this phenomenon may be linked to power relationships (see above), it could also be that the child is not intimidated yet is simply trying to please the researcher.

Is it necessary to clarify a response?

For a variety of reasons it may be necessary to clarify the response a child makes. Particularly where communication gestures require interpretation, the researcher will need to take steps to validate inferences (Detheridge, 2000). In addition, children with SEN may overuse a 'don't know' response (Begley, 2000) and have difficulty sustaining attention. Where the data gathering has been recorded in some form, it may be necessary for the interactions to be analysed independently. If there is any doubt about how to interpret the child's response, it may be desirable to find an alternative way of responding. Even if this means starting the whole process again, the researcher has a duty to ensure that the special educational need does not, in itself, prevent the young child from giving an authentic response.

Reporting Findings

When reporting findings it is important to ensure that the young child with SEN is not only presented appropriately to a wider audience, but that the findings are reported in a form easily understood by the children themselves and carers involved in the research. The findings may need to be conveyed in a variety of ways, including visually, orally or via sign language. The medium may include the use of a collection of photographs, video footage or a sequence of images with speech bubbles, sign language or computer packages.

Conclusions and summary

Undertaking ethical research with young children is always challenging; this chapter has outlined the further difficulties when the children have special educational needs. It is the duty of the researcher to find suitable methods to unlock a route to communication. The 'key' may take many forms, as children with SEN are a very diverse group. Each child will need to be considered on an individual basis when the researcher determines the most appropriate research methods; this is to ensure that the voice of each child is heard.

Key points to remember

- It is important to identify exactly how children communicate – the key is spending time with them and their carers.

- The research needs to be beneficial to the child.

- The research should take place in a familiar situation with familiar people at a time to suit the child.

- In gaining informed consent, according to the level of severity and type of SEN, researchers should consider:
  - how to present information about the research
  - consider how we (or whether in fact we can) establish whether this information has been understood
  - how to know whether they really are happy to participate (rather than simply trying to please us)
  - how we can record this consent
  - the role of the parents or caregivers within this process.

- The research methods should aim to find a 'best fit' with the needs of the individual child, although this will require time and effort.

- The research process should empower the children, who should take an active part in the research process from the design stage to the reporting stage, to whatever extent is possible.

- Responses from young children with SEN should be validated as far as possible and clarification sought if necessary.

- Children should be presented appropriately in findings and fully informed of outcomes.

Points for reflection and discussion

1. What are the differences (if any) in ethical considerations for children with: (a) learning difficulty; (b) physical disability; and (c) sensory impairment?

2. 'Physical, social, cognitive and political distances between the adult and child make their relationship very different from adult relationships' (Graue & Walsh, 1998: 96). Often, an adult researching another adult will try to find a 'common ground' to reduce the distance between researcher and subject. As an adult researcher is socially very different from a child, what are the pros and cons of trying to 'close the gap'/build a rapport with a SEN child as subject?

Further reading

See references below relating to specific need and method.

Useful websites

ACE centre: http://www.ace-centre.org.uk/

References

Begley, A. (2000) 'The educational self-perceptions of children with Down Syndrome', in A. Lewis & G. Lindsay (eds), *Researching Children's Perspectives*. Buckingham: Open University Press, pp. 98–110.

BERA (2004) *Revised Ethical Guidelines for Educational Research*. Southwell: BERA.

BPS (2009) *Code of Ethics and Conduct*. Leicester: BPS.

Campbell, A. & Groundwater-Smith, S. (eds) (2007) *An Ethical Approach to Practitioner Research*. Abingdon: Routledge.

Chinner, S., Hazell, G., Skinner, P., Thomas, P. & Williams, G. (eds) (2002) *Developing Augmentative and Alternative Communication Policies in Schools: Information and Guidelines*. Headlington: ACE Centre Advisory Trust.

Clark, A. (2004) 'The Mosaic Approach and research with young children', in V. Lewis, M. Kellett, C. Robinson, S. Fraser & S. Ding (eds), *The Reality of Research with Children and Young People*. London: Sage, pp. 142–56.

Denscombe, M. (1998) *The Good Research Guide: For Small-Scale Social Research Projects*. Buckingham: Open University Press.

Department for Education and Skills (DfES) *The Special Educational Needs Code of Practice*. London: HMSO.

Department of Education Northern Ireland (1998) *Code of Practice on the Identification and Assessment of Special Educational Needs*. Ireland: DENI.

Department of Health (1991) *The Children Act 1989 Guidance and Regulations: Volume 6, Children with Disabilities*. London: HMSO.

Detheridge, T. (2000) 'Research involving children with severe learning difficulties', in A. Lewis & G. Lindsay (eds), *Researching Children's Perspectives*. Buckingham: Open University Press, pp. 112–21.

Doyle, D. (2007) 'Transdiciplinary enquiry: researching with rather than on', in A. Campbell & S. Groundwater-Smith (eds), *An Ethical Approach to Practitioner Research*. Abingdon: Routledge.

Graue, M.E. & Walsh, D.J. (1998) *Studying Children in Context: Theories, Methods and Ethics*. London: Sage.

Knight, A., Clark, A., Petrie, P. & Statham, J. (2006) *The Views of Children and Young People with Learning Disabilities about the Support They Receive from Social Services: A Review of Consultations and Methods*. London: Institute of Education, University of London, Thomas Coram Research Unit.

Lewis, V., Kellett, M., Robinson, C., Fraser, S. & Ding, S. (eds) (2008) *The Reality of Research with Children and Young People*. London: Sage.

Morris, J. (2002) *A Lot to Say*. London: Scope.

Morrow, V. (n.d.) 'The ethics of social research with children'. Available at: http://www.ciimu.org/webs/wellchi/workshop_1.htm (accessed 26 July 2011).

Moss, J. (2008) 'Visual methods and policy research', cited in J. Murray (2011) 'Knock, knock! Who's there? Gaining access to young children as researchers: a critical review', *Educate*, 11(1): 91–109.

Murray, J. (2011) 'Knock, knock! Who's there? Gaining access to young children as researchers: a critical review', *Educate Journal*, 11(1): 91–109.

SERA (2005) *Scottish Educational Research Association Ethical Guidelines for Educational Research*. Edinburgh: SERA.

Thomson, P. (ed.) (2008) *Doing Visual Research with Children and Young People*. Abingdon: Routledge, pp. 59–73.

4

Ethical Research with Children and Vulnerable Groups

Colette Gray

Chapter overview

This chapter aims to identify some of the potential dilemmas and conflicts inherent in research involving children and vulnerable groups. Specifically, it aims to review the research practices that led to calls for ethical guidelines, to consider potential barriers to work and research involving children and vulnerable groups, and to explore participatory research practices involving young children.

Introduction

The ethical rigour required of research involving children and vulnerable groups has changed dramatically in the last two decades. Informed by the United Nations Convention on the Rights of the Child (UN, 1989), researchers and policy makers are now tasked with ensuring that children and young people are given freedom of expression on all matters that affect their lives. They are also charged with responsibility for ensuring the mental and physical health, safety and well-being of all research participants. The tensions created by these competing demands underpin the discourse of this chapter. It begins by exploring some of the unethical research practices that led to demands for greater ethical rigour in the care of research participants then continues with an examination of the barriers that preclude marginalised and vulnerable groups from participating in the research process.

The Evolution of Research Ethics

The notion that children require legislative protection is far from new and has existed in one form or another for more than 400 years (see, for example, the Poor Relief Act 1597, the Factory Acts of 1833/1878, the Forster Education Act 1870). In 1914, Eglantine Jebb, the founder of Save the Children, promoted an International Charter that asserted the rights of children and the duty of the international community to place children's rights at the forefront of planning. The Declaration of the Rights of the Child (1923), or the Declaration of Geneva as it became known, was adopted a year later by the League of Nations (1924). An expanded version of the Charter was adopted by the United Nations in 1959 and informed the watershed United Nations Convention on the Rights of the Child (UN, 1989).

Surprisingly, however, ethics in research involving children and vulnerable groups is a relatively new area of investigation (Gray & Carville, 2008; Robert-Holmes, 2005). Connolly (2003) attributes the dearth of interest in this subject to the fact that, for many years, researchers mistakenly believed that methodological integrity and ethical integrity were one and the same. Although both are essential for the veracity of the research, they are easily distinguished. Methodology refers to the theoretical perspective of a researcher. For example, a researcher might explore childhood issues from a sociological, ecological, phenomenological or psychological perspective. The methods or tools of enquiry used by these differing groups of researchers tend to reflect their methodological traditions and may include, among many other methods, clinical trials, laboratory experiments, intervention studies, observations, interviews, drama, story boards, stories, drawing, photographs, cameras, bookmaking, tours or map making. These approaches are not mutually exclusive. On the contrary, in many instances a researcher will explore an issue using a range of methods to triangulate[1] the findings. In contrast to the methodology, research ethics focus on the conduct and behaviour of the researcher. This latter point is discussed in greater detail throughout the chapter. To place today's ethical codes of practice in context it is useful to explore their origins.

Current ethical codes of practice in research are rooted in the Nuremberg Code (1949), established in response to the atrocities of experimentation perpetrated in Nazi concentration camps during the Second World War. The Code included three core features:

- Voluntary consent must be obtained from all research subjects.

- Research studies must be undertaken for the good of society.

- Unnecessary physical and mental suffering must be avoided.

It was argued that the prominence given to the issue of voluntary consent made it impossible for researchers to conduct research on young children, on children and adults with special needs, and on adults with mental health problems (Gray & Carville, 2008). In response to these and other criticisms the Code was modified in the Helsinki Declaration (1964–89) to permit research with 'incompetents' subject to strict controls. It soon became apparent that the code was not being rigorously enforced. Throughout the 1960s and 1970s researchers were roundly criticised for employing unethical practices in studies involving vulnerable children and particularly children with special needs.

From a review of 22 medical studies, Beecher (1966: 37) concluded that most involved 'experimentation on a patient not for his benefit but for that, at least in theory, of patients in general'. By way of example, adult skin grafts were attached to the chest wall of children being treated for congenital heart disease to examine the effect of removing the thymus gland on children's growth and development. Another study sought to determine whether an antibiotic used in the treatment of acne would cause liver dysfunction if given to young children. It did.

More recently, unethical investigative practices were uncovered at Birmingham's Diana Princess of Wales Children's Hospital and the Alder Hey Children's Hospital in Liverpool. Without seeking parental consent, between 1988 and 1998 medical researchers in both hospitals harvested the organs and tissues of babies who died at their hospitals. The same hospitals were also found to have sold thymus glands removed during heart surgery from live children to a pharmaceutical company for money (BBC News, 2001). In 2010 a doctor was struck off the medical register for fabricating and misreporting his results to create the appearance of a possible link between the measles, mumps and rubella (MMR) vaccine and autism (Sanchez & Rose, 2010). The same doctor is alleged to have paid children as young as five years of age, attending a birthday party for one of his children, £5 each for a sample of their blood. Their parents later complained that neither their nor their child[ren]'s consent was sought prior to the blood withdrawals. Accepting that the children were too young to understand what was happening, the doctor defended his unorthodox methods claiming they served the greater good. Although we have focused on medical malpractice it would be quite wrong, as the following exemplar demonstrates, to assume that unethical practices are the sole preserve of medical research.

 Case study

The Case of Genie

Discovered in California in the early 1970s, Genie (a pseudonym) had been subject to dreadful deprivation and neglect by her abusive father. Genie was discovered when her partially-sighted mother took her to a local social services department to enquire about payments for the blind. Fascinated by the child's withdrawn and hunched demeanour, a social worker guessed that Genie was about six years old and might have Autism. In fact, Genie was thirteen years old, unable to speak, had no social skills and was not potty trained. It is unclear whether Genie had special needs that affected her learning and early development or if her living conditions caused her to have special needs. What is known is that for thirteen years Genie was raised in isolation in one bedroom of her parent's house. Tied to a potty for most of the day or in a cot with a wire mesh hood, Genie's father growled like a dog and barked at her if she made a noise. He committed suicide before he could be charged with child neglect.

Although there are conflicting accounts of what happened next the evidence suggests that the primary abuse Genie received at the hands of her parents was compounded by the secondary abuse she received at the hands of psychological investigators. Indeed, researchers were so fascinated by this living experiment that they fought to study every facet of Genie's life and she was subject to rigorous and continued testing. Her ability to develop attachments and learn language were topics of particularly intense and prolonged investigation. These studies were deemed to be so intrusive that by the late 1970s a lawsuit was filed banning all psychologists from coming within a 30-mile vicinity of Genie. This was followed by a court order making it illegal for her whereabouts to be disclosed to researchers.

Group activity 1

Make a list of the potential risks this research posed to Genie, the researchers and the wider public. Can this type of research ever be justified?

The requirement for the regulation and governance of research studies was acknowledged with the publication of the watershed United Nations Convention on the Rights of the Child (UN, 1989), mentioned above. The UNCRC established children's rights to provision, protection and participation; it changed the way children were viewed by researchers. It also heralded an important shift away from children being treated as research *subjects* to children being viewed as research *participants* with rights. Article 12 of the Convention calls for state parties to:

> [A]ssure to the child who is capable of forming his or her own views the right to express those views freely in all matters affecting the child, the views of the child being given due weight in accordance with the age and maturity of the child.

Article 13 of the Convention respects 'Children's right to express their views in the way they wish', while Article 36 calls for 'Children's right to protection from all forms of exploitation, this includes protection from exploitation through research processes'. To help children realise their rights, the Convention recommends the provision of age-appropriate assistance for very young children and children with disabilities.

The UNCRC has been ratified by 52 nations, the exceptions being Somalia and the United States (US), although the US does implement some aspects of the Convention. The passing of the Children Act 1989 and the Children Bill 2004 in the UK added further weight to government assertions that children's views and perspectives can and must be heard on issues that affect them. While these conditions are fundamental to good practice, a number of professional bodies including the British Psychological Society (BPS, 2009), the British Sociological Society (BSS, 2002) and the British Educational Research Association (BERA, 2010) produce their own ethical guidelines for practitioners. Members who breach these ethical codes may be subject to a disciplinary hearing and in the most serious cases struck off their respective professional register.

 Group activity 2

The UNCRC calls for children to be given a voice on issues that affect their lives. Identify and discuss potential barriers to the inclusion of young children in early years research.

Is it appropriate to include them in each of these areas:

- Gender differences in the toy choices of boys and girls?
- Leadership styles in the pre-school sector?
- Hours of TV viewing in young children?

Access and Consent

Despite gaining enhanced status in society, children's participation in research projects and policy-making remains within the gift of their adult carers. As McDowall Clark (2010: 97) points out, 'adults have more resources and authority and therefore have power over children's lives'. Decisions about access and consent frequently hinge on the issue of age and competence. Although scientific studies indicate that babies and children have an innate capacity to understand and process information from their earliest years (Gopnick et al., 1999; Brierley, 1994), young children are frequently considered too young to participate in the research process.

This may explain why even the most cursory review of the literature reveals a paucity of studies actively involving young children; their exclusion is attributed to age-related competence. James & James (2008) believe this explanation confuses two quite distinct issues. Whereas age is easily calculated, competence proves more difficult to determine. This may be due, at least in part, to the fact that competence is fluid and subject to the effects of contextual and situational factors. By way of example, Lyon (2002) explored children's understanding of oath-taking in court and found their responses were considered competent when questions were presented in concrete rather than in abstract terms. Compared to their poor performance on abstract statements about what constitutes a liar, even the youngest child could correctly identify true and false statements. Support for the notion that young children can provide accurate and component accounts of events that affect their lives comes from research into a range of salient issues including abuse by nursery school teachers (Bee & Boyd, 2010), transition to school (Dockett & Perry, 2004), divorce (Pruett & Kilne Pruett, 1999), smacking (Phillips & Alderson, 2003) and bullying in school (Oliver & Candappa, 2003).

Given the confusion that surrounds the notion of children's competence, it is reassuring to note that access to children and vulnerable groups is closely guarded by 'gatekeepers'. Adult gatekeepers typically include early years professionals, classroom teachers, school principals, education authorities and social workers. Each of these groups is charged in law with a duty of care towards their young charges. According to the Children Act 1989, the level of this duty of care is measured as being that of a 'reasonable parent'. Gatekeepers have, however, frequently been described as overprotective, intransigent and difficult by researchers attempting to access the views of young children or vulnerable groups (McLeod, 2008; Gray & Carville, 2008).

The overprotective stance adopted by some gatekeepers has led to accusations that they have silenced and further marginalised atypical groups of children. For example, with funding from Guide Dogs for the Blind this author undertook a large-scale investigation into the mobility and life experiences of children and young people with a visual impairment (VI) in Northern Ireland (NI). The names and addresses of mainstream schools with (a) child(ren) with a VI was supplied by each of the five local education authorities in NI on the condition that no effort would be made by the research team to contact the children or their parents. Without access to pupils with a VI, this author was unable to verify or refute teacher assertions that pupils with a VI enjoyed mainstream school, were fully integrated into all aspects of school life and were well liked by their peers and teachers (Gray, 2009). Attempts at interviewing young people with a VI attending a Saturday morning club organised by the Royal National Institute for the Blind proved equally frustrating. Keen to voice their views on the lack of provision available for children with a VI, a few parents tended to dominate the conversation. After a number of false starts each parent was invited to withdraw to another part of the room where they could observe but not participate in the discussion; several parents who had issues with the lack of provision available for children with a VI declined this offer on the basis that 'their child needed them to be at their side' (Gray & Carville,

2008: 224). Similarly, Savage & Callery (2007) observed parents frequently interrupting their children's responses to questions from professionals concerning their cystic fibrosis. As Curtis et al. (2004) pointed out parental interference in the research process can restrict the opportunity for the researcher and young interviewee to engage in a meaningful dialogue about matters that affect young lives. Of equal concern, when parents interrupt the conversation, redirect it or interpret their child's meaning they can inadvertently distort and invalidate the results. Curtis et al. give the example of teachers who create a false-positive impression by excluding dissenting pupils from contributing to an evaluation.

Parents can also give, refuse or withdraw permission for their child to participate in research. At the last minute, one of my dissertation students was distressed to find that parental permission was withdrawn for her small-scale study into the benefits of multi-sensory sessions for children with profound disabilities. Following good practice, consent from the placement provider, therapist and parents was secured at an early stage of the project to observe the children during several multi-sensory sessions. Parental permission was withdrawn after a parent whose child was involved in the study complained to others that the research was intrusive and strongly advised them to withdraw their consent. The study was altered to exclude the children and redesigned to explore practitioners' views on multi-sensory sessions through a questionnaire survey. Distance and availability frequently restrict access to children with specific disorders such as autism, Down's syndrome and attention deficit hyperactivity disorder. This can make it difficult for a researcher/student to identify and include a representative group who share in common a particular disorder in the research process. Over the years a number of my students have been forced to abandon or redesign their original study because they were unable to access statistically significant numbers of children with specific disorders.

Clearly, it would be impossible to anticipate all of the factors that might frustrate the research process. Nevertheless, in order to gain access and consent from gatekeepers a researcher should be prepared to clearly articulate:

- the purpose of the study – i.e. what do you intend to do?

- the methods employed – do you intend to use interviews/ observations/surveys?

- the time frame involved – how long will you keep each child and how often will they be involved in the study?

- the measures taken to protect the child's confidentiality and anonymity – will you use pseudonyms and will you remove all identifying features to protect the child's identity?

- protection of the data – how will it be stored and who will see/have access to the data?

Despite their best efforts some researchers find it impossible to access particular participant groups. In that circumstance the aims of the study should be revisited and a back-up plan devised.

 Group activity 3

Read the following scenario, list potential gatekeepers and identify the following: the value of the research for the participant group, how consent will be sought, and how confidentiality, anonymity and data protection will be assured. In the event that permission is refused, develop a back-up plan.

Compare your list with that of others in your group.

> For her research project a student intends to study gender differences in the play activities of pre-school children with special needs. She would like to observe the children in her current placement – a special needs nursery school. Time is very tight because it took her a while to identify her subject area. She is in placement only for a short time and is working to a deadline. Given the lack of literature on the topic, she is considering observing the play of the most severely disabled children.

Obtaining Consent

Although adult gatekeepers are responsible for making decisions about children's participation in research, as pointed out in Article 12 of the UNCRC, every effort should be made to seek *the views of the child*. Gaining informed consent from young children with a limited vocabulary demands careful consideration.

To gain consent from pre-school children with and without a disability, in several studies I employed a tool box of methods (Gray & Winter, 2008, 2011) informed by the Mosaic approach (Clark & Moss, 2001; Clark et al., 2005). The methods adopted included the use of an artefact (Molly, a rag doll), 'thumbs up' and 'thumbs down' stickers, smiley faces, drawings, disposable cameras and audio recording devices. The children's understanding of the process was subsequently assessed by a playgroup assistant, who asked each child to tell her about the research and whether they wanted to be involved in the study. In this study consent was considered to be a process rather than a one-off indication of agreement. Respecting the children's right to change their minds and to withdraw from the project, the issue of consent was revisited at every stage of the project. None of the children in this project elected to withdraw.

In contrast, several children in Skanfors' (2009) ethnographic study of two- to five-year-old children in pre-school changed their minds. She notes how some children were able to verbalise their wishes by saying no while others asserted control by either moving away from her, by failing to respond to her questions, by hiding or by ignoring her. Terming these approaches 'say no' and 'show no', Skanfors (2009: 10) concluded that researchers should continue to employ sensitivity and their 'ethical radar' throughout the research process.

Participatory Research

As previously discussed, the publication of the UNCRC (1989) and the growth of the child's rights movement fuelled expectations that children can and must be consulted about matters that affect their lives. According to Lewis & Porter (2004: 19) this led to a 'veritable torrent' of government initiatives undertaken to give voice to the child. Policy-makers have been particularly keen to involve children and young people as service-users in discussions on government policies (Kellett, 2005; Brownlie et al., 2006). As well as improving the lives of children, participatory research with children has the capacity to highlight their concerns, increase their self-esteem and develop their ability to investigate and explore issues of interest to them (Kellett, 2005, 2006).

Notwithstanding its many benefits, Dockett (2008: 13) points out that participatory research with children can be fraught with difficulty:

The reality of researching with children and young people is that it is a time-consuming, resource-intensive, often 'messy' process that requires considerable time and commitment to work through with different agencies (such as project workers), talk with children and young people, provide briefing and debriefing sessions, organise travel and provide ongoing support. All of these aspects are critical to building strong and responsive relationships with children and young people.

To reduce these shortcomings, a number of researchers involve children in some but not all aspects of the research process. Indeed, the very term 'participation' can be used to describe a broad continuum of involvement. On the one hand it can simply mean taking part, being present, being involved or being consulted; on the other it can denote a transfer of power so that participants' views have influence on decisions (Boyden & Ennew, 1997). Kirby et al. (2003) consider participation under six dimensions: the level of participation; the focus of decision-making; the content of decision-making; the nature of the participation activity; the frequency and duration of participation; and the children and young people involved.

A number of authors have developed models or frameworks to illustrate the difference between full, partial and tokenistic levels of participation. Hart (1992), for example, adapted Arnstein's (1969) metaphor of a ladder of participation to illustrate the nuances implied by the terms participation and non-participation (see Figure 4.1). Shier (2001) offers a more developed five-step model with manipulation

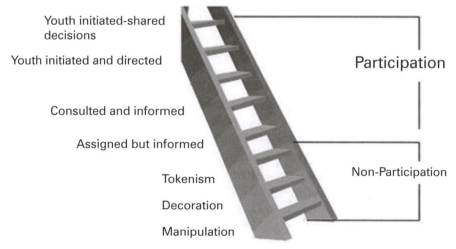

Figure 4.1 Hart's (1992) ladder of participation

at the lowest level and child-initiated or shared decision-making at the pinnacle (see Figure 4.2). Each step is accompanied by questions organised under three headings: openings, opportunities and obligations. According to Shier's model, research that meets the demands of steps 1 to 3 has achieved the minimum levels of participation required by the UNCRC.

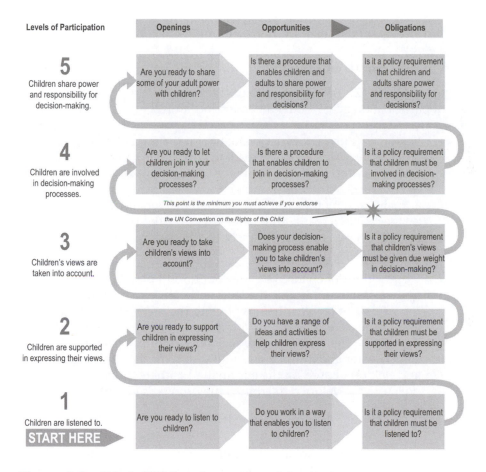

Figure 4.2   Shier's (2001) pathways to participation

Opponents of hierarchical models of participation believe them to be merely descriptive tools that fail to take account of the subject matter under investigation, the extent of participation required and the practicality of involving pre-verbal or vulnerable groups at higher levels of participation. In exploring the meaning of participatory models, Cornwall (2008) asks who is participating, why are they participating and for what benefits? Rather than present participation as a hierarchical step-wise process, other commentators describe it in terms of a continuum, a circle or a jigsaw puzzle. Kirby et al. (2003) offered an alternative non-hierarchical model of participation with no one level assumed to be 'better' than another; instead, circumstances determine the type of participation.

 Group activity 4

Using Shier's (2001) pathways to participation determine the level of participation achieved by the following projects:

1. Researchers undertook an evaluation of the impact of a literacy programme on the reading and spelling performance of 150 children (half of whom received and half of whom did not receive the programme). Each child completed tests administered by the class teacher then marked and analysed by the research team. At the initial stage of the process permission was given by the school, the parents, and the children involved.

2. Observations of children's behaviour during playtime was undertaken to determine the level and nature of bullying in the school. To gain further insight into the issue, small-group interviews were conducted with groups of boys and girls in the school. The children were selected at random from the class register and permission sought from the school, parents and children. Based on the information gathered a new school policy was developed to address the problems identified.

At this point I will use an example from my own research to determine how the reality of conducting a participatory study with pre-school children maps onto the stages outlined in Shier's (2001) pathways to participation. My research project involved 36 children (18 with and 18 without a known disability) attending four pre-school settings in NI (Gray & Winter, 2011). Permission to undertake the project was sought at the initial stages of the project from the playgroup leaders, nursery school principals, parents and children. Respecting the children's right to change their mind and withdraw from the process, we revisited the issue of consent at every stage of the project. Using a circle time approach to generate discussion, in each setting I encouraged the children to select the subject of the research from a range of topics and to chose the methods of enquiry from a toolbox of potential methods such as smiley face stickers, drawing, photographs and walking diaries. Over a period of weeks, working in small groups of two (each dyad included a child with and a child without a known disability) the children identified what they most and least liked in their pre-school setting. To gain a more rounded picture, several dyads chose to interview staff and children in their setting. The results were collated by me and to ensure their accuracy were presented and discussed with the children who listened carefully and corrected them as necessary.

At this juncture issues such as anonymity and confidentiality required careful consideration. For example, three groups of children asked if they could have their own names attached to their work. This issue was discussed at length with staff who expressed their opposition. In the event a compromise was reached: it enabled the children to select their own pseudonym or use their own first name; in all instances surnames were omitted. Permission was refused in two settings for the children to use digital cameras. At the children's request, staff retained all of the pictures taken by the children using disposable cameras, their drawings and any other materials generated as a result of the study. Children's participation is in essence shaped by the overt and subtle influences of their adult gatekeepers. The same approach was used in each of the participating settings in order for consistency to be maintained. Debriefing sessions at the end of the project were conducted using a circle time approach to gain some insight into children's thoughts on the process.

Ownership of the dissemination stage of the process was retained by the children involved, who presented their findings to their parents, peers and pre-school staff during their end-of-year 'graduation' ceremony in the form of collages and through role-play. An examination of Shier's model (2001) suggests that the first three stages were achieved with the children encouraged to express their views and their opinions given serious consideration. Although our research is arguably commensurate with stages four and five of the model, in our experience the children's wishes were frequently ignored or viewed as subordinate to adult concerns. From this example it might be concluded that: hierarchical models offer useful descriptive tools but are limited in terms of explanation; participatory research with young children remains within the gift of adult gatekeepers; compromise and negation are integral aspects of participatory studies; and power sharing is a worthy aspiration but in reality adults make the final decisions.

Conclusions and summary

This chapter has considered how past and recent research malpractice has fuelled demands for a code of practice to be put in place, one that ensures the ethical rigour of research involving children and vulnerable groups. Allied with concern for the protection and care of children and vulnerable groups and informed by Article 12 of the UNCRC (1989), a new participatory movement has evolved to give children a voice in matters that have an impact upon their lives. Honouring and facilitating children's participation presents researchers with a new set of challenges. These range from gaining access to children and vulnerable groups through to ownership of the data. Such issues are examined in the body of this chapter; guidance and examples are offered to minimise some of the frustrations inherent in the process.

Key points to remember

- At the outset of the project, consider the ethical implications of the research – who will be involved and how will the participants benefit from your research?

- Before approaching a gatekeeper clearly identify:
    - the aims of the research – what are you investigating?
    - the methods employed – interviews/observations/surveys?
    - the time frame involved – how long will you keep each child and how often will they be involved in the study?
    - the measures taken to protect the child(ren)'s confidentiality and anonymity
    - protection of the data – how will it be stored and who will see/ have access to the data?

- Consider how you will gain the child(ren)'s consent.

- Where appropriate, actively involve children in aspects of the research.

Points for reflection and discussion

1. Read 'Involving Children and Young People in Research', available at: http://kids.nsw.gov.au/uploads/documents/InvolvingChildrenandYoungPeopleinResearch.pdf.

2. What is your theoretical perspective? What methods or tools do you prefer to use when working with young children?

3. Make a list of the important transitions and events that marked your progress from early childhood through to adulthood.

4. You have written consent from both the staff and parents to conduct a small-scale project into the healthy eating options of Key Stage 1 children. One child refuses to let you have a peek into her lunchbox. You have adult permission and a deadline to meet; what would you do? Compare your solution with those given by other members of the group.

Further reading

Hill, M. (2005) 'Ethical considerations in researching children's experiences', in D. Harcourt, B. Perry & T. Waller (eds) (2011) *Researching Young Children's Perspectives*. Routledge.

Robert-Holmes, G. (2005) *Doing Your Early Years Research Project: A Step-by-Step Guide*. London: Paul Chapman.

Skanfors, L. (2009) 'Ethics in child research: children's agency and researchers "ethical radar"', *Childhoods Today*, 3(1): 1–22.

Useful websites

Engaging Young Children in Research (2008): a compendium of papers and reflections from a think tank co-hosted by the Australian Research Alliance for Children and Youth and the New South Wales Commission for Children and Young People on 11 November 2008.

Whyte, J. (2006) *Research with Children with Disabilities. National Disability Authority*. Full report available at: http://www.nda.ie/cntmgmtnew.nsf/0/851DE72FE32677F0802571CB005A165B?OpenDocument.

Note

1. Triangulation refers to the use of more than one approach to enhance confidence in the findings.

References

Arnstein, S. (1969) 'A ladder of citizen participation', *Journal of the American Institute of Planners*, 35(4): 214–25.

BBC News (2001) 'Organ scandal background'. Available at: http://news.bbc.co.uk/1/hi/1136723.stm.

Bee, H. & Boyd, D. (2010) *The Developing Child: With My Development Lab*, 12th edn. London: Pearson Education.

Beecher, H. (1966) 'Ethics and clinical research', *New England Journal of Medicine*, 274: 1354–60.

Boyden, J. & Ennew, J. (1997) *Children in Focus: A Manual for Participatory Research with Children*. Stockholm: Rädda Barnen.

Brierley, J. (1994) *Give Me a Child Until He Is Seven: Brain Studies and Early Education*, 2nd edn. London: RoutledgeFalmer.

British Education Research Association (2011) Online at: http://www.bera.ac.uk/files/2011/08/BERA-Ethical-Guidelines-2-11.pdf.

British Psychological Association (2009) Ethics and Standards. Online at: http://www.bps.org.uk/what-we-do/ethics-standards/ethics-standards.

British Sociological Society (2002) Equality and Diversity. Online at: http://www.britsoc.co.uk/equality/.

Brownlie, J., Anderson, S. & Ormston, R. (2006) *Children as Researchers: SEED Sponsored Research*. Scottish Executive website at: http://www.scotland.gov.uk/insight.

Clark, A., Kjørholt, A.T. & Moss, P. (eds) (2005) *Beyond Listening: Children's Perspectives on Early Childhood Services*. Bristol: Policy Press.

Clark, A. & Moss, P. (2001) *Listening to Young Children: The Mosaic Approach*. London: National Children's Bureau and Joseph Rowntree Foundation.

Connolly, P. (2003) *Ethical Principles for Researching Vulnerable Groups*. Belfast: Office of the First Minister and Deputy First Minister.

Cornwall, A. (2008) 'Unpacking participation: models, meanings and practices', *Community Development Journal*, 43(3): 269–83.

Curtis, K., Roberts, H., Copperman, J., Downie, A. & Liabø, K. (2004) 'How come I don't get asked no questions? Researching hard to reach children and teenagers', *Child and Family Social Work*, 9(2): 167–75.

Dockett, S. (2008) 'Engaging young children in research', *Involving Children and Young People in Research*, pp. 52–63. Compendium of papers and reflections from a Think Tank co-hosted by the Australian Research Alliance for Children and Youth and the New South Wales Commission for Children and Young People on 11 November 2008.

Dockett, S. & Perry, B. (2004) 'Starting school perspectives of Australian children, parents and educators', *Journal of Early Childhood Research*, 2(2): 171–89.

Fine, G.A. & Sandstrome, K.L. (1988) *Knowing Children. Participant Observation with Minors*, Sage University Paper Series on Qualitative Research Methods No. 15. Beverley Hills, CA: Sage.

Gray, C. (2009) 'A qualitatively different experience: mainstreaming pupils with a visual impairment in Northern Ireland', *European Journal of Special Needs Education*, 24(2): 169–42.

Gray, C. & Carville, S. (2008) 'Ethical research practices across disciplinary boundaries: the process of research involving children with a visual impairment', *Child Care in Practice*, 14(2): 217–28.

Gray, C. & Winter, E. (2008) *Real and Perceived Ethical Barriers to Participatory Research and Children with Special Needs.* Paper presented at the 19th Early Childhood Education Research Association Annual Conference, Strasbourg, 26–29 August.

Gray, C. & Winter, E. (2010) 'Hearing voices: participatory research with pre-school children with and without disabilities', *European Early Childhood Education Research Journal*, 18(3).

Gray, C. & Winter, E. (2011) 'The ethics of participatory research involving children with special needs', in D. Harcourt, B. Perry & T. Waller (eds), *Researching Young Children's Perspectives*. London: Routledge, pp. 26–37.

Gopnick, A., Meltzoff, A. & Kuhl, P. (1999) *How Babies Think.* London: Weidenfeld & Nicholson.

Greene, S. & Hill, M. (2005) 'Researching children's experience: methods and methodological issues', in S. Green & D. Hogan (eds), *Researching Children's Experiences: Approaches and Methods*. London: Sage, pp. 1–21.

Hart, R. (1992) *Children's Participation: From Tokenism to Citizenship.* Florence: UNICEF International Child Development Centre.

James, A. & James, A. (2008) *Key Concepts in Childhood Studies.* London: Sage.

Kellett, M. (2005) *Children as Active Researchers: A New Research Paradigm for the 21st Century?* London: ESRC National Centre for Research Methods.

Kellett, M. (2006) *Pupils as Active Researchers: Using Engagement with the Research Process to Enhance Creativity and Thinking Skills in 10–12 Year Olds.* Paper presented at the British Educational Research Association Annual Conference, University of Warwick, 6–9 September.

Kirby, P., Lanyon, C., Cronin, K. & Sinclair, R. (2003) *Building a Culture of Participation: Involving Children and Young People in Policy, Service Planning, Delivery and Evaluation. Research Report.* London: Department for Education and Skills.

Lewis, A. & Porter, J. (2004) 'Interviewing children and young people with learning disabilities: guidelines for researchers and multi-professional practice', *British Journal of Learning Disabilities*, 32(4): 191–7.

Lyon, T. (2002) 'Child witnesses and the oath', in H.L. Westcott, G.M. Davies & R.H.C. Bull (eds), *Children's Testimony: A Handbook of Psychological Research and Forensic Practice*. Chichester: Wiley, pp. 254–60.

McDowall Clark, R. (2010) *Childhood in Society: For Early Childhood Studies.* Exeter: Learning Matters.

McLeod, A. (2008) *Listening to Children: A Practitioner's Guide.* London: Jessica Kingsley.

Oliver, C. and Candappa, M. (2003) *Tackling Bullying: Listening to the Views of Children and Young People*, Thomas Coram Research Unit, Institute of Education, University of London, Research Report RR400, National Foundation for Educational Research. DfES Publications Ref. No.: RR400.

Phillips, B. & Alderson, P. (2003) 'Beyond "anti-smacking": challenging violence and coercion in parent–child relations', *International Journal of Children's Rights*, 115: 175–97.

Pruett, K.D. & Kline Pruett, M. (1999) 'Only God decides: young children's perceptions of divorce and the legal system', *Journal of the American Academy of Child and Adolescent Psychiatry*, 38(12): 1544–50.

Robert-Holmes, G. (2005) *Doing Your Early Years Research Project: A Step-by-Step Guide.* London: Paul Chapman.

Sanchez, R. & Rose, D. (2010) 'Dr Andrew Wakefield struck off medical register', *Sunday Times*, 25 May.

Savage, E. & Callery, P. (2007) 'Clinic consultations with children and parents on the dietary management of cystic fibrosis', *Social Science and Medicine*, 64: 363–74.

Shier, H. (2001) 'Pathways to participation: openings, opportunities and obligations', *Children and Society*, 15(2): 107–17.

Skanfors, L. (2009) 'Ethics in child research: children's agency and researchers "ethical radar"', *Childhoods Today*, 3(1): 1–22.

United Nations (1989) *The Convention on the Rights of the Child*. Geneva: Defense International and the United Nations Children's Fund.

5

Ethical Researching in Other Cultures

Ioanna Palaiologou

Chapter overview

The contemporary issue of researching other cultures and its challenges is addressed in this chapter. There are two types of researchers in other cultures: in one the researcher is an insider (part of the culture), while in the other the researcher is an outsider, i.e. is not part of the culture. Both entail challenges and difficulties, as individuals often cannot divorce themselves from their own cultural context. The aim of this chapter is to increase understanding of how cultures shape our identity and therefore how culture shapes the researcher's perspectives. The challenges of researching other cultures are examined and some of the ethical challenges researchers might face are elaborated.

Introduction: The Insider and Outsider Researcher

In studies such as those of Aries (1986), Bloch (1992), James and Prout (1997), Christensen & James (2011) and Lewis & Lindsay (2000), it is emphasised that the Western perspective and concept of childhood is barely three or four centuries old; childhood is seen as a distinctive period and a separate phase in life, characterised either by the religious perspective of innocence or the perspective of the apprentice (to be prepared for the real world and work), or through sexuality (the psychoanalytical concept). For many years, as has been stressed elsewhere in this book, childhood was viewed as a period in which the development aspect was to be enhanced and protected. A number of contemporary studies (Bloch, 1992; James & Prout, 1997; Kjørholt, 2001, 2002; Prout, 2000, 2003; Rinaldi, 2005; Clark et al., 2005), alongside the introduction of children's rights by the UNCRC (1989), brought a broader view of childhood. The importance of the UNCRC is that children are viewed as full individual human beings, holders of rights, who are to be actively involved in gaining and enjoying their rights. There is a change from the view that children are the dependents or property of parents. The UNCRC acknowledges the fact of children's vulnerability and that they are in need of protection yet they also have strengths and capacities. Children are also now viewed as active members of society, able to contribute their views, to be involved in cultural activities, and able to take an active role in their societies; they have rights to free expression, to be consulted, to be heard and to participate.

However, it is essential to acknowledge that there are cultural differences in the constructions of childhood. These differences need to be taken into consideration when researching cultures other than the researcher's own.

There have been numerous attempts to define culture. However, these mainly emphasise the traits that characterise what aspects constitute each respective culture. For example, White claims that:

> [C]ulture consists of tools, implements, utensils, clothing, ornaments, customs, institutions, beliefs, rituals, games, works of art, language, etc. (1959: 3)

The number of differing definitions demonstrates the difficulty of actually defining 'culture'. They focus on describing the characteristics of a culture, such as its knowledge, beliefs, arts, morals, law, customs and many other capabilities and habits acquired by a person as a member of a society, ethnicity and gender (Tylor, 1958; Kottack, 1994).

Consequently, one of the main challenges faced by researchers when conducting research within other cultures is learning to understand these complexities. However, although Kottack (1994) claims that culture is learned, it cannot be ignored that culture shapes our nature and our sense of identity and thus affects the relationships between our social and cultural groupings and the environment in which each of us lives.

From a psychological point of view, it is difficult to distinguish what an individual conceives him/herself to be from that individual's cultural context. 'Culture' is a complex concept. It might be related to a feature as local and individual as membership of a family, a sports or a music group that defines an individual's aspirations, values, interests and habits. In a broader frame, it could embrace religious affiliations, social class or ethnicity. Studies on the impact of culture on the construction of self have shown that it plays a significant role in the formation of a person's identity and determines one's actions and behaviours (Hill et al., 1989; Hogg & Vaughan, 1995; Kelly, 1995).

For example, Hsu (1986) claims that an individual cannot distinguish him/herself from the society and culture in which they are living. He claims that 'self' is embedded in a multi-layered model, a series of concentric rings, as shown in Figure 5.1. The outermost ring represents the influence of the external world: the culture, society,

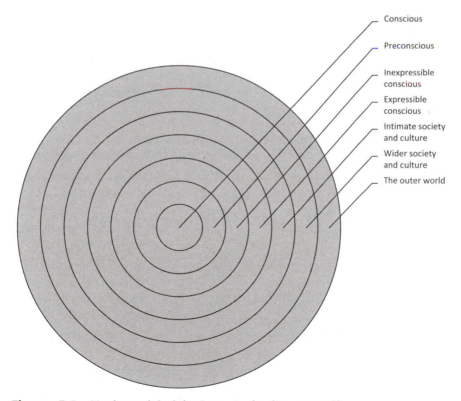

Conscious

Preconscious

Inexpressible conscious

Expressible conscious

Intimate society and culture

Wider society and culture

The outer world

Figure 5.1   Hsu's model of the impact of culture on self

values and beliefs. The innermost ring represents the influence of the unconscious mind in Freudian terms. According to Hsu, our unconscious determines our behaviour, although without our conscious awareness of it. At the intermediate levels within his model, society and culture exert a strong influence upon individuals. He also claims that the third level of intimate society and culture is particularly resistant to change.

Other studies such as those of Tajfel (1978, 1982), Tajfel & Turner (1986), Devos (1986), Bharati (1986) and Abrams & Hogg (1990a, 1990b) have shown the formation of our identity in relation to culture and society; all suggest that the social groups to which we belong are an integral part of our concept of self. Such a perception might raise issues about the nature of the research project itself and about where it may or may not be appropriate to impose a type of research enquiry onto another culture.

Abrams & Hogg (1990a), for example, claim that social groupings such as religion or nationhood are instrumental in providing their members with identity. They consider this 'social identity' and claim that our social identity defines and evaluates individuals. For example, national identities, such as Welsh, Scottish or English, have their own distinctions as to what constitutes a Welsh, Scottish or English person. It also assumes appropriate behaviour that defines a person and their actions. For example, at a football match between two nations, the supporters of each team tend to group together and behave in a certain way, singing the same songs or their national anthem; in many cases they wear the same colours, representing those of their national flag or their team's strip.

These studies raise an important point about whether to consider the role of a researcher as an insider (part of the culture being studied) or an outsider (not part of that culture). There are issues about any biases of the researcher and how these may be overcome, as well as the participation of children in the research. It also raises a number of questions and ethical challenges around the methods the researcher is choosing to use with children; the methods may be in conflict with the cultural, religious or ethnic habits of the children, their families and their society. A further dimension relates to the researcher's focus in the project and how data are interpreted. There is no identification of the subjects, thus ideological neutrality is preserved. However, the researcher may be exposed to the fluid needs and influences of the cultural group under research.

The discussion about our concept of 'self' was offered in order to demonstrate that the construction of this concept has an impact on a researcher in the process of researching another culture as an insider; it also determines outcomes as an outsider. For example, there may be behaviours or data that are ignored because the researcher defines him/herself with these behaviours or characteristics and evaluates him/herself in similar terms (insider researcher); in contrast, certain behaviours or characteristics, rather than their causes, are more likely to be emphasised (outsider researcher). Our social and cultural identity prescribes behaviour we consider appropriate within our social groups. In that sense, researchers need to bear in mind that the cultural group to which each belongs is an integral part of who they are; at an unconscious level, as Hsu claims, it plays a role in determining our own and our children's perspectives. An ethical challenge when researching within other cultures is how the researcher may acknowledge and address a need to make adjustments, either external, i.e. methods, or internal, i.e. the values and axiology of the research.

The Challenge of Cultural Relativism

The dominant view, when approaching other cultures, is cultural relativism; it contrasts with ethno-centrism, which holds 'one's culture as best and to judge the behaviour and beliefs of culturally different people by one's standards' (Kottack, 1994: 48) or 'the habit or tendency to judge or interpret other cultures according to the criteria of one's own culture' (Seymour-Smith, 1986: 97).

Cultural relativism refers to the position that values and standards of cultures differ. It promotes the idea of diverse respect (Kottack, 1994: 48). 'Cultural relativism involves understanding another culture in its own terms sympathetically enough so that the culture appears to be a coherent and meaningful design of living' (Greenwood & Stini, 1977: 182).

Parekh states that culture is:

> [A] body of belief and practices in terms of which a group of people understand themselves and the world they organise their individual and collective lives around. (2000: 2–3)

Thus, on a broader level, cultural relativism concerns respecting cultural diversity, understanding differences in ways of living, and avoiding making judgements.

Bolton adds that:

> [W]e are all culture bound – physically, socially, psychologically and spiritually. We might change that culture, but can never make ourselves 'free' thus the diversity in terms of ways of living, opinions, views and approaches to social phenomena. (2010: 67)

Similarly, different cultures have different moral codes (Rachels, 1993). Our own way of living seems natural, 'right' and appropriate in our social context. The concepts of 'right' and 'wrong' differ from culture to culture. For example, each culture has different views about children and work. There are some cultures where work is viewed as a good way for children to learn about life and the world around them at the same time as contributing to society. Work is seen as preparation for adult life, therefore children are encouraged to participate in work. In many societies there is a tendency for it to be seen as 'normal' for children of disadvantaged groups (lower classes or ethnic minorities) to do jobs that, to another culture, seem difficult and dangerous for their age. The question rather concerns the factors that lead households to make decisions involving their children working outside the control of those households than to what extent a job is hazardous and prevents children from following their development and education. The customs of different cultures and societies are distinct and different from one another. In a culturally relativistic approach, which claims that there exist no universal standards of right or wrong, the idea is to respect other people's traditions, beliefs, habits, customs and values.

The pioneering work of William Graham Summer made the point thus:

> [T]he right way is the way which ancestors used and which has been handed down. The tradition is its own warrant. It is not held subject to verification by experience. The notion of right is in the folkways. It is not outside of them, of independent origin, and brought to test them. In the folkways, whatever is right, is right. This is because they are traditional, and therefore contain in themselves the authority of the ancestral ghosts. When we come to the folkways we are at the end of our analysis. (1906: 28)

Cultural relativism challenges our belief in the universality of views, customs, ideas and practices. It promotes, in effect, the notion that there is no such thing as global ethics; there are only the various codes that people are using to communicate and lead their lives.

To summarise: different cultures have different codes, different aspects of what is right and wrong. There is no objective standard that can be used to judge one societal code as 'better' than another. The moral code of our society has no special status: it is merely one among many. The moral code of a society determines what is right or wrong within that society: if the moral code of a society says a certain action is right then that action is indeed right, at least within that society.

However, cultural relativism may be criticised as an ideal situation; it should not forbid us from criticising the codes of other societies, as doing so would prevent us from criticising our own codes. For example, traditions exist that are, to outside eyes, hazardous or exploitative, and should not be tolerated as they appear to contravene another society's perceptions of human dignity and protection.

 Case study

Female genital mutilation

This is one of the most highly political areas of women's health. World-wide, it is estimated that well over 120 million women have been subjected to the procedure. Supporters claim it is an important part of cultural and religious life. Some compare it to the practice of male circumcision, more widely accepted in the Western world, while opponents say that not only is it potentially life-threatening, it is also an extreme form of oppression of women.

In certain countries where it is more widely practised, it is nevertheless officially illegal; those who persist in the practice in Senegal face a prison term of between one and five years, for example. However, it persists, quietly, within the family and out of sight of officials.

Female circumcision is mainly carried out in western and southern Asia, the Middle East and large areas of Africa. It is also known to take place, contrary to the law, among immigrant communities in the USA, Canada, France, Australia and Britain. In total it is estimated that as many as two million girls a year are subjected to genital mutilation.

▶

Why is female genital mutilation carried out?
Female genital mutilation conforms to several cultural beliefs. The aim of the process is to ensure a woman remains faithful to her future husband. Some communities consider girls ineligible for marriage if they have not been circumcised. Girls as young as three undergo the process; the age at which the operation is performed varies according to country and culture. Girls who have not been circumcised may be considered 'unclean' in many cultures, and may be treated as harlots by other women. Many men believe the folklore saying they will die if their penis touches a clitoris.
(Adapted from BBC website: http://www.bbc.co.uk/health/ physical_health/conditions/female_genital_mutilation.shtml)

Examples such as this demonstrate the appeal of cultural relativism. Even though it is not infallible, it is an attractive concept because it is based on a genuine insight that many of the practices and attitudes we think so natural are really products of one's culture. However, in situations such as the above case study these practices are intolerable as they carry a risk of harm. It is important to distinguish between the views that customs of other societies are inferior to our own on the one hand, and that on the other the customs of other societies are hazardous to health or to mental, spiritual and moral development or are exploitative.

The Challenge for the Researcher

In light of the above discussion, several ethical challenges are faced by researchers when researching either other cultures (outsiders) or their own (insiders). In both circumstances the main challenge concerns the limitation of biased approaches. It should be noted that this is part of a much wider debate concerning not only the issue itself of researching cultures, but also the question of what constitutes 'not bad' approaches and who holds the power to impose ideas, theories, policies or practices. Put simply, there have been and are many different societies in the world, each of which has its own culture, its own way of living and behaving, and its own system of norms, values and beliefs. It is not difficult for most of us to recognise this – contact with another society/culture is usually enough to alert us to the many sorts of differences. We can call this the recognition of plurality or diversity. The difficulty arises when we start to make judgements of the value or truth of key elements of the research. Fundamental questions arising from such a view are:

- What are the 'best' or the 'right' ways of acting (the epistemology of research)?

- Whose system of thought or belief is the most 'true' (the axiology and ontology of research)?

For example, there is a great deal of research into gender stereotypes. One instance is the study carried out by Spence et al. (1975), who investigated large samples of American college men and women; they described the following differences between males and females:

Males	**Females**
Independent	Emotional
Assertive	Warm to others
Aggressive	Creative
Dominant	Excitable
Like maths and science	Feelings easily hurt
Mechanical aptitude	Need approval

In an earlier study Mead (1935) looked at three primitive tribes in New Guinea and found that sex roles were culturally bound. In her sample, in one of the tribes – the Tchambuli – women were independent, assertive, made decisions about the economic organisation of the tribe and took key decisions; the men, on the other hand, took few decisions, looked after the food and were deeply involved in artistic activities.

The findings of these two studies are contradictory. Does this mean that one of the two studies is 'wrong'? On the contrary: the two different gender stereotypes found in the studies prove the fact that culture plays an important role in research. Results therefore vary, depending on the cultural context of the study; as Bolton (2010) phrased it, they are 'culturally bound'.

A major implication in terms of ethical practice is to question the way in which dominant versions of what is 'good' research and how to achieve it have been determined. For example, in the dominant European and North American experience and literature, there is a tendency to see the world in such dichotomous terms as:

modern v. traditional

civilised v. primitive

developed v. not developed

industrial, urban v. agricultural, rural

rational, scientific, technological v. irrational, unscientific, non-technological

democratic v. undemocratic.

The first of these pairs has in the past been associated with Europe and North America, the West; the second, with the developed world. Both associations ignore the millennia of other, far earlier, highly developed civilisations. In addition, there has been a strong tendency to see the first set as having not only 'truer'-superior knowledge but also more efficient, effective, political, economic and social systems producing a higher quality of life. The modern Western way has been seen by some as providing a universal model of an ideal society. Furthermore, it has been able to make a claim for universal status because of the current economic, military and political power of the West.

Within contemporary discussions on development there is much questioning and criticism of what is seen as a dominant Eurocentric view of the world, alongside suggestions for what needs to be done to redress the imbalance. This has applied equally to discussion about rights and whether there is such a thing as a universal list of human rights, and whether what is contained in the various international human rights instruments is primarily driven by Western cultures and politics.

It is within this context of the critique of Western economic, political and cultural dominance that the researcher sets his/her mind when researching other cultures.

Moreover, as was shown in the example of gender stereotypes mentioned above, the social construction and the experience of childhood vary between societies and cultures. In essence, among cultures there are issues with children's participation. It is clear that differences exist among cultures, especially Western and Eastern cultures, regarding the role of parents and family in shaping the views of the child; in this way a child's socialisation varies, as what is considered the 'norm' in one society it is not so in another.

Consequently, the dominant view in research into the participation of children should not be about isolating or uprooting the child from its culture. The view of an individual and of rights as resting in the individual is essentially part of the historical development of Western capitalism; other traditions exist, for example in Hindu and Islamic culture and law where identity and status are rooted in the family and the community. It should be noted that different traditions and cultures are coming to terms with modernity and are further developing their own norms of law and relationships among individuals, communities and people; they need to do so at their own pace.

Key Issue of Ethical Research with Children from Other Cultures: The Right *Not To* . . .

In light of the above, research with children from other cultures should comply with ethical practice as discussed throughout the book and, in particular, in Chapter 2. Here was emphasised **the right *not to* participate** – in the complexity of the arguments around how children may participate and be heard, the right not to participate is often ignored. However, if we want to demonstrate cultural awareness and diversity, we need to understand that to some cultures, the right not to participate is central.

Acknowledging that right as an essential principle in ethical practice, it is suggested that a key to ethical research with children from other cultures is to consider research as a continuum, divided into categories in terms of its likely effect on children. This continuum is illustrated in Figure 5.2.

Central to research is the knowledge and understanding of children's lives, experiences, learning and development, as well as how these can be furthered; thus research is undertaken. Ethical research needs to consider the impact of culture and for the researchers to think in a continuum of dimensions of different values (axiology) or set of cultural realities (ontology), rather than as a universal set of values and 'truths' (hegemony). With this in mind, before researchers embark on a choice of methods (epistemology) they need to question the nature of research from three key ethical perspectives. Firstly, it must be asked whether the research is positive and/or beneficial in that it ensures that all children gain opportunities for self-realisation. Finding the

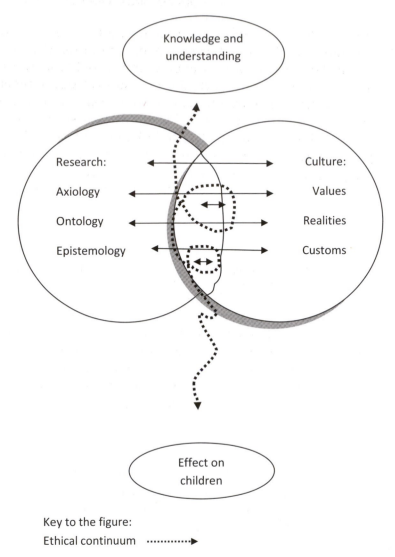

Figure 5.2   Ethical continuum in researching other cultures

right balance between children's cultural codes and research codes that suit the needs, interests and customs of their culture is the second priority. Finally, as explored elsewhere in this book and in particular in Chapters 4, 5, and 10, there is the empowerment of children. Young children are often at risk of being socially oppressed by adults. Ethical practice in that sense is the protection of children and the continuum from dependency towards supporting the self-regulation, self-organisation, determination and control of their lives, which involves listening to what children themselves want rather than an adult's views of their best interests.

Distinguishing factors in research are the nature of the research, the types and conditions of the research taking place, the long- and short-term effects of the research with children, and their opportunities to choose whether to be part of the research, i.e. the right *not to* participate and to leave the process. Sensitivity to children's culture are foregone indicators of where research falls along this continuum.

Conclusions and summary

This chapter has aimed to discuss ethical implications when researching other cultures. It is important to understand, as has been emphasised throughout this book, that there is no such notion as 'global ethics', as these would deny autonomy to an individual's cultures and societies. In the whole discourse of ethical practice regarding research with children, there is an underlying risk that the development of assumed universal ethics may reinforce divisions not only between cultures and societies but also hierarchies of cultures, as well as inequalities of practice. Researching children from cultures other than the researchers' should be based on the creation of a debate on cultural coalitions to promote and protect children's rights and cultural identities. Ethical practice in researching with children from other cultures is a continuum, divided into criteria in terms of its likely effect on children. Distinguishing criteria include the right not to participate, the right to represent each individual's culture and the right to each individual's own perception of this.

Key points to remember

- Each culture and society possesses its own rationality and coherence, thus the ideas we have for ourselves govern the way we live our lives although there exist different ways for each culture.

- Different cultures have different perspectives on what is 'good' and what is 'right'.

- It is difficult for the researcher to divorce him/herself from his/her beliefs and cultural contexts. Our cultural identity prescribes our behaviours and influences the ways 'good' and 'right' are perceived.

- Ethical practice researching other cultures should be viewed as a continuum, where the key elements consist of examining whether the research is positive and beneficial for children and is empowering children.

- Key issues of ethical research with children from other cultures involve their right not to participate, and respecting the autonomy and agency of the child.

Points for discussion and reflection

- Outline ways in which your individual cultural beliefs may be different in the context of your work or researching other cultures.

- How do you see gender or ethnicity affecting the way in which we conduct research with children?

- Discuss whether social constructions and the experience of childhood vary between societies and cultures, and why.

Further reading

Alderson, P. & Morrow, V. (2011) *The Ethics of Research with Children and Young People: A Practical Handbook*. London: Sage.

Christensen, P. & James, A. (2011) *Research with Children* (2nd edn). London: Routledge.

Parker, B. (2000) *Rethinking Multiculturalism: Cultural Diversity and Political Theory*. Cambridge, MA: Harvard University Press.

References

Abrams, D. & Hogg, M. (1990a) *Social Identification: A Social Psychology of Intergroup Relations and Group Processes*. London: Routledge.

Abrams, D. & Hogg, M. (1990b) 'Social identification, self categorization and social influence', *European Review of Social Psychology*, 1: 195–228.

Aries, P. (1986) *Centuries of Childhood. A Social History of Family Life*. New York: Random House.

Bharati, A. (1986) 'The self in Hindu thought and action', in A.J. Marsella, G. Devos & F.L.K. Hsu (eds), *Culture and Self: Asian and Western Perspectives*. London: Tavistock.

Bloch, M. (1992) 'Critical perspectives on the historical relationship between child development and early childhood research', in S. Kessler & B. Swadener (eds), *Reconceptualising the Early Childhood Curriculum*. New York: Teachers College Press.

Bolton, G. (2010) *Reflective Practice. Writing and Professional Development* (3rd edn). London: Sage.

Christensen, P. & James, A. (2011) *Research with Children* (2nd edn). London: Routledge.

Clark, A., Kjørholt, A.T. & Moss, P. (2005) *Beyond Listening: Children's Perspectives on Early Childhood Services*. Bristol: Policy Press.

Devos, G. (1986) 'Dimensions of the self in Japanese culture', in A.J. Marsella, G. Devos, G. & F.L.K. Hsu (eds), *Culture and Self: Asian and Western Perspectives*. London: Tavistock.

Greenwood, P.J. & Stini, W.A. (1977) *Nature, Culture, and Human History: A Bio-cultural Introduction to Anthropology*. New York: Harper & Row.

Hill, T., Lewicki, P., Czyzewska, M. & Boss, A. (1989) 'Self-perpetuating development of encoding biases in person perception', *Journal of Personality and Social Psychology*, 57: 373–87.

Hogg, M.A. & Vaughan, G.M. (1995) *Social Psychology: An Introduction*. Hemel Hempstead: Prentice-Hall/Harvester Wheatsheaf.

Hsu, F.L.K. (1986) 'The self in cross-cultural perspective', in A.J. Marsella, G. Devos & F.L.K. Hsu (eds), *Culture and Self: Asian and Western Perspectives*. London: Tavistock.

James, A. & Prout, A. (1997) *Constructing and Reconstructing Childhood* (2nd edn). London: Falmer.

Kelly, G.A. (1995) *The Psychology of Personal Constructs*. New York: Norton.

Kjørholt, A.T. (2001) '"The participating child": a vital pillar in this century?', *Nordissk Pedagogic*, 21: 65–81.

Kjørholt, A.T. (2002) 'Small is powerful: discourses on "children and participation"', *Norway, Childhood*, 9(1): 63–82.

Kottack, C.P. (1994) *Anthropology: The Exploration of Human Diversity* (6th edn). New York: McGraw-Hill.

Lewis, A. & Lindsay, G. (eds) (2000) *Researching Children's Perspectives*. Buckingham: Open University Press.

Mead, M. (1935) *Growing Up in New Guinea*. Harmondsworth: Penguin.

Parekh, B. (2000) *Rethinking Multiculturalism. Culture Diversity and Political Theory*. Cambridge, MA: Harvard University Press.

Prout, A. (2000) 'Children's participation: control and self-realisation in British late modernity', *Children and Society*, 14: 304–31.

Prout, A. (2003) 'Participation, policy and the changing conditions of childhood', in C. Hallet & A. Prout (eds), *Hearing the Voices of Children: Social Policy for a New Century*. London: RoutledgeFalmer.

Rachels, J. (1993) *The Elements of Moral Philosophy*. London: McGraw-Hill.

Rinaldi, C. (2005) *In Dialogue with Reggio Emilia*. London: Routledge.

Seymour-Smith, C. (1986) *Macmillan Dictionary of Anthropology*. London: Macmillan.

Spence, J.J., Helmreich, R.L. & Stapp, J. (1975) 'The personal attributes questionnaire: a measure of sex role stereotypes and masculinity-feminity', *JSAS Catalog of Selected Documents in Psychology*, 4: 127.

Summer, W.G. (1906) *Folkways*. Boston: Ginn & Co.

Tajfel, H. (1978) 'The achievement of group differentiation', *Differentiation Between Groups: Studies in the Social Psychology of Intergroup Relations*. London: Academic Press.

Tajfel, H. (1982) *Human Groups and Categories*. Cambridge: Cambridge University Press.

Tajfel, H. & Turner, J.C. (1986) 'The social indentify theory of intergroup behaviour', in S. Worchel & W.G. Austin (eds), *Psychology of Intergroup Relations* (2nd edn). Chicago: Nelson Hall.

Tylor, J. (1958 [1871]) *Primitive Culture*. New York: Harper Torchbooks. In J. Moore (1997) *Visions of Culture*. London: Altamira Press.

United Nations (1989) *The Convention on the Rights of the Child*. Geneva: Defence International and the United Nations Children's Fund.

White, L.A. (1959) *The Evolution of Culture: The Development of Civilization to the Fall of Rome*. New York: McGraw-Hill.

Part 2

Ethical Issues in Policy and Practice

6

Ethics, Policy and Every Child Matters

Barry Powell

Chapter overview

This chapter seeks to engage readers with the fragmentation of social policy over the last four decades and possible continuing developments from the Coalition government. Social policy areas such as housing, education, health and social work have become compartmentalised and reflect the growing atomisation of British society (Lonne et al., 2009: 123). The impact of this on children can be seen directly in the case of Victoria Climbié and the subsequent Laming Report (2003). Sent by her mother to live with her aunt in Europe, Victoria's death was a signifier of, and catalyst for, the subsequent Every Child Matters (ECM) agenda and Children Act. The development of the Children Act 2004, with sections 10–12 placing a duty on those working with children to share information to protect them, seems to suggest 'joined-up' working (Hudson, 2005: 229). However, services at a local level are now themed, with social workers, educationalists and healthcare workers providing services to both adult and child groups dichotomously (Featherstone et al., 2010: 5). ECM and other child development initiatives such as Sure Start reflect the drive towards devolution in the United Kingdom, with delivery the responsibility of each of the four nations and regions within those areas. Thus countervailing forces are at work.

Joined-up thinking, professional responsibility and ethics, along with tighter central management targets, are in juxtaposition and contradiction with an increasingly segmented society; they continue to feed emphasis on blaming the individual through the 'cycle of deprivation' thesis (Parton, 2009: 73) and concerns about the efficacy of policy. Ethics are seemingly a background issue, as political and societal forces react only when cases such as that of Victoria Climbié and, most recently, of Baby P become apparent. Yet safeguarding children and implementing the aims of Every Child Matters is what practitioners are working towards and on which their progress is measured. The current chapter seeks to engage readers as critical practitioners who are able to: trace the historic and substantive issues; outline why changes in the social fabric might allow certain issues to recur; and, finally, think beyond their immediate role and locate themselves in the landscape as actors for ethical change.

ECM – The Policy Background and Fall-out

There has indeed been a frenzy of policy documents, with regard to early years practice, generated by Every Child Matters (Taylor, in Broadhurst et al., 2009: 30–31). However, missing from all of the documentation is an ethical stance other than the 'common-sense' assumptions that children should be protected and nurtured. The practical application of the wishes of Lord Laming and those who have invested political, legislative and emotional capital in him is almost completely devoid of a truly normative standpoint. An example of this can be gleaned by undertaking a word search of Lord Laming's inquiry into the murder of Victoria Climbié, the Every Child Matters Green Paper and Lord Laming's subsequent progress review of ECM following the death of Baby Peter. Nowhere in the documents are the words 'ethical' or 'ethics' found in the body of these works (Laming, 2003; Chief Secretary to the Treasury, 2003; Laming, 2009). In the recent Munro Reports (2010, 2011a, 2011b) a similar word search relates 'ethical' only to social work practice and to the wider neo-liberal context in which social policy operates. This may have two immediate explanations. Firstly, Lord Laming and those who worked with him felt that their work is implicitly ethical. This assumption sees no disjuncture between the aims of what followed – the ECM agenda, on the one hand, and failings that lead to child abuse on the other. The period since the death of Victoria Climbié has seen Karen Matthews successfully hide her daughter for a length of time in order to elicit a ransom fee while Vanessa George, a nursery worker, abused children while at work in Plymouth. It will be noted that female perpetrators are in the foreground of such cases, even though behind them were, arguably, more influential males; the gender aspect of this debate will not be discussed here. However, the subtext of the present argument is that there exists a fault line in the thinking of those such as Laming, who believe their world-view is shared by all. This laudable moral standpoint, a 'common-sense' given, is clearly not shared by the adults mentioned in the two examples above. Indeed, most incidents connected with the welfare of children are decontextualised.

As Broadhurst et al. (2009: 251–2) point out, the social context of the deaths of Victoria Climbié and Baby Peter are ignored, as are the issues faced by the borough in which they both died – Haringey. For example, as Broadhurst et al. (2009: 249–50) note, Haringey is the eighteenth-most deprived area in England and Wales, with a substantial proportion of its children eligible for free school meals. These are just two of the socio-economic indicators of deprivation suggested by Broadhurst et al. (2009) with which successive governments have struggled to get to grips for the last thirty years. This point was not lost in the report into Victoria Climbié's death (Laming, 2003: 109). However, the recommendations failed to recognise structural issues, in contrast to the public enquiry into the death of Maria Colwell in 1973, which caused an equal amount of public concern (Parton, 2004: 82).

This leads us to the second immediate reason why Laming omits the context: the socio-economic reality is too risky politically to confront directly. Thirty years of opprobrium for most of those who work in public services and at the forefront of social policy initiatives, including those who work with young children, along with constraints in funding and autonomy, mean that it is inexpedient to tackle growing inequality (see Grover, in Broadhurst et al., 2009: 55–7; Hoyle, 2008). Therefore, upskilling those who work in pre-school education (Baldock et al., 2009: 105–12), accompanied by the managerialisation (and potential downskilling) of professionals such as social workers (Parton, 2004: 88–9), is evident in various documents. At the same time, the pathologising of those from lower socio-economic backgrounds as inadequate parents continues in parallel, as illustrated by Broadhurst et al. (2009: 253; Parton, 2009: 73). The strongest recommendation from Laming was a national database, ContactPoint, of all aged under 18. This project was terminated by the Coalition agreement under the notion of civil liberties (Coalition Agreement, 11 May 2010: 6). Nevertheless, White et al. (2010) suggest that political and economic retrenchment from IT-led developments are flawed; however, as noted by Featherstone et al. (2010), the reinvigoration of professionals' involvement with children and families called for by Eileen Munro in her reports on social work, as commissioned by the Coalition government, seems to continue the omission from the role of neo-liberal economics its societal effects (Featherstone et al., 2010). The thesis of the cycle of deprivation expounded by Sir Keith Joseph in the 1970s seems to have become integral to the analytic framework of social policy.

Joseph's notion was that those brought up in households of material and spiritual poverty replicate the same lives as those of their parents and aspire to nothing but un- or under-employment for their own children. Thus the poor parenting and limited life chances of those who are mothered and fathered by such parents need to be addressed (Parton, 2009: 73). The ten-year Blair administration (1997–2007) took measures to remedy this perceived malady, unlike the previous Conservative regime; the latter saw the cycle as a way of justifying the inbuilt inequality of capitalism and its partial withdrawal of welfare from such families (Alcock et al., 2008: 395–7). However, New Labour's practical application of policies built upon the cycle of deprivation leaves a vacuum in terms of ethics and social policy. There is indeed a policy agenda, but it is one driven by events and personalities, always reactive and never plumbing the bases of inequalities in British society; in addition, it avoids tackling the flaws in the dominant idea that individuals through paid employment in a free-market society are responsible for their own destinies. This idea clearly divides New Labour from Old Labour, which, at least politically, gave credence to such structural factors as class and the inequalities generated in a free-market economy. To this end, New Labour had more in common with the previous Conservative administrations, and continued to develop what Jessop calls a 'workfare state', as contrasted with the welfare state that existed between 1945 and 1979 (Jessop, in Lewis et al., 2000: 171–85). Coalition policy developments on welfare continue this line of thinking.

Group activity 1

Examine the distribution of wealth (and even locate yourself in an income bracket) by accessing http://www.ifs.org.uk/wheredoyoufitin/welcome.php?x=59&y=19.

The media often report about the effect of taxes on wealth innovation. This is usually in response to the feeling of those who own media concerns that they are unduly harshly taxed. In addition, the wealth of top personalities in sport and entertainment is often discussed. After looking at the website, consider these points:

- What percentage of the population earns over £50,000 per year?

- What is the median income?

Next, undertake research into the income of the top 1 percentile of earnings and the bottom 10 per cent. Consider the disparities and the effect these disparities might have on children born into poor households.

Children, Harm and Welfare

While not wishing to diminish the importance of situational factors that disadvantage children and, in extreme cases, lead to headline-making news (of which more will be discussed later) it is important to understand certain facts about those children who perish in circumstances that attract the attention of the law. In 2007–8, 43 of the 69 children who were murder victims were killed by their parents (Coleman, 2009: 12). Children under the age of one are the most-at-risk group, particularly when males aged 16–20 (Coleman, in Povey, 2009: 13) are excluded from the statistics covering murders per million of the population. However, the statistical picture is somewhat confusing. For example, the NSPCC website (2009) notes that more than 100 die per year due to abuse or neglect, yet the Ofsted figure is in excess of this. With such contradictory information, it is unclear how the policies enacted since 2004 reflect evidence-based detail, or how the policies have informed practice. It is only since January 2009 that those under 16 have been included in the British Crime Survey; this offers some explanation for the increase in knee-jerk reactions by governments over time.

Previous child deaths that provoked a government response include those of Denis O'Neill who died at the hands of foster parents in 1945, Maria Colwell who was killed by her stepfather in 1973, and Kimberley Carlisle and Jasmine Beckford who died at the hands of their step-parents in the 1980s. However, the evidence from recent incidents where children have been abused suggests that the policy environment, while animated, lacks an ethical standpoint that includes those adults lacking the initiative to act as a government would wish. This is to say, the government is failing to engage universally with parents, including those who clearly do not share the same ideas on what constitutes a positive start for children. The discourse of ECM thus excludes the participation of the very people/parents who need to be included while, at same time, using techniques of surveillance to ensure that they behave appropriately towards children in their care (Hoyle, 2010; Chief Secretary to the Treasury, 2003: 51–66). As noted, the past thirty years of social policy have seen a move back to individual responsibility, a reduced role for the state in providing welfare and a greater reliance on market mechanisms. This has been more than evidenced in the shape of policies affecting children and young people. For adults, this has meant that paid employment is seen as the key to economic success (see Grover, 2009: 55–72). Those without work have been subjected to a reinvigoration of the Victorian notion of lowered eligibility (ibid.: 249): those out of work should receive no more than slightly less than the lowest-paid worker in similar circumstances. Such an attitude towards claims to welfare has come to haunt areas such as Haringey, which, as mentioned earlier, suffers from high levels of deprivation; the results are that those living on benefit or low incomes are penalised and, by default, so are their children. Indeed, this limiting of services was noted by Laming (2003: 10–11) although was never politically challenged.

While some couples with children on benefits have seen their incomes rise, the idea is clearly to encourage parents, whatever the formation of their families (lone parents, reconstituted families or traditional nuclear families) to develop a work ethic and participate in an increasingly global market. Add the factors of globalisation and immigration and boroughs like Haringey have a potent mix of local issues through which national governments struggle to steer a policy (Parton, 2004: 84–6). Indeed, the Blair/Brown administrations placed paid employment at the centre of social policy. In so doing they have been even more hard-line than the Conservative administrations (1979–97) which, while disapproving of lone parents (especially lone young mothers), did not impose the idea of paid work as the key to success to the same extent as did New Labour (Baldock et al., 2009: 28–9) or has the Coalition government.

Children, especially younger ones, have no control over the income of their parents. They have no exit from and no voice in the market society into which they are born; they struggle to make their own histories and not necessarily those of their own choosing. The deficiencies of the market-based, employment-oriented society are exposed as failing some children; inequalities are not necessarily redressed, even by governments such as New Labour. Both New Labour and its commitment to addressing poverty and the Coalition government which speaks of fairness have fallen short. Those who work in the field of childcare and early years are left with an erratic set of agendas within which to work. The various modulations are still being felt in areas covered by documents such as the Children and Young People's Workforce Strategy (DCSF, 2008).

 Group activity 2

Look at one recent issue connected with harm to children where an official enquiry has taken place and compare it to a past incidence. Assess the following:

- the respective backgrounds to both

- the use of language in both enquiries

- the recommendations.

In doing so, compare and contrast any subsequent changes in policies.

Modernisation, the Workforce and New Public Management

New Public Management (NPM) has become a tool via which to restructure the delivery of welfare services. The welfare state, a post-Second World War political consensus, was by the mid-1970s viewed as anachronistic. At this point, the paternalistic notions of welfare administered by bureaucrats whose professionalism had remained relatively unchallenged was seen as patronising and also as stifling to individual enterprise (Clarke & Newman, 1997). The state had encouraged dependency, according to this reading of welfare as it was between 1945 and 1979. The idea of the 'welfare scrounger', perpetuated by the media, had also made a claim on the public imagination (Clarke & Newman, 1997: 32). Welfare professionals were seen as self-regarding and protective of their boundaries; the ills welfare had sought to cure were, for some at least, still prevalent. Teachers, doctors, social workers and other welfare professionals were seen not to be delivering the better society envisaged by Beveridge.

It was felt that there was a need for welfare professionals to be exposed to the world of markets and competition. In private enterprise products have to be competitive, responsive to customer wants and desires, and reasonably priced. For Conservatives of the Sir Keith Joseph ilk, this was missing from the land of welfare. There was a need to substitute the romantic idea of the welfare worker with ideas that drew upon the workings of private enterprise (Clarke et al., 2007: 28–36). Therefore, what has become evident in the alliance of overhauling the children's workforce and monitoring the deviant benefit-claiming poor parent is an enhancement of the 'cycle of deprivation' theory. At this point it may be asked what this has to do with ethics and social policy. Answered simply, the documents developed since the ECM and the Children Act 2004 can be neither understood nor placed into context without their being viewed from this policy perspective.

New Public Management or NPM has, as a method of controlling and responsibilising public service workers, since 1979 become the modus operandi of governments. Targets, reporting, league tables and inspection pervade all those agencies cited in Laming's original inquiry into the death of Victoria Climbié. This was done apparently to make agencies such as social work, police and the NHS, to name but a few, more responsive to their customers – in other words, it was a way of controlling the state sector. Hood describes NPM as:

> [A] shorthand name for a set of broadly similar administrative doctrines which dominated the bureaucratic reform agenda in many OECD group of countries from the late 1970s onwards. (Hood, 1991: 3–4)

NPM has its variants from this description, yet the one to which the UK gives primacy is savings in time and money in the production of welfare. Latterly, Senior et al. (2007) have proposed that New Labour has moved to Modernisation in terms of the criminal justice system. The differences between NPM and Modernisation are too finely nuanced to be discussed at length here; however, both discourses have been enacted.

Indeed, the panoply of agencies managing and surveying public service workers, the individuals who observe and work with problematic parenting, leads to a conclusion that the state and its social policy lack an ethical compass. The proposed idea of 'joined-up thinking' espoused by Tony Blair appears not to have any substance; even under Gordon Brown the government failed to subject all of its legislation to the child impact assessment as championed by the United Nations Convention on the Rights of the Child (UNCRC) (Payne, 2007: 472).

It has been mentioned that unless social class is included more strongly in the equation, then the failure subsequently to instigate the ideas that are at the heart of Laming's thinking cannot be understood (Hudson, 2005: 234). The argument seeks thereby not to diminish the minutiae of professional judgement and professionals working with each other on a day-to-day basis, but instead to frame those interactions in the context of a class-based, capitalist society. White (in Broadhurst et al., 2009: 93–110) describes how two different readings of the same note between two professionals in different fields came to play a part in Victoria Climbié's death. A subsequent reclassification of Victoria as a 'child in need', rather than one who required more urgent attention under the heading of 'child protection' on the basis of an interpretation of a doctor's statement, had a fatal corollary. This is just one small piece of a complicated jigsaw peculiar to Victoria's case yet with echoes in others (Parton, 2004). Despite the grand ideas behind joined-up thinking (see Hudson, 2005), the imposition of management techniques imported from the private sector, a raft of initiatives, development plans and aims, and the work of the many professionals who saw Baby P, the outcome for him was the same as that of Victoria Climbié. The current vogue for using market mechanisms to instigate change in welfare is merely a replication of class inequalities being conducted from within the field of welfare. Indeed, this whole chapter has been framed within the context of negative rights, that is being free to carry out one's own business and, in this case, freedom from being killed when one is not a fully reasoning human being. Thus positive rights in terms of entitlements have not been introduced; social divisions are at best cementing themselves or even becoming worse (Baldock, 2009: 47–9; Grover, in Broadhurst et al., 2009: 63–6). While ECM's five outcomes suggest a set of positive rights for children, there is no way for individual children to claim them in a society that has social policies increasingly framed upon negative rights. In addition, the role of devolution has not been taken into account.

The account by Baldock et al. (2009) of devolution in relation to the early years agenda gives an instructional description that sets the backdrop towards raising further issues about a coherent, ethically based social policy. As Baldock et al. (2009) note, the component parts of the union, i.e. Scotland, Wales and Northern Ireland, have framed their own early years policies. For example, Wales appointed a Children's Commissioner in 2001 after opposition from New Labour and the previous Conservative government (Baldock et al., 2009: 94; Hudson, 2005: 232–3). Other changes in the principality focused on teacher training, with less reliance on familial bonds in childminding. Scotland hosted the first integrated services department for young children in Strathclyde during the 1980s, and has now embarked on workforce development. In Northern Ireland, the most troubled part of the union, there are partnerships transcending national boundaries. Baldock et al. (2009: 100) note that there is an all-Ireland service for children with autistic disorders. However, there are cultural divides in the union, not to mention the divides within each of the component parts. The devolution of power, along with the fragmentation of social policy and the effects of globalisation, leaves the coherent development of children's services as a mammoth task.

One of the paradoxes of New Labour was its need to micro-manage while giving greater powers to the constituent nations of the United Kingdom. The Coalition government seeks to devolve – yet without a budget. This leads to the conclusion that is, therefore, not a conclusion as such, but more of a recapitulation of the confusing state of current UK politics.

Conclusions and summary

In this chapter policy seems to be contradictory and paradoxical in nature towards children, not only since 1997 but in the last thirty years, due to the effects of neo-liberalism. This denotes a switch from a welfare state to a 'workfare' state (Jessop, in Lewis et al., 2000). An example of contradiction is inherent in one of the outcomes of ECM, which centres on a positive right – achieving economic well-being. Economic well-being is centred around paid employment and protecting the 'free market', elements that might have little direct relevance to parenting. Furthermore, while the government claims a commitment to

UNCRC, it carries out no child impact assessment on all of its proposed legislation (Payne, 2007). Welfare reform aimed at the 'welfare scrounger' may directly affect children. Recent governments have juxtaposed the rights of children with the parents' necessity to work, when politically expedient. The government has sought not only to devolve power to the nations that make up the United Kingdom; it has also encouraged regional powers. However, with this have come targets, performance measurement and the making responsible of those invested with power, hence an inversion of the criticisms by the media: the media have power without responsibility, yet workers in local authorities and in the devolved state seem to hold responsibility without power. That Laming's initial report into the death of Victoria Climbié led to public castigation of relatively inexperienced workers is apparent.

All of this highlights the dilemmas for anyone working with young children, alongside the weight of responsibility they bear. In the absence of a clear ethical dimension to social policy, they are able to act only through their professional associations, unions and other related organisations. Recent governments can point to consultation, certainly with the latter, in framing their policies; however, the lack of consistent child impact assessments is a serious omission. The clash over the death of Baby P in the House of Commons in November 2008 only serves as a reminder that policy is made by politicians who have their own interests at heart. Self-interest is what drives the free market in twenty-first-century Britain; the protection of the market, a negative right, seems to supersede the positive rights of the child in social policy. This fragmentation of a common social policy interest, allied with devolution, an increasingly globalised economy and workforce, and the residue of a welfare state, does not bode well for children. This is the context in which the ECM agenda operates and hopes to effect change. However, it might well lead to more of the same operating conditions for those who work with children and, more importantly, for children themselves unless there is a social, political and economic paradigm shift.

Key points to remember

Key points to remember are:

- the recurring issues in critical incidents to have influenced children's policy

- the effects of an increasingly disparate set of communities that make up British society today

- the role played by inequality in making Every Child Matters outcomes an ambitious and possibly unachievable aim. In fact, does every child matter when assessing social policy?

Points of discussion and reflection

1. Consider the communities you serve and how easy it is to meet the five outcomes of Every Child Matters within your communities.
2. What knowledge do you have of social policy and how it affects your setting?
3. In what ways do you think further knowledge of social issues could further your work?

Further reading

Dorling, D. (2010) *Injustice – Why Social Inequality Persists*. Bristol: Policy Press.
Titmuss, R. (1970) *Social Policy – An Introduction*. London: George Allen & Unwin.
Wilkinson, R. & Pickett, K. (2010) *The Spirit Level – Why Equality Is Better for Everyone*. London: Penguin.

Useful websites

Child Poverty Action Group: http://www.cpag.org.uk
Institute for Fiscal Studies: http://www.ifs.org.uk
Poverty Organisation: http://www.poverty.org

References

Alcock, C., Daly, G. & Griggs, E. (2008) *Introducing Social Policy* (2nd edn). Harlow: Pearson Longman.
Baldock, P., Fitzgerald, D. & Kay, J. (2009) *Understanding Early Years Policy* (2nd edn). London: Sage.
Banks, S. (2006) *Ethics and Values in Social Work* (3rd edn). Basingstoke: Palgrave Macmillan.

Baverstock, A., Bartle, D., Boyd, B. & Finlay, F. (2008) 'Review of child protection training uptake and knowledge of child protection guidelines', *Child Abuse Review*, 17: 64–72.

Broadhurst, K., Grover, C. & Jamieson, J. (2009) 'Conclusion: safeguarding children', in K. Broadhurst, C. Grover & J. Jamieson (eds), *Critical Perspectives on Safeguarding Children*. Chichester: Blackwell, pp. 248–59.

Chand, A. (2008) 'Every child matters? A critical review of child welfare reforms in the context of minority ethnic children and families', *Child Abuse Review*, 17: 6–22.

Chief Secretary to the Treasury (2003) *Every Child Matters*, Cm 5860. London: TSO.

Clarke, J. & Newman, J. (1997) *The Managerial State*. London: Sage.

Clarke, J., Newman, J., Smith, N., Vidler, E. & Westmarland, L. (2007) *Creating Citizen-Consumers*. London: Sage.

Coleman, K. (2009) 'Homicide', in D. Povey (ed.), *HMSO Statistical Bulletin Homicides: Fire-arm Offences and Intimate Violence 2007-08 (Supplementary Volume 2 to Crime in England and Wales)* (3rd edn). London: HMSO.

Conservative Liberal Democrat Coalition Negotiations Agreement Reached (2010) Online at http://www.conservatives.com/News/News_stories/2010/05/Coalition_Agreement_published.aspx (accessed 17 July 2011).

DCSF (2008) *2020 Children and Young People's Workforce Strategy*. Nottingham: DCSF Publications.

Driscoll, J.J. (2009) 'Prevalence, people and processes: a consideration of the implications of Lord Laming's Progress Report on the protection of children in England', *Child Abuse Review*, 18: 333–45.

Featherstone, B., Broadhurst, K. & Holt, K. (2010) 'Thinking systemically – thinking politically: building strong partnerships with children and families in the context of rising inequality', *British Journal of Social Work* (first published online 7 June 2011, accessed 17 July).

Grover, C. (2009) 'Child poverty', in K. Broadhurst, C. Grover & J. Jamieson (eds), *Critical Perspectives on Safeguarding Children*. Chichester: Blackwell, pp. 55–72.

Home Office (2008) *Consultation on the British Crime Survey Extension to Cover Under 16s*, Response from the Home Office December 2008. Online at: http://www.homeoffice.gov.uk/rds/pdfs08/consult-bcsu16-response08.pdf (accessed 28 December 2009).

Hood, C. (1991) 'A public management for all seasons?', *Public Administration*, 69: 3–19.

Hoyle, D. (2008) 'Problematizing Every Child Matters', *The Encyclopaedia of Informal Education*. Online at: http://www.infed.org/socialwork/every_child_matters_a_critique.htm (accessed 23 July 2009).

Hoyle, D. (2010) 'ContactPoint. Because every child matters?', in *The Encyclopaedia of Informal Education*. Online at: http://www.infed.org/socialwork/contactpoint.htm (accessed 17 July 2010).

Hudson, B. (2005) 'User outcomes and children's services reform: ambiguity and conflict in the policy implementation process', *Social Policy and Society*, 5(2): 227–36.

Jessop, B. (2000) 'From KWNS to the SWPR', in G. Lewis, S. Gewirtz & J. Clarke (eds), *Rethinking Social Policy*. London: Sage, pp. 171–84.

Laming, Lord (2003) *The Victoria Climbié Inquiry: Report of an Inquiry by Lord Laming*, Cm 5730. London: TSO.

Laming, Lord (2009) *The Protection of Children in England: A Progress Report*, HC330. London: TSO.

Lonne, B., Parton, N., Thompson, J. & Harries, M. (2009) *Reforming Child Protection*. Abingdon: Routledge.

Munro, E. (2010) *The Munro Review of Child Protection: Part One: A Systems Analysis*. Online at: http://www.education.gov.uk/munroreview/downloads/TheMunroReviewofChildProtection-Part%20one.pdf (accessed 14 July 2011).

Munro, E. (2011a) *The Munro Review of Child Protection: Interim Report: The Child's Journey*. Online at: http://www.education.gov.uk/munroreview/downloads/Munrointerimreport.pdf (accessed 14 July 2011).

Munro, E. (2011b) *The Munro Review of Child Protection: Final Report: A Child-Centred System*. Online at: http://www.education.gov.uk/munroreview/downloads/8875_DfE_Munro_Report_TAGGED.pdf (accessed 17 July 2011).

NSPCC (2009) *Child Killings in England and Wales*. Online at: http://www.nspcc.org.uk/Inform/research/Briefings/child_killings_in_england_and_wales_wda67213.html#Who_kills_children? (accessed 28 December).

Oftsed (2009) *The Annual Report of Her Majesty's Chief Inspector of Education 2008, Children's Services and Skills 2007/08*, HC1114. London: TSO.

Oliver, B. (2008) 'Reforming the children and young people's workforce: a higher education response', *Learning in Health and Social Care*, 7(4): 209–18.

Parton, N. (2004) 'From Maria Colwell to Victoria Climbié: reflections on public inquiries into child abuse a generation apart', *Child Abuse Review*, 13(2): 80–94.

Parton, N. (2009) 'From Seebohm to think family: reflections on 40 years of policy change of statutory children's social work in England', *Child and Family Social Work*, 14: 68–78.

Payne, L. (2007) 'A children's government in England and child impact assessment', *Children and Society*, 21: 470–5.

Senior, P., Crowther-Downey, C. & Long, M. (2007) *Understanding Modernisation in Criminal Justice*. Maidenhead: Open University Press.

White, S. (2009) 'Arguing the case in safeguarding', in K. Broadhurst, C. Grover & J. Jamieson (eds), *Critical Perspectives on Safeguarding Children*. Chichester: Blackwell, pp. 93–110.

White, S., Wastell, D., Broadhurst, K. & Hall, C. (2010) 'When policy o'erleaps itself: the "tragic tale" of the integrated children's system', *Critical Social Policy*, 30(3): 405–30.

7

Ethics in Multi-agency Working

Ioanna Palaiologou

Chapter overview

It is continually emphasised that where children are concerned, multi-agency working is essential. Research into multi-agency work has demonstrated some successful factors as well as certain challenging issues that come with this type of work. Consequently, a number of ethical challenges arise. This chapter aims to discuss these issues and the different ways of working in partnership: 'joined-up' working. It will also address the ethical implications in the era of working in partnership in order to conclude that the joined-up ideology can move beyond the traditional mono-, inter- and multi-agency approaches towards working together. It will be suggested that trans-agency approaches to joined-up work in early childhood can be effective; also, the chapter addresses a number of ethical challenges faced by professionals when the various agencies work together.

Introduction

The field of early childhood has seen a vast number of rapid changes in terms of policies, legislation, guidance and curricula in the last decade, to name just a few: *Every Child Matters* (DfES, 2003), the Children Act 2004, the Childcare Act 2006, *The National Framework for Children, Young People and Maternity Services* (DfES/DoH, 2004), *Children and Young People in Mind: The Final Report of the National CAMHS* (DCSF/DoH, 2008), *The 21st Century School: A Transformation in Education* (DCSF, 2008). These policies and others have brought a number of changes in the development of services in early years. In particular, emphasis has been placed on the welfare of the child and families. There is a shift away from traditional-style public services towards a 'joined-up services' and 'multi-agency teamwork' ideology. There are many studies (Anning, 2005; Siraj-Blatchford et al., 2007; Fitzgerald & Kay, 2008; Anning et al., 2010; Gasper, 2010) trying to investigate multi-agency work in early years, addressing the barriers and the benefits, looking at how to work in multi-disciplinary teams, how to develop skills among professionals, how to address issues of communication, how to achieve effective problem-solving and how to share knowledge in the multi-professional work environment.

All of these studies aim to investigate models of multi-agency work and address the complexity and the challenges of multi-professional work.

In extensive studies certain authors (Warmington et al., 2004; Anning, 2005, Anning et al., 2010) offer useful, detailed definitions that loosely encompass most of the structures and practices described in the current literature. These are:

- *Inter-agency working*: involving more than one agency, working together in a planned and formal manner rather than simply through informal channels of communication.

- *Multi-agency working*: joint planning or, possibly, a form of replication, resulting from the lack of a coherent policy.

- *Joined-up working*: policy or thinking referring to deliberately conceptualised and coordinated planning that takes account of multiple policies and varying agency practices.

In addition, *Every Child Matters: Change for Children* (DfES, 2007) identifies three models of multi-agency working:

- *Multi-agency panel*: in this type, members are not permanently part of the panel. Rather, they identify with and remain employed by their home agencies. The panel meets regularly, usually the team around the child.

- *Multi-agency teams*: these teams are more permanent and have more of the sense of being a team, with recruits or seconded members, a team leader and a team identity.

- *Integrated services*: the team is co-located, usually part of community-based service providing inter-disciplinary services to children and families.

Since the concepts of working together or joined-up ideology were introduced and began to be implemented in children's services, a vast number of pieces of research attempted to examine effective ways and models of this type of work. In doing so, they identified a number of challenges in such an environment. Atkinson et al. (2001) and Atkinson et al. (2007) demonstrated the following key challenges:

- complexity in terms of funding and resources, roles and responsibilities, competing priorities, communications among professional and agency cultures and management;

- conflicting professional and agency cultures, conflicting policies and procedures, finding accommodation, staffing, turnover of personnel, difficulties in ensuring agency commitment, in particular involving the health sector.

Extensive research (Roaf & Lloyd, 1995; Watson et al., 2002; Anning, 2005; Warmington et al., 2004; Allen, 2003; Anning et al., 2010; Fitzgerald & Kay, 2008; Gasper, 2010; Siraj-Blatchford et al., 2007) has demonstrated that cross-professional collaboration may be problematic in nature and could potentially lead to conflict (Challis et al., 1998: 17) because of a number of barriers to effective collaboration created by professional identity and culture; however, researchers have also stressed the benefits and the success factors for children and families.

As may be seen from the above discussion, there is a wealth of research into effective multi-agency work. All conclude that multi-agency work is complex and challenging. Table 7.1 attempts to provide a summary of the challenges and success factors of multi-agency work.

Table 7.1 Challenges to and success factors in multi-agency work

Challenges	Successes
Agencies' aims and objectives	Common aims and objectives
Budgets and finances	Sharing access to funding
Resources	Sharing access to resources
Confusion re: roles and responsibilities	Understanding roles and responsibilities
Competing priorities	Leadership drive
Barriers in terms of physical spaces	
Communication	Communication and willingness
Professional and agency cultures	
'Barriers' of differences of professional culture and identity	Understanding roles and responsibilities
Management	Involving the relevant personnel
Training opportunities	
Time investment	

Ethical Challenges in Multi-agency Work

Table 7.1 shows that there are several success factors in multi-agency work – and also a number of challenges. Within these challenges, ethical issues arise.

Flinders (1992) developed an approach for thinking about ethics throughout research, a method that can be applied to work environments. He suggests four ethical axes along which it may be possible to foresee ethical problems. They are utilitarian, deontological, relational and ecological ethics, as described here:

- *Utilitarian* ethics examine the positive and negative consequences of ethical dimensions.

- *Deontological* ethics emphasise conforming to ethical codes of practice.

- *Relational* ethics focus on relationships and the rules or laws that underpin these relationships.

- *Ecological* ethics 'strive to situate independent relationships' (p. 112) within contexts and people.

Such an approach may be applied in key aspects of multi-agency work, as demonstrated in Figure 7.1.

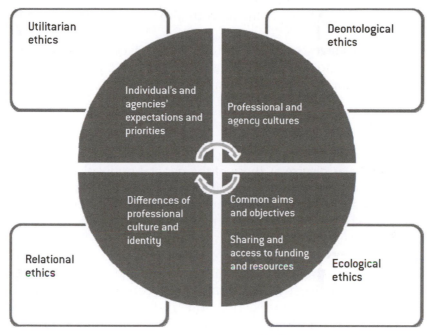

Figure 7.1 Flinder's ethical code applied in multi-agency work

Although Flinder's work is appealing and may be applied in the work environment, ethical issues within multi-agency work present pause for thought. Firstly, it can hardly be expected that professionals move out of the zone of the relative comfort of their own professional identity. However, it is required as a success factor in multi-agency work for them to move into a zone where they have to share deontological codes and build relationships with professionals from other agencies. All four axes (i.e. the utilitarian, deontological, relational and ecological ethics) are consequently problematic in their implementation. Secondly, professionals who have been valued in their own respective contexts (ecological ethics) and for their 'agency' knowledge (deontological ethics) are required to move into a new and unknown work environment, there to cooperate with people from other agencies (relational ethics); this is likely to be experienced as an unwelcome distribution to an otherwise predictable and protected mode of work (utilitarian ethics).

Whitmarsh suggests that:

> [T]ensions exist in multi-agency working. They are often caused by misunderstandings about shared language, shared information and mutual practices relating to them. (2007: 87)

She therefore suggests the Aristotelian model of ethics, based on reflection (what do we know?), clarification (what is the problem?) and consideration (how can the issue be addressed?).

She points out that:

> In a multi-agency team, the code of ethical beliefs and values of the team may be as diverse as those of the general population. Tackling this dilemma requires us to stop thinking in dualistic terms: that is, to halt the dialectic in which something is either true or it is not. Instead, we need to begin thinking more in terms of ethical behaviour as an interaction can vary according to its context. (2007: 93–4)

In that sense, working in partnership requires rigorous consideration of methods of practice, the examination and common understanding of the problems, and reflection on individuals' and agencies' expectations and priorities, as well as on the aims and objectives of the multi-agency work.

Consequently, ethical practice in multi-agency work is concerned with identifying what is needed in terms of strategy then developing a fresh strategy around the practice. It needs to be a mode of enquiry that enables professionals to initiate and pursue their actions through ethical lenses. In such an approach, problems are identified and formed by the needs of practice and professionals, where the strategy is carried out through practice using predominantly the methodologies and specific methods familiar to professionals. Such a view places the primacy of practice at the heart of ethical considerations in multi-agency work. However, such an approach raises two key issues. Firstly, it does not consider the causality of multi-agency work and secondly, there are alternative medial forms of communication among individuals and agencies.

Moving Beyond Multi- or Inter-agency Work: 'Trans-agency' Work

As has been demonstrated from the above discussion and examination of a number of studies (Roaf & Lloyd, 1995; Watson et al., 2002;

Atkinson et al., 2001; Anning, 2005; Warmington, 2004; Allen, 2003; Anning et al., 2010, Fitzgerald & Kay, 2008; Gasper, 2010; Siraj-Blatchford et al., 2007) multi-/inter-agency work requires professionals to develop practices as a means through which they can support the children and families while attempting to ensure that the best level of practice is achieved. It was felt that whereas multi-/inter-agency work is concerned with interactions among professionals from different agencies, the focus would shift onto ways in which these interactions occur, i.e. their causality.

This section aims to discuss the key findings of a research project (Palaiologou, 2011) that attempted to apply a different way of working with different agencies based on the principles of trans-disciplinary work. The project revealed that in a trans-agency environment the ethical challenges are limited; it is more likely that problems arising from the barriers of professional cultures and identities may be overcome. However, prior to this discussion, it is necessary to differentiate between three terms: multi-disciplinary work, inter-disciplinary work and trans-disciplinary work. As mentioned previously, there are three common levels of integration among disciplines and thus agencies represented by multi-, inter- and trans-disciplinarity.

To begin with, multi-disciplinary (multi-agency) approaches deal with an issue or problem from the perspectives of a range of disciplines and agencies. However, one of the problems demonstrated by research in the field is that each discipline works in a self-contained manner, with little cross-communication among them and or synergetic outcomes (Palaiologou, 2010). Multi-disciplinary collaboration does not challenge the structures of agencies and organisations and does not require any changes in the methods, strategies or actions.

Galliers (2003, 2004) believes multi-disciplinary work offers a 'mechanistic pooling' of approaches, with little in the way of knowledge and sharing of information. In such an approach, no matter how hard we seek to achieve ethical practice, it is doomed to be problematic because of the very nature of multi-disciplinary work.

Let us turn now to inter-disciplinary work. This type is concerned with approaches to an issue or problem from a range of disciplines (agencies); however, in this case the contributions of the various disciplines are integrated to provide a holistic or systemic outcome (Palaiologou, 2010). Effective inter-disciplinarity requires new modes of thinking by individuals as it cuts across the traditional discipline-based academic structures, i.e. training, professional standards and systems of reward, resources and allocation. Despite its most important benefits in providing a collaborative ethos to support children and families, it involves intellectual and practical challenges. These may be more difficult to achieve and hence less common than multi-disciplinary work (Bruce et al., 2004). However, Fazenda argues that:

> [I]n the name of inter-disciplinarity established routines are condemned and abandoned, and slogans, nicknames, and working hypotheses are created which many times are impoverished and ill considered. (1995: 7)

Inter-agency work can demonstrate a 'distractive eclecticism' of pseudo-inter-disciplinary or pluri-disciplinary approaches that often do not embrace real inter-disciplinarity; on the contrary, they substitute a synergy of contents of subject areas (Lenoir, 1997; Lenoir et al., 2000, 2001).

Thus this research project attempted to investigate another type of work that has evolved from inter-disciplinarity: trans-disciplinary work or, as it is called in the project, 'trans-agency work'. While inter-disciplinary work involves several disciplines and agencies, trans-disciplinarity implies crossing the boundaries between disciplines and agencies. It defines a mediation space between them (Palaiologou, 2011). Trans-disciplinarity focuses on the organisation of knowledge around complex domains, rather than on the disciplines and subjects, in its aim to transcend structures.

From an examination of existing research into multi-/inter-agency work summarised in Table 7.2, the most common characteristics of multi-/inter-agency work are presented in the first two columns; the third column presents the findings of this project as characteristics for trans-agency work.

In a trans-agency environment it is felt that the working together, joined-up philosophy of the children's services may have the potential to develop effective means of addressing the increasingly complexity of problems with children and families other than through the orthodox means of multi- or even inter-agency work.

It was found that the effectiveness of the trans-disciplinary approach is based on the preparedness of all participants (all agencies, the public and the politicians, and, in the case of the project, the local authority) to work in an atmosphere of transparency, trust and openness, trying

Table 7.2 Summary of characteristics of multi-, inter- and trans-agency work

Multi-agency work	Inter-agency work	Trans-agency work
Involvement of a number of disciplines	Addresses complex problems	Tackles complexity
Communication is linear, parallel, sequential	Develops inter-relationships	Challenges knowledge that derives from agencies and tackles fragmentation of agency boundaries
Fragmentation of boundaries, professional cultures and indemnities	Opens a dialogue and inter-communicative actions	Willingness to understand languages of different agencies
Separate set of values, methods and strategies	Encourages interaction between agencies	Non-linearity
No intention of synergy after the problem is solved	Negotiates the boundaries of agencies	Reflexivity
Outcome(s) the sum of the individual parts	Linear process	Transcending agency structures
	Transferring knowledge among agencies involved	Accepts local contexts, uncertainty
	Weaknesses alter disciplines' borders and identities across agencies	It is context-specific
	Fragmentation in the boundaries of agencies	Requires inter-communicative action
	Lack of flexibility	Unifies knowledge beyond agencies
		Individuals from different agencies work as a team within a mutually accepted system of organisations with an overall set of system goals
		Transcends constructions of knowledge, procedures
		A common system of axioms for a set of agencies involved in the process
		Comprehensive discourse
		Facilitation of long-term dialogue of agencies between specialists

to balance personal interests with interests for the common good (Palaiologou, 2011).

This section aims to explore the ethical implications and challenges of this type of work rather than discussing the research itself. Thus we present in Table 7.3 a summary of the key findings of the research then move on to discuss the ethical issues.

It was found that, apart from the effects that trans-agency work has both on the professionals and on the children and their families in terms of the effectiveness of solving problems or tackling difficult social issues, this type of work attempts to integrate major ethical challenges that multi- or inter-agency work cannot integrate. They involve the collaboration process, sharing a common language, sharing information, acknowledging the boundaries of agencies, and sharing the allocation of funding, space and management by encouraging these to be decided collaboratively by the individuals involved in the whole team. It was shown that trans-agency work involves the integration of resources, consisting of spatial integration, chronological integration and training integration.

As trans-disciplinarity and trans-agency work are context-specific, their type of work is based on communicative actions; their work is underpinned by rationality, which is localised. Given this, trans-agency work employs ethical forms of working. Trans-agency working starts not from the basis of what we know, but how we communicate what we know (Nowotny et al., 2001; Newell & Galliers, 2000). Team members of other professions enter into the process of negotiation, contributing what they know; how they can communicate it allows professionals from each agency to express their views and proposals. The result of such a type of communication results in making sense together and establishing mutual understanding. A trans-agency culture of ethical collaboration is based upon reflection on the consequences of actions and the development of the ability to deal with any expected or unexpected effects.

Ethical Challenges of Trans-agency Work

Many professions view the development of practices as a means by which they can provide information and support to children and families while attempting to ensure that a level of best practice is achieved. It was felt that whereas inter-agency work is concerned with interactions among professionals from different agencies, the focus

Table 7.3 Challenges and success factors for multi-, inter- and trans-agency work

Challenges	Success of multi- and inter-agency work	Success of trans-agency work
Agencies' aims and objectives	Common aims and objectives	Common and mutually accepted system of axioms for a set of agencies
Budgets and finances	Sharing access to funding	It is context-specific
Recourses	Sharing access resources	Unification
Confusion about roles and responsibilities	Understanding roles and responsibilities	Individuals from different agencies work as a team within mutually accepted systems and organisations with an overall set of system goals
Competing priorities	Leadership drive	Transcending structures beyond agencies and individuals act responsibly
Barriers in terms of physical spaces		Flexibility, mobilisation
Communication	Communication and willingness	Long-term dialogue among agencies and among specialists
Professional and agency cultures		Transcending fragmentation of agency and culture
'Barriers' of differences of professional culture and identity	Understanding roles and responsibilities	Willingness to understand professional culture and identity
Management	Involving the relevant personnel	Reflexivity; no linearity
Training opportunities		Unification of training beyond agency needs
Time investment		Acceptance of local contexts and uncertainty

should be shifted to the specific ways in which those interactions occur and the causality of these actions.

This type of work encompasses ethics involving, as Nicolescu (1996) claims, the discovery of bridges between different areas of knowledge and different beings. The principal task is the elaboration of a new language, logic and concepts of genuine dialogue. Trans-disciplinarity moves beyond multi- or inter-disciplinary work to a new understanding. It raises the questions not only of problem-solving but problem choice; it seeks the mutual understanding of a problem and aims to arrive at a common solution. The language of the team members must also be recognised, as it is a content-specific negotiation link with the concept of communicative action.

Trans-disciplinarity is at the same time an attitude and a form of action, a mode of thought and action. It thus entails ethical challenges, although these can be overcome through long-term dialogue among different agencies.

It was found that a main ethical challenge comes within the professionals. In trans-agency work, professionals are confronted with the fact that the structures within agencies may militate strongly against trans-disciplinary activity. As trans-agency work challenges the near-monastic existence retained within agency boundaries, a shift to an environment where these boundaries are transcended may prove challenging to some professionals.

The scepticism that professionals may bring to the possibility of engagement in trans-disciplinary work is exacerbated by the perception that trans-disciplinary work requires the dissolution of the distinctiveness of an agency. While it is accepted that no agency has a monopoly on knowledge and practice, ethical thoughtfulness needs to be in place regarding professionals' insecurities. The ethical challenge of ethical work in a trans-agency environment is not only its potential effect on children and families (external), but also the ethical implications for the professionals (internal).

In addition, trans-agency work demands the systematic use of methods and strategies. These must be based on the invention of new dialectics and capacities for translating them across different agencies that by nature are bounded by systems of knowledge production. Here is where the internal pressures and ethical implications arise for the professionals. Professionals are trained according to the security of their knowledge and practice, while trans-agency work requires them to develop, as Charlie Leadbeater (2004) suggests, 'useful ignorance' rather than sure knowing. What holds people back from taking risks, according to Leadbeater, may often be their knowledge rather than their ignorance. However, employers praise professionals for their knowledge, so asking professionals to be 'usefully ignorant' and valuing them for this brings a conflict; it requires the adoption of learning dispositions that have not yet been rewarded by the employers or policies. This internal conflict consequently becomes an ethical challenge in trans-agency work, as it might affect the causality of the actions of the work.

Conclusions and summary

This chapter has discussed the challenges and success of multi-agency work. It is evident that professionals are faced with a number of ethical issues in such an environment. The main challenges are information sharing and communication, as well as the barriers of professional identities and cultures. The findings of a research project have been presented as an alternative perspective on ethical practice in multi-agency work. It has suggested, as a resolution, a shift instead towards trans-agency work, because successful and effective trans-agency work develops an ethos based on communicative actions and deals with the dynamics of communication in teamwork. It also relies on the comprehension of problem areas; it analyses and tries to investigate ways of tackling the complexities of problems, based on involvement, dialogue and cross-agency intercommunication towards arriving at results.

Key points to remember

- Multi- or inter-agency work aims to solve complex social needs of children and families.

- Multi- or inter-agency work involves a number of agencies' coming together to address a specific issue or concern regarding children and/or their families.

- A number of pieces of research have demonstrated the successes and challenges of these types of work. The challenges mainly involve professional identities and cultures, agency boundaries and structures, communication and resources.

- Ethical challenges evolve around the key challenges of multi- or inter-agency work and focus mainly on communication, sharing information and the variety of beliefs and codes.

- Trans-agency work attempts to provide a different way of working. Indeed, it is a challenging way, as it requires professionals to move beyond their comfort zones and work in such a manner that the boundaries of their own agency are transcended.

- Although trans-agency work has effective results, in attempts to develop a trans-agency ethos of work there are ethical challenges in terms of the professionals' sense of identity.

Points for discussion and reflection

1. Consider the notion of 'working together' and discuss what this means in your own practice.
2. Consider and reflect on the ways information is shared in your own practice. Can you address any challenges, barriers and factors of success?
3. Consider the ethical challenges of your day-to-day work with other professionals.

Further reading

Anning, A., Cortell, D., Frost, N., Green, J. & Robinson, M. (2010) *Developing Multi-professional Teamwork for Integrated Children's Services*. Maidenhead: Open University Press.
Gasper, M. (2010) *Multi-agency Working in the Early Years: Challenges and Opportunities*. London: Sage.
Siraj-Blatchform, I., Clarke, K. & Needham, M. (eds) (2007) *The Team Around the Child: Multi-agency Working in the Early Years*. Stoke-on-Trent: Trentham Books.

References

Allen, C. (2003) 'Desperately seeking fusion: on "joined up thinking", "holistic practice" and the new economy of welfare professional power', *British Journal of Sociology*, 54: 283–306.
Anning, A. (2005) 'Investigating the impact of working in multi-agency service delivery settings in the UK on early years practitioners' beliefs and practices', *Journal of Early Childhood Research*, 3(1): 19–50.
Anning, A., Cortell, D., Frost, N., Green, J. & Robinson, M. (2010) *Developing Multi-professional Teamwork for Integrated Children's Services*. Maidenhead: Open University Press.
Atkinson, M., Jones, M. & Lamont, E. (2007) *Multi-agency Working and Its Implications for Practice: A Review of the Literature*. London: CfBT, Education Trust.

Atkinson, M., Wilkin, A., Scott, A. & Kinder, K. (2001) *Multi-agency Activity: An Audit of Activity*, Local Government Association Research Report 17. Slough: National Foundation for Education Research.

Bruce, A., Lyall, C., Tait, J. & Williams, R. (2004) 'Interdisciplinary integration in Europe: the case of the Fifth Framework programme', *Futures*, 36(4): 457–70.

Challis, L., Fuller, S., Henwood, M., Klein, R., Plowden, W., Webb, A., Whittingham, P. & Wistow, G. (1998) *Joint Approaches to Social Policy*. Cambridge: Cambridge University Press.

DCSF (Department for Children, Schools and Families) (2008) *The 21st Century School: A Transformation in Education*. London: DoH.

DCSF/DoH (Department for Children Schools and Families/Department of Health) (2008) *Children and Young People in Mind: The Final Report of the National CAMHS*. London: DoH.

DfES (Department for Education and Skills) (2003) *Every Child Matters*. London: HMSO.

DfES (Department for Education and Skills) (2007) *Every Child Matters: Change for Children*. London: HMSO.

DfES (Department for Education and Skills) (2004) *Children Act*. London: HMSO.

DfES (Department for Education and Skills) (2006) *Childcare Act*. London: HMSO.

DfES/DoH (2004) *The National Framework for Children, Young People and Maternity Services*. London: DoH.

Fazenda, I. (1995) 'Critical-historical review of interdisciplinary studies in Brazil', *Association for Integrative Studies Newsletter*, 17(1): 2–9.

Fitzgerald, D. & Kay, J. (2008) *Working Together in Children's Services*. London: Routledge.

Flinders, D. (1992) 'In search of ethical guidance: constructing a basis for dialogue', *Qualitative Studies in Education*, 5(2): 101–13.

Galliers, R.D. (2003) 'Change as crisis or growth? Towards a trans-disciplinary view of information systems as a field of study: a response to Benbesat and Zmud's call for returning to the IT artifact', *Journal of the Association for Information Systems*, 4(6): 337–51.

Galliers, R.D. (2004) 'Trans-disciplinary research in information systems', *International Journal of Information Management*, 24(1): 99–106.

Gasper, M. (2010) *Multi-agency Working in the Early Years: Challenges and Opportunities*. London: Sage.

Leadbeater, C. (2004) *Open Innovation and the Creative Industries*. Guest lecture presented at the Creative Industries Faculty, Queensland University of Technology, Brisbane, Australia.

Lenoir, Y. (1997) 'Some interdisciplinary instructional models used in the primary grades in Quebec', *Issues in Integrative Studies*, 15: 77–112.

Lenoir, Y., Geoffroy, Y. & Hasni, A. (2001) 'Entre le "trou noir" et la dispersion évanescente: quelle cohérence épistemologique pour l'interdisciplinarité? Un essai de classification des différentes conceptions de l'interdisciplinarité', in Y. Lenoir, B. Rey & I. Fazenda (eds), *Les Fondements de l'interdisciplinarité dans la formation à l'enseignement*. Sherbrooke: Editions du CRP, pp. 85–110.

Lenoir, Y., Larose, F. & Geoffroy, Y. (2000) 'Interdisciplinary practices in primary education in Quebec – results from ten years of research', *Issues in Integrative Studies*, 18: 89–114.

Lenoir, Y., Rey, B. & Fazenda, I. (eds) (2001) *Les Fondements de l'interdisciplinarité dans la formation à l'enseignement*. Sherbrooke: Editions du CRP.

Newell, S. & Galliers, R.D. (2000) 'More than a footnote: the perils of multidisciplinary research collaboration', in *Proceedings: AIS Americas Conference, Long Beach, CA, 10–13 August*, Vol. III, pp. 1738–42.

Nicolescu, B. (1996) *Manifesto of Transdisciplinarity*, English trans. K.-C. Voss and R. Baker, Reports of First World Congress of Transdisciplinarity Convento de Arrábida in Portugal (1994) and Locarno Congress, Switzerland (1997). Paris: Editions du Rocher.

Nowotny, H., Scott, P. & Gibbons, M. (2001) *Rethinking Science: Knowledge and the Public in an Age of Uncertainty*. Cambridge: Polity Press.

Palaiologou, I. (2010) 'The death of a discipline or the birth of a trans-discipline: subverting questions of disciplinarity within Education Studies undergraduate degrees', *Education Studies*, 36(2): 269–82.

Palaiologou, I. (2011) *Investigating Alternatives of 'Joined Up' Ideology: The Need for Trans-disciplinary Collaboration*. Paper presented at 13th Annual Conference of Early Childhood Education, Thessaloniki, Greece, January.

Roaf, C. & Lloyd, C. (1995) *Multi-agency Work with Young People in Difficulty*. Oxford: Oxford Brookes University.

Siraj-Blatchford, I., Clarke, K. & Needham, M. (eds) (2007) *The Team Around the Child: Multi-agency Working in the Early Years*. Stoke-on-Trent: Trentham Books.

Warmington, P., Daniels, H., Edwards, A., Leadbetter, J., Martin, D., Brown, S. & Middleton, D. (2004) *Conceptualizing Professional Learning for Multi-agency Working and User Engagements*. Paper presented at British Educational Research Association Annual Conference, University of Manchester, 16–18 September.

Watson, D., Townsley, R. & Abbot, D. (2002) 'Exploring multi-agency working in services to disabled children with complicated health needs and their families', *Journal of Clinical Nursing*, 11: 367–75.

Whitmarsh, J. (2007) 'Negotiating the moral maze: developing ethical literacy in multi-agency settings', in I. Siraj-Blatchford, K. Clarke & M. Needham (eds), *The Team Around the Child: Multi-agency Working in the Early Years*. Stoke-on-Trent: Trentham Books.

Loss, Bereavement and Ethics

Sarah James

Chapter overview

This chapter discusses the challenging area of helping children to cope with bereavement in early years settings. For many years young children were considered almost immune from the full experience of bereavement because of their stage of development, or else it was considered right, or ethically justifiable, to protect children from the harsh reality of this form of permanent loss. Whatever the justification, excluding children in such ways is challenged by theories and models of loss and bereavement. These acknowledge the active and continuing nature of grief, and the ways in which young children – and their families and wider social communities – can be supported and nurtured. The chapter also relates early years social and emotional goals to the need for *proactive* death awareness learning opportunities. It aims to enable the reader to understand the professional and theoretical contexts in relation to bereavement and the early years, including the associated – and often complex – ethical underpinnings and dynamics. In doing so it attempts to raise awareness of early years bereavement issues, to relate early years bereavement issues to policy and curricular contexts and to elevate understanding among early years professionals of the need to facilitate both bereavement support and death awareness learning opportunities in early years settings.

Loss, Bereavement and Mortality Data

It is a very difficult and salient fact of life that many children – of all ages – are affected by the death of someone close to them. Annually, approximately 20,000 children in the UK lose a parent through death, which is equivalent to a parental death every 27 minutes (Office for National Statistics (ONS), cited in Children and Young People's Services Scrutiny Panel (CYPSSP), 2006: 4). In the US, statistics indicate 'up to 1.2 million children, about 4 per cent of the total child population, will lose a parent through death by the age of 15' (Young and Papadatou, in Parkes et al., 1997: 197). When bereavement through the loss of a sibling as well as a parent is included, the UK figure is set at between 3 and 5 per cent of children (ONS, cited in CYPSSP, 2006: 4); and by the ages of 11 to 16, 78 per cent of children have known the death of a 'first or second degree relative or close friend' (Harrison & Harrington, 2001: 159).

Another very significant and more commonplace form of loss affecting young children is that of divorce and, similarly, separation, the impacts of which may be profound. Where family units – whether based on marriage, civil partnership or cohabitation – are affected by a breakdown in the relationship between two adults, it can be very difficult for children to understand and cope with. The essential features of attachment and separation anxiety are discussed further below, but it is as well to be reminded of the rate of divorce which, for 2008 in England and Wales, was 11.2 per 1,000 married couples (which is actually at its lowest since 1979), with men and women in their late twenties having the highest divorce rate (ONS, 2010). In 2007, 20 per cent of children affected by the divorce of their parents were less than five years old (Royal College of Psychiatrists, 2009). Empirical data exist which indicate that the living arrangements for children following divorce or separation can have a substantial impact on children in both the shorter and longer terms, for which 'parenting plan models offering multiple options for living arrangements following separation and divorce more appropriately serve children's diverse developmental and psychological needs' (Kelly, 2007: 35).

For very young children, the first experience of bereavement is usually through the loss of a pet, a grandparent, a mother's miscarriage or the stillbirth or neonatal death of a sibling. The stillbirth rate in the UK for 2007 equates to almost one in every 200 babies, while the neonatal death rate in 2007 was 3.3 per 1,000 births (Confidential Enquiry into Maternal and Child Health (CEMACH), 2009: 19). Loss through early (first trimester) miscarriage affects around one in four pregnancies

(Atkins, 2010). Given these statistics, especially those for miscarriage, stillbirth and neonatal mortality, it is thus highly likely that young children will encounter bereavement through such a loss affecting their family units; knowing how to support bereft young children and their families understandably presents specific challenges for early years professionals. As for young children themselves, the mortality rate in 2008 for children 5 years or under in England and Wales combined is 10.1 per 1,000 (ONS, 2009: 3). Of all UK childhood deaths, 'around 30–40% are unexpected', predominantly from environmental causes such as road traffic accidents (CEMACH, 2008: 90). Childhood mortality rates obviously differ quite considerably globally, with low socio-economic status being a clear indicator worldwide (Victora et al., 2003). In addition to the experiences of bereavement caused by the death of a young child's sibling, parent, pet or other relative or friend, it is thus a tragic reality that early years settings will occasionally experience the death through illness or accident of one of the children in their care.

Socio-cultural Contexts

In the UK, as with many westernised nations such as the US (Mitford, 1998), death and mourning have differing traditions and practices, and the degree to which death and related rituals and customs are embedded in community life varies considerably and regionally. What might be termed the 'English way of death' (Litton, 2002) has changed significantly over time and in relation to both local and religious traditions, as well as to class and social status (Walter, 1994; Wienrich & Speyer, 2003). Indeed, religious and cultural traditions probably account for the greatest variation in funerary customs in multicultural societies such as the UK, and these – as with secular traditions – are changing (Howarth, 2007; Seale, 1998). Ten or more years ago most funerals in England, for example, were cremations following a simple service with an evident religious underpinning, depending on the deceased and his or her family's wishes. Today, the 'English funeral', if there is such a thing, increasingly reflects a postmodernist preference for individualistic funerals, initially popularised by the gay community in the 1980s (Levine, in Dane & Levine, 1994; Holloway et al., 2010). It is now fairly 'mainstream', therefore, for high-street funeral directors to offer a wide variety of services and products for a personalised, individual funeral. Thus horse-drawn carts or motorcycle side-carriages carrying a wicker coffin for an eco-funeral are as familiar now to most people as is the 'traditional' black hearse cortège to the crematorium. The extent to which children – especially young children – are included in English funeral traditions varies; however, it is evident that the post-Edwardian belief of many, i.e. that some children are too young to understand and should thus be kept away from funerals (especially due to the risk that they might 'misbehave'), is changing towards far more inclusive practices (Holland, 2004).

In contrast to Western funeral customs and traditions there are many cultural traditions that are wholly inclusive and community-centred. Traditional, rural Jamaican funerals and 'death rituals', for example, include the whole community, with a 'nine night' wake and maximised support for the grieving extended family (Marshall & Sutherland, 2008; Wardle, 2000). Prior to the funeral itself the men of the community dig the deceased person's grave, while the women cook in the open. The inside of the grave is then lined with cement to form a vault and the closest members of the family cover the vault's plastered walls with paintings and scriptural quotations pertinent to the deceased. After the casket is lowered into the vault, which may be on family or communal land, the family then seals the vault and creates a headstone – all without the services of a monumental mason or funeral director. Children of all ages will have been involved in, or witnesses to, the whole process, including visiting the deceased prior to his or her burial, and will be part of the extended grieving rituals of their community. Jamaican children therefore grow up witnessing death rather than being protected from it. Children in countries or communities where death is more hidden or taboo, however, tend not to grow up seeing people dead or dying, or attending funerals, wakes or other mortuary rituals. By the time children reach upper primary school their sense of needing to ask about death may be acute yet silent – unless given voice (Jackson & Colwell, 2001; James, 2002, in press).

In the UK, until relatively recently, sex education held a 'taboo' status similar to that of death, whereas in Victorian society, the reverse was true: death and mourning were highly ritualised and inclusive of children, with sex classified as strictly taboo, in 'polite society' at least (Berridge, 2002; Litton, 2002). Around the world, the way in which communities and cultures approach and 'celebrate death' or the life of someone who has died varies enormously (Metcalf & Huntington, 1991; Morgan, 1997) although a degree of catharsis is – to a greater or lesser extent – a common theme or process (Berman, 2007; Holloway, 2007). This is further discussed below in relation to bereavement models. The same degree of variation may also be said of the grieving process. It is generally considered that a radical change in the grieving or mourning traditions during the First World War in the UK is at least in part responsible for the dramatic change in the post-Victorian era, when public, relatively exuberant displays of mourning were suppressed for fear of their affecting army recruitment. The sheer numbers of young men dying in the trenches would – if mourned in traditional Victorian style – have plunged British society into dysfunctional despair. As bodies were not repatriated from the trenches this era in history also saw a significant change in funerary customs, with death memorialised *in absentia* (Ariès, 1976; Gorer, 1965). The overall effect on postwar British mourning traditions was a dramatic departure from prewar customs. It saw the emergence of the 'stiff upper lip' characteristic that continued into the Second World War and beyond, and is now considered a national trait (Walter, 1997). The post-First World War era coincided with rapid and dramatic developments in medical provision – occurring also in the US (Mitford, 1998) – which led to both birth and death moving from the home and community to a new, clinical domain, the hospital. In 2007, only 2.7 per cent of births in England and Wales took place in the home (National Childbirth Trust (NCT), 2008). The majority of deaths occurred in clinical settings, despite the fact that 'fewer people are able to die at home than would wish to do so' (Grande et al., 1998: 565). In a recent study in the US, however, a discernible rise was noted in the number of children with chronic, terminal illnesses dying at home in preference to a clinical setting; evidence in Sweden also confirms a rise in the numbers of children with a malignant condition dying at home (Surkan et al., 2006). With ever-increasing advances in home-based palliative care, as well as what appears to be a postmodernist construction of death (Seale, 1998) towards 'natural death' (Wienrich & Speyer, 2003) and a 'good death' (Bradbury, 2000), caring for a dying child at home is likely to become more commonplace. Somewhat ironically, therefore, there may – in the next few decades – be witnessed a return to more home-centred values relating to dying and death, similar to those prior to the First World War in Britain.

Childhood mortality in Victorian Britain was significantly higher than it is now, thus children in possibly the majority of families would have been familiar with mourning a sibling, if not a parent (Schlüter, 2008). Nowadays, despite the statistical evidence showing that bereavement during childhood is more prevalent than may have been thought, society remains largely in a post-First World War social framework that finds discussing death difficult and upsetting, and thus wishes to protect children – especially young children – from this harsh fact of life often hidden from them.

Bereavement in Early Years Settings

Young children in early years settings have both specific and generic needs in relation to bereavement and understanding death. Until recently it was widely assumed that pre-school children were too young, or too developmentally immature, to 'understand death', and this was underpinned by influential research (for example, Childers & Wimmer, 1971; Nagy, 1948); this generally suggested that only children at around or beyond the age of seven or eight are capable of understanding the universality and finality of death. Such children were frequently looked after by friends while family funerals were being held, for fear they might find the event upsetting, or – perhaps more truthfully – for fear they might make their presence felt too noticeably in an essentially formal and reserved adult ritual (Cranwell, 2007; Holland, 2004). This is an obvious ethical issue:

> Under 5 or 6, a child may not be able to understand that death is permanent nor that it happens to every living thing. A 4-year-old may be able to tell others confidently that 'my daddy's dead' and may even be able to explain how 'he was hit by a car and he died'. However, the next sentence may be: 'I hope he'll be back before my birthday' or 'He's picking me up tonight'. (Winston's Wish, n.d.)

Longitudinal research conducted by Vianello & Marin (1987), however, challenges previous developmentalist assumptions relating to children's understanding of death:

> [A]t the age of 4–5, most children reveal a particularly well-structured understanding of death, implying the substantial comprehension that they do not consider death as something which may happen only to others, but also to their parents and to themselves and that death is irreversible, universal and consists in the cessation of vital functions. (Vianello & Marin, 1987: 97)

Developmentalist and social constructivist perspectives on young children's understanding of death or their potential to understand death thus appear dichotomous. As with other areas of life education with an ethical dimension, therefore, the provision of death awareness education in early years settings probably reflects, to a greater or lesser extent, such theoretical underpinnings. The degree to which young children in early years settings, and in their home environments, need or even have a *right* to loss and bereavement support and death education that will help scaffold their understanding of death and bereavement, thus enabling their grieving to unfold and be acknowledged, is arguably a key ethical issue.

Research evidence exists relating to the long-term impact of early loss. Tracey's (2008) qualitative study on the feelings and experiences of women whose mothers died when they were young children identified the following, profound observations:

> The loss of a mother in early life remains a 'live' issue in the hearts and minds of survivors . . . Throughout their lives, daughters continually yearn for their mother – the inescapable loss is never far away from the surface. Everything in life holds a different meaning because, as time goes on, the deep and lasting implications of the death and loss of a mother are realised. (Tracey, 2008: 139)

Such research evidence implies a strongly ethical basis for long-term bereavement support for families and throughout bereaved children's education, including when a child's mother has died at or shortly after a child's birth (Black, 1998; Tracey, 2008).

Death Education – for Every Child Matters

Just as young children need formative, inclusive support to grieve, they also need more generic learning opportunities within the curriculum to explore death as a natural event and concept. Keeping pets such as hamsters is not as popular as it used to be in educational settings, although there are many early years settings that do keep hamsters or goldfish. When a hamster or goldfish dies, it may be tempting, possibly in deference to a belief in children's inability to understand death 'fully', and/or to protect their feelings, to purchase a seemingly identical hamster or goldfish. A more constructivist alternative would be to explain to the children that 'Hammy' had sadly died overnight, to allow the children to look at and stroke Hammy (with the usual health observations) and to extend the moment into a wider learning opportunity, including child-centred ritual burial. Similarly, when a child (or adult) finds a dead baby bird that has fallen from its nest, extending such moments can facilitate invaluable learning opportunities for children. There are also many excellent stories for young children that can complement such an event (or initiate similar learning opportunities when there is no pet bereavement in the setting), for example *Goodbye Mousie* (Harris, 2004) and *Badger's Parting Gifts* (Varley, 1992).

More details of books for young children are available online from child bereavement charities such as Winston's Wish (see end of chapter). Perhaps the most significant early years book relating to death and bereavement is the Miffy book, *Dear Grandma Bunny* (Bruna, 2006). This tells the story of when Miffy's grandmother dies. Grandma is seen lying in her bed as if asleep, yet the simple verse assures us Miffy knows this not to be the case. She sees her Grandpa and other family members crying and does not know quite what to think or feel. Later, as Miffy's first time, the reader sees her grandmother lying in her coffin and the funeral itself. This is in my opinion a gem of a book for the very young and for many primary children. In this classic, simple yet profound story, Miffy is included fully; she is encountering new emotions and rituals she does not yet fully understand (adult readers, too, can empathise with her). It is also seen how Miffy is able to maintain a bond with her grandmother that is both natural and poignant. In short, the story exemplifies two key issues: firstly, the importance and benefits of enabling young children to be fully included in family bereavements; secondly, that death education, i.e. the facilitation of enabling people to learn about and begin to understand death and dying, is both beneficial and inclusive. *Dear Grandma Bunny* is possibly one of the best books to read to young children in relation to both bereavement support and – formatively and proactively – as a story to initiate death awareness learning; to extend the development of emotional literacy, and to help young children to gain social agency in relation to death and bereavement. This complements the Statutory Framework for the Early Years Foundation Stage Early Learning Goals and Educational Programmes (DCSF, 2008) relating to personal, social and emotional development (PSED) for which:

> Children must be provided with experiences and support which will help them to develop a positive sense of themselves and of others; respect for others; social skills; and a positive disposition to learn. Providers must ensure support for children's emotional well-being to help them to know themselves and what they can do. (DCSF, 2008: 12)

Among others, one of the key early learning goals in this respect is for children to '[r]espond to significant experiences, showing a range of feelings when appropriate' (DCSF, 2008: 12).

Young Children and Grief

Grieving occurs where an attachment has formed, therefore all people 'grieve' to a greater or lesser extent when an attachment is vulnerable or severed. In this respect a child's feelings of loss or grief are hard to distinguish, as they may well be with adults. 'Loss and bereavement' emotions and related professional issues go hand in hand, with school and early years settings accordingly producing policies and pastoral support. When something of intrinsic value is lost, as in *Dogger*, the much-loved book by Hughes (2009), for example, the loss is suffered because complex emotional attachments to the object are suffered. In terms of monetary value the bereaved may also feel affected; financial compensation does not usually alleviate the severed emotional or 'sentimental' ties. Losing a person through separation, including through adoption, divorce, emigration or the end of a friendship, as well as through death, is frequently far more difficult to cope with or understand, depending on individual circumstances and other complex variables. Influenced by Charles Darwin's work *The Expression of the Emotions in Man and Animals* (1872, cited in Parkes, 2009), Bowlby (1980, 1990) developed Darwin's observations. Taking the theories further, Bowlby noted that humans form significant attachments, the varying patterns and experiences of which will, he believed, determine an adult's psychological well-being. Attachment theory is now recognised as relevant to all social animals, not only to humans (Parkes, 2009). Separation anxiety is thus considered a natural response in infants and young children, the manifestations of which – in behaviourist terms – function to elicit reunion. While aspects of Bowlby's work may be open to criticism by some social scientists for its biological determinism (Machalek & Martin, 2004), separation anxiety is without doubt a common experience in early years settings. The degree to which childhood experiences of separation and grief may affect one's mental health in later life as well as at the time is well documented (Black, 1998; Black & Young, 1995, cited by Young & Papadatou, in Parkes et al., 1997; Parkes, 2009). In addition to children affected by separation through the death of someone close to them, the high rates of separation and divorce, as discussed earlier, clearly resonate with the need for both proactive as well as responsive pastoral care and emotional literacy development for young children. This implies longer-term ethical considerations for those working in early years settings, and further highlights the need for proactive as well as reactive education and support, given the potentially enduring nature of bereavement and separation.

Bereavement Models

In addition to theories on attachment and separation, as discussed above, many have emerged which both significantly enhance our understanding of grief processes and help in the provision of more empathic and individualised support. How young children manifest their emotions and experiences of bereavement (and other forms of loss) will vary significantly, depending, for example, on age, perhaps gender, and cultural environments. It may be stated that very young children have little or no understanding of permanent separation and therefore require very gentle yet clear and honest support. In early years settings, as in primary schools, it is vital that clear rather than euphemistic language be used, since children often have very literal understandings. Thus, if a child is told 'we have lost Grandpa', for example, they will try to help 'find' him. If Grandpa is described as having 'fallen asleep', it is not unusual for children to develop sleep anxieties themselves (Holland et al., 2005). Children aged between 2 and 5 may also, as may adults, develop 'magical thinking', in which, for example, a young child may become convinced that his or her actions (or inactions) have somehow caused the death of the person to whom they are so attached (Webb, 2010). Furthermore, young children 'may build up fantasies far worse than the reality if they are not given the facts from adults who are trying to protect them' (Holland et al., 2005: 61). It is common for the sadness felt by young children to occur in 'brief bursts of emotion, perhaps while playing, [which] often goes unrecognised by others' (Young & Papadatou, in Parkes et al., 1997: 198), or for children to resume play quite happily after a period of relatively brief but profound sadness. Grief in young children may seem to be 'punctuated' when compared with the more sustained ways in which adults grieve. Recognising this may prevent inaccurate assumptions being made about how young children seem to be coping with their loss. Similarly, in addition to the emotional impact of a child's own experience of bereavement, many children will also be aware of and affected by the grief and emotion of other close family members.

Current models and theories on loss and bereavement may be described in relation to three main approaches: grieving as a passive experience; as an active experience, and as an ongoing or continuing experience (Holland et al., 2005: 43). The seminal work of Elizabeth Kübler-Ross *On Death and Dying* (1969) identified the now well-known 'Five Stages of Grief' model, in which those dying or bereft are described as frequently experiencing denial, anger, bargaining, depression and acceptance (Kübler-Ross, 1969, 1973). Kübler-Ross's model is retrospectively considered by many to be a *passive* model (Holland et al., 2005), in which those experiencing loss will normally progress in a linear manner from one stage to the next, with the end goal of acceptance equating to what some refer to as 'closure'.

Depending on circumstances, levels of support and other factors, some, including children, may become effectively stuck or trapped in a particular stage, which could necessitate therapeutic intervention.

Building on Kübler-Ross's work, successive and complementary models identify more active bereavement 'journeys': the Dual Process model of Stroebe & Schut (1999) describes the healthy means in which someone experiencing grief in an 'adaptive way' will benefit from oscillating between the stressor of loss orientation (i.e. active grieving) and the stressor of restoration orientation, or respite from the grieving process (Stroebe & Schut, 1999: 197). As in Kübler-Ross's model, however, some individuals may become trapped within one of the two stressors, with possible detriment to mental health and well-being.

The more recent of significant bereavement models is known as the Continuing Bonds model (Klass et al., 1996); it suggests that healthy grieving should not terminate with 'closure' and detachment (and the facilitation of new emotional bonds), but with a healthy, albeit changing, *continuing* relationship with the person who has died. This understanding of grieving seems to resonate more with many people's accounts of their grieving processes, including those of children, yet is not invulnerable (see Points for Discussion and Reflection below).

Bereavement Support Agencies

When a child or a member of the wider early years community becomes ill, or is affected by serious and potentially life-threatening illness, it is advisable to seek support and guidance from one of the many regional and national bereavement support agencies and charities. In many instances the advice offered will at the very least reassure the person seeking guidance that the actions being taken or proposed are appropriate. It is likely a person will be referred to resources for both children and professionals and be recommended proactive interventions. Some charities, such as Winston's Wish (see Useful websites below), are able to offer individually tailored support, in which a highly trained bereavement professional will begin working with a child and his or her family, ideally during the time when an illness affecting the family member is still *potentially* terminal. In watching *The Mummy Diaries* produced by Winston's Wish (2007) and freely available online, it can be seen that children of all ages, including the very young, benefit enormously in terms of their understanding and experience of the bereavement process.

Many such organisations offer free downloadable materials that are both age-specific and generic, including professional resources to enable educational and care settings to produce policies and to order resources. Training opportunities are also increasingly available, and are to be highly recommended: it is clearly desirable that members of early years staff receive proactive, rather than reactive, training in loss and bereavement.

☐ Conclusions and summary

Loss – in any form – is always hard to bear, be it that of a sentimental item, the end of a transitional phase or that of a person in our lives through separation, divorce or death. Probably the hardest challenge for early years settings is the death of a child in its care, as well as any form of bereavement affecting the early years community. Contrary to much of the thinking of the last century, young children need to be given appropriate, guided bereavement support by all those who share in their care and education, with particular emphasis on enabling what might be termed a 'healthy' continuing bond (Parkes, 2009; Holland et al., 2005). While much of the support might need to be at an individual level, this ought also be considered a whole-community focus in which other children in the setting need to be included in order to enable their emotional and social development. In addition to the need for continuing support when a child is bereaved, there is also a very strong case – linked to the Framework for the Early Years Foundation Stage (DCSF, 2008) – for proactive death awareness learning opportunities to be included in the delivery of early years curricula (James, 2011).

Key points to remember

- Research evidence suggests that the experience of early loss and bereavement can have a profound effect during both childhood and adulthood.

- Proactive measures to support young children are far more enabling compared with reactive, ad hoc approaches.

- In addition to supporting young children's experiences of loss and bereavement, scaffolding death education opportunities in early years settings will enable the process of understanding loss and grief as a normal – albeit very challenging – part of life.

- Research supports the belief that an active, continuing bonds model promotes healthy grieving.

- Loss and bereavement training is highly recommended for early years professionals, as is the development of an associated policy within early years settings.

Points for discussion and reflection

1. How old were you when you first encountered death? How did it affect you, and what support did you get? Is the inclusion or exclusion of young children in or from death rituals and customs an ethical issue?

2. What, in your experience, do you think young children understand about death? As an adult, what do *you* 'understand' about death? Is it ethical to exclude someone, such as a young child, from proactive bereavement support and associated learning opportunities just because – at the time – he or she is considered unable to 'understand'?

3. What might be the impact on a surviving child (i.e. where a sibling has died) who is told 'Your sister/brother would never have done that'? In an early years setting, how might a positive, continuing bond for a bereft child be supported and enabled?

Further reading

Bruna, D. (2006) *Dear Grandma Bunny*. London: Egmont Books.
Holland, J., Dance, R., MacManus, N. & Stitt, C. (2005) *Lost for Words: Loss and Bereavement Awareness Training*. London: Jessica Kingsley.
Webb, N.B. (ed.) (2010) *Helping Bereaved Children: A Handbook for Practitioners*. New York: Guildford Press.

Useful websites

Winston's Wish
Website: http://www.winstonswish.org.uk
Tel (helpline): 08452 030405
Tel (general enquiries): 01242 515157

Child Bereavement Network
Website: http://www.childbereavementnetwork.org.uk
Tel: 020 7843 6309
Fax: 020 7843 6053

Child Bereavement Charity
Website: http://www.childbereavement.org.uk
Tel: 01494 446648
Fax: 01494 440057
Email: enquiries@childbereavement.org.uk

References

Ariès, P. (1976) *Western Attitudes Toward Death: From the Middle Ages to the Present*. London: Marion Boyars.

Atkins, L. (2010) 'NHS "must lessen trauma of miscarriages"', *Guardian G2*, 2 March, p. 14.

Berman, J. (2007) *Dying to Teach: A Memoir of Love, Loss and Learning*. Albany, NY: State University of New York Press.

Berridge, K. (2002) *Vigor Mortis: The End of the Death Taboo*. London: Profile Books.

Black, D. (1998) 'Coping with loss: bereavement in childhood', *British Medical Journal*, 316: 931–3.

Bowlby, J. (1980) *Attachment and Loss*. New York: Basic Books.

Bowlby, J. (1990) *A Secure Base: Parent-Child Attachment and Healthy Human Development*. New York: Basic Books.

Bradbury, M. (2000) 'A good death', in D. Dickenson, M. Johnson & J. Katz (eds), *Death, Dying and Bereavement*. London: Sage.

Braithwaite, A. (2001) *When Uncle Bob Died (Talking It Through)*. London: Catnip.

Bruna, D. (2006) *Dear Grandma Bunny*. London: Egmont Books.

Childers, P. & Wimmer, M. (1971) 'The concept of death in early childhood', *Child Development*, 42: 1299–301.

Children and Young People's Services Scrutiny Panel (CYPSSP) (2006) *Bereavement Support: The Key Issues for Bereaved Children and Young People*. Shrewsbury: Shropshire County Council.

Confidential Enquiry into Maternal and Child Health (CEMACH) (2009) *Perinatal Mortality 2007: United Kingdom*. London: CEMACH.

Cranwell, B. (2007) 'Adult decisions affecting bereaved children: researching the children's perspectives', *Bereavement Care*, 26(2): 30–3.

Dane, B.O. & Levine, C. (eds) (1994) *AIDS and the New Orphans: Coping with Death*. Westport, CT: Auburn House.

Department for Children, Schools and Families (DCSF) (2008) *Statutory Framework for the Early Years Foundation Stage: Setting the Standards for Learning, Development and Care for Children from Birth to Five*. Nottingham: Department for Children, Schools and Families.

Gorer, G. (1965) *Death, Grief and Mourning in Contemporary Britain*. London: Cresset Press.

Grande, G.E., Addington-Hall, J.M. & Todd, C.J. (1998) 'Place of death and access to home care services: are certain patient groups at a disadvantage?', *Social Science and Medicine*, 47(5): 565–79.

Harris, R.H. (2004) *Goodbye Mousie*. New York: Aladdin Paperbacks.

Harrison, L. & Harrington, R. (2001) 'Adolescents' bereavement experiences: prevalence, association with depressive symptoms, and use of services', *Journal of Adolescence*, 24: 159–69.

Holland, J. (2004) 'Should children attend their parent's funerals?', *Pastoral Care in Education*, 22(1): 10–14.

Holland, J., Dance, R., MacManus, N. & Stitt, C. (2005) *Lost for Words: Loss and Bereavement Awareness Training.* London: Jessica Kingsley.

Holloway, M. (2007) *Negotiating Death in Contemporary Health and Social Care.* Bristol: Policy Press.

Holloway, M., Adamson, S., Argyrou, V., Draper, P. & Mariau, D. (2010) *Spirituality in Contemporary Funerals: Final Report.* Swindon/Hull: Arts and Humanities Research Council/University of Hull.

Howarth, G. (2007) *Death and Dying: A Sociological Introduction.* Cambridge: Polity Press.

Hughes, S. (2009) *Dogger.* London: Red Fox Books.

Jackson, M. & Colwell, J. (2001) 'Talking to children about death', *Mortality*, 6: 321–5.

James, S. (2002) 'Death in the Curriculum'. Unpublished MA paper, University of Hull.

James, S. (2011) *Bruna, Miffy and Death: Enabling Children to Gain Social Agency through Fiction.* Conference paper, Death, Dying and Disposal [DDD10], Nijmegen, The Netherlands, 9–12 September.

Kelly, J.B. (2007) 'Children's living arrangements following separation and divorce: insights from empirical and clinical research', *Family Process*, 46(1): 35–52.

Klass, D., Silverman, P.R. & Nickman, S.L. (eds) (1996) *Continuing Bonds: New Understandings of Grief.* Washington, DC: Taylor & Francis.

Kübler-Ross, E. (1969) *On Death and Dying.* New York: Simon & Schuster/Touchstone.

Kübler-Ross, E. (1973) *On Death and Dying.* London: Routledge.

Litton, J. (2002) *The English Way of Death: The Common Funeral Since 1450.* London: Robert Hale.

Machalek, R. & Martin, M.W. (2004) 'Sociology and the second Darwinian revolution: a metatheoretical analysis', *Sociological Theory*, 22(3): 455–76.

Marshall, R. & Sutherland, P. (2008) 'The social relations of bereavement in the Caribbean', *Journal of Death and Dying*, 57(1): 21–34.

Metcalf, P. & Huntington, R. (1991) *Celebrations of Death: The Anthropology of Mortuary Ritual* (2nd edn). Cambridge: Cambridge University Press.

Mitford, J. (1998) *The American Way of Death Revisited.* London: Virago Press.

Morgan, J.D. (1997) *Readings in Thanatology.* Amityville, NY: Baywood.

Nagy, M. (1948) 'The child's theories concerning death', *Journal of Genetic Psychology*, 73: 3–27.

National Childbirth Trust (NCT) (2008) 'New National Statistics: Big Increase in Home Births Across UK', 9 December 2008. Online at: http://www.nctpregnancyandbabycare.com/press-office/press-releases/view/118 (accessed 2 June 2010).

Office for National Statistics (ONS) (2009) *Mortality Statistics: Deaths Registered in 2008.* Newport: Office for National Statistics.

Office for National Statistics (ONS) (2010) *Divorces: England and Wales at 29-Year Low.* Online at: http://www.statistics.gov.uk/cci/nugget_print.asp?ID=170 (accessed 17 July 2010).

Parkes, C.M. (2009) *Love and Loss: The Roots of Grief and Its Complications.* Hove: Routledge.

Parkes, C.M., Luangani, P. & Young, B. (eds) (1997) *Death and Bereavement Across Cultures.* Hove: Routledge.

Royal College of Psychiatrists (2009) *Mental Health and Growing Up.* Online at: http://www.rcpsych.ac.uk/mentalhealthinfo/mentalhealthandgrowingup/divorceandseparation.aspx (accessed 17 July 2010).

Schlüter, C. (2008) *Home and Family Life in Victorian England: Reflections on Urban Middle-class and Working-class Relationships*. Munich: Verlag.

Seale, C. (1998) *Constructing Death: The Sociology of Dying and Bereavement*. Cambridge: Cambridge University Press.

Stroebe, M. & Schut, H. (1999) 'The dual process model of coping with bereavement: rationale and description', *Death Studies*, 23(3): 197–224.

Surkan, P.J., Dickman, P.W., Steineck, G., Onelöve, E. & Kriecbergs, U. (2006) 'Home care of a child dying of a malignancy and parental awareness of a child's impending death', *Palliative Medicine*, 20: 161–9.

Tracey, A. (2008) *Surviving the Early Loss of a Mother: Daughters Speak*. Dublin: Veritas.

Varley, S. (1992) *Badger's Parting Gifts*. London: Picture Lions.

Vianello, R. & Martin, L.M. (1989) 'Children's understanding of death', *Early Child Development and Care*, 46(1): 97–104.

Victora, C.G., Wagstaff, A., Armstrong Schellenberg, J., Gwatkin, D., Claeson, M. & Habich, J.-P. Ar (2003) 'Applying an equity lens to child health and mortality: more of the same is not enough', *The Lancet*, 362: 233–41.

Walter, T. (1994) *The Revival of Death*. London: Routledge.

Walter, T. (1997) 'Emotional reserve and the English way of grief', in K. Charmaz, G. Howarth & A. Kellehear (eds), *The Unknown Country: Death in Australia, Britain, and the USA*. Basingstoke: Palgrave Macmillan.

Wardle, H. (2000) 'Subjectivity and aesthetics in the Jamaican nine night', *Social Anthropology*, 8(3): 247–62.

Webb, N.B. (ed.) (2010) *Helping Bereaved Children: A Handbook for Practitioners*. New York: Guildford Press.

Wienrich, S. & Speyer, J. (eds) (2003) *The Natural Death Handbook* (4th edn). London: Rider.

Winston's Wish (2007) *The Mummy Diaries*, DVD. London: Channel 4.

Winston's Wish (n.d.) 'How age can affect a child's understanding of death and dying'. Online at: http://www.winstonswish.org.uk/page.asp?section=00010001000200020001 (accessed 20 May 2010).

Ethics in Studying Early Years

Gary Beauchamp and Chantelle Haughton

Chapter overview

Given that the number of university students in Early Years programmes has increased and they are in work placements, the current chapter discusses how students may be helped in implementing good ethical practices when in settings where they are studying children.

The chapter will also examine how students will be able to plan an effective research project allowing a variety of voices (including those of children, parents and practitioners) to be heard. It will differ from earlier chapters in that its focus is on practical guidance for students on how to plan an ethical research project *prior* to undertaking research within an early years setting – the application of which is covered in earlier chapters.

Introduction

Any course of early childhood study involves examining theoretical perspectives of child development, the ideas of established thinkers, and perhaps videos of young children in learning situations and at play. In addition, students gain practical experience in a variety of early years settings. When undertaking their placements, it is suggested, most students approach their time in settings with the mindset of a practitioner who is there to support the growth of the children in their care. When they observe a child, the 'lens' through which they observe is that of someone who is examining the individual and identifying how best to aid their development. The challenge of adopting the lens of researcher when required lies in being able to refocus the 'practitioner' perspective and adopt a more objective, detached view of the child – although, as outlined elsewhere in this book, all research should be for the benefit of the child. It will be argued that there is much that can and needs to be done towards developing this researcher persona (with its variety of lenses and associated skills) prior to undertaking research in early years settings.

Perhaps the hardest part of the process is the potential or perceived loss of a 'caring' perspective. There is no suggestion that researchers do not care about the children who are subjects of the research, nor that they shirk responsibility if they see adverse situations developing – especially as the methods of reporting and reacting to such situations are varied and should be known in advance. In reality, a practitioner is able to conduct caring research, yet only if the role of researcher is adopted from the outset and if the children understand the basis of their relationship with you, the researcher. The particular nature of early years research has its own unique characteristics reflecting the nature and developmental stage(s) of those being researched. Perhaps the first step in making the transition to researcher is to examine the *purpose* of your presence in the classroom or early years setting. Although it may seem slightly contrary, it may be safer and easier to consider first what you are *not* there to do.

A dilemma students may face is how to negotiate with the practitioners in the setting the purpose of data collection/observation visits (as a 'researcher' you will be mostly unavailable to offer a helping hand with play activities, etc.). You will need to establish *ethical partnerships* with practitioners from the outset; then it is understood how you will spend your time in the setting, also with the aim that your research/ learning experience will be valued and supported.

 Group activity 1

Make a list of things that you will **not** do when undertaking research in early years settings, compared with other types of visit.

Think about how you will approach such aspects with the practitioners in the settings you plan to visit.

As you may expect, the next step is to consider what you *are* there to do. The list could be long; however, the key features could include:

- planning

- selecting a topic or area of study: macro-, meso-, micro-perspectives

- considering the wording of your working title

- choosing an age group

- planning the best use of time

- arranging access to settings

- undertaking research – behaviour in setting/relationships

- keeping field notes, records and storage of data

- analysing data

- reporting findings.

Compiling this list is a start towards not only considering how to make the transition from practitioner to early years researcher, but also developing the set of skills required to undertake such research effectively. The remainder of this chapter will consider key ethical considerations under each of the bullet points. It should be noted that actual research methods appear elsewhere in this book, thus will not be addressed here.

Planning

The early stages of most studies involve reviewing existing literature to determine what is already known. This may involve reading a variety of sources, such as academic articles, official reports (by government agencies), inspection findings, summary reports and possibly dissertations. These sources vary greatly in explaining how they considered the ethical implications of their respective work. Some, such as dissertations, may make an explicit mention of ethics; others, such as inspection reports, may make no mention at all. This does not imply that such work is unethical; merely that the importance of recording such decisions varies. It is important to realise that *all* work undertaken in settings, including your own, has ethical implications. While reading the literature, it is also possible to examine what research methods were used and their levels of success. It may be possible to adapt an existing set of methods; equally, though, the research you read may lead you to conclude that certain methods have not worked. Before deciding to adopt methods used by others, you need to take note of key factors (such as sample size, age and social context of the children involved in the research) and see if they match your own plans. As Groundwater-Smith & Campbell (2007: 172) point out: 'practitioner research is contingent upon the contexts in which it is undertaken . . . what may be appropriate in one setting may require a different resolution in another'.

Having reviewed the literature, you should also explore the impact of your presence on a setting, however familiar it may be to you and however much time you have spent there. It is worth considering in a very early phase whether it is important to know the setting and the children. Think about whether you will be able to make unbiased judgements and observations when you know the setting and children well. In addition, decide whether the young children who are familiar with you appreciate that your role may have changed; they may be puzzled why you do not now respond to them in the same way as you have before. How would you explain this to them? Alternatively, are you able to make such judgements when you do not know the setting or the children? In addition, depending on the length and focus of your visits to early years settings, you will need to consider relevant policies in place. Awareness of child protection policies and procedures will be required, thus you should familiarise yourself with the procedure to be followed. In preparation, you need to know to whom to report matters of concern/disclosures. Consideration of this issue would link with your selection of research methods (for example, observations may mean you spend more time in the setting and have more direct contact with children, parents and staff).

All of the above will need to be considered carefully at an initial stage of research. You may decide that it is preferable to avoid the temptation to go to a setting you know well. Your study should be driven by the best methodology for answering your research questions, rather than ease of access to a setting. At every stage of planning your research there are, however, ethical considerations. A selection of key events in conducting research are considered below.

Selecting a Topic or Area of Study – Macro-, Meso-, Micro-perspectives

In selecting a topic to investigate it is necessary to consider the potential impact and implications at all levels. Perhaps the most obvious is to ask whether it is appropriate for the age of the child(ren) involved. In addition, you need to ask if it is appropriate for their setting. All such decisions need to be considered at the micro-, meso- and macro-levels. For instance, the micro-level could be the impact on a particular child, class or group of children in a setting; the meso-level could be the school or setting context; and the macro-level could be the county or even the national context. This process would work in both directions in that, even if working with a small group of very young children at a micro-level, policy and practice at the meso-level (for instance, school policies) and macro-level (for instance, the Children Act and Every Child Matters) will have to be considered. The possible impact of other factors such as ethnicity, gender and culture (those of both the researcher and the researched) need to be considered on these three levels.

In seeking a topic to research, you should also consider what Coady (2005) labels the 'risk/benefit equation'. In this situation the 'risk' in undertaking research would be that to children in the study, and the potential 'benefit' to *all* children – or to society as a whole. No ethical researcher would knowingly put a child at risk, yet the concept of risk needs to be considered.

 Group activity 2

In a group, make a list of the first words that come into your head when you think of 'risk'. Organise them into groups/topics and discuss how they may have an impact on your choice of research topic.

The concept of risk is perhaps most obvious in medical research, where there are risks of physical as well as psychological harm. The same concerns are faced by educational researchers, especially those working with vulnerable groups, such as young children (see Chapters 3 and 4). Allen (2005: 21) lists some of the risks in educational research:

- negative impact upon academic results

- negative impact upon the employability or reputation of educators

- exposure to criminal, civil or other proceedings

- emotional or psychological distress

- negative impact upon family relationships.

Together with areas identified in the task above, it should be apparent that selecting a topic has many ethical implications that need to be considered.

Emotional Involvement

One additional risk requiring consideration is the risk to *you*. Although all researchers hope to be suitably objective, it is advisable to think about how you will manage your own emotional response to what you see and hear and what you find. Robert-Holmes (2007: 58) offers sensible advice when he suggests that the inexperienced researcher should 'stick to research topics which are relatively emotionally safe. Any potential risks can be minimised early on at the planning stage of the research.' The earliest stage that this can be considered is when you are in the process of choosing an area or topic to investigate. As part of this process, and during the research, you will inevitably consider your own experiences; however, it is important that you do not 'unconsciously focus upon unresolved personal issues' (West, 1996, cited in Robert-Holmes, 2007: 58). This will also be true below when considering how research is reported, especially if it does not accord with your own views or expectations.

Working Title and Research Question(s)

Having identified a topic, the wording of the title also has ethical considerations. In many areas, such as special educational needs (see Chapter 3) and ethnicity, definitions or ways of labelling groups have changed with differing social values and new legislation. It is necessary to check that your title reflects accurately current thinking, also that it does not display a negative image or stereotype.

Group activity 3

Each member of the group should write down her/his prospective title and put it into a box. Draw one out at random and read it to the group.

Discuss the wording to determine whether it contains any inappropriate language or stereotyping. In addition, decide if it has a clear research focus, giving details of the age group and topic being researched.

Age Group

An important ethical consideration is whether you are looking at the most appropriate age group in your research. All students on early years courses will have undertaken some study of child development, which should guide decisions about what age group to research – although this should always be checked with the setting. It is important to allow enough time to seek research opportunities within relevant settings and age groups. Part of this consideration, which will also affect the methodology selected for a study, will be the emotional maturity of the children with whom you seek to work. Although in theory they may be ready to help you, their responses may vary considerably: the setting is the best guide. Irrespective of whatever theory may say, the needs of the individual child must come first.

Another consideration affected by age is the statutory and curriculum framework within which the children may be working. Although there are common statutory guidelines, such as when a child starts school, there are also other, more localised, factors (such as the impact of the Foundation Phase in Wales – as distinct from the Foundation Stage in England) that should be considered. Settings may not be able to accommodate your requests because they are not appropriate for the age of the child or the curriculum framework in which they operate. Again, the more thoroughly prepared you are, the easier it is prevent such factors from having a negative impact on your work.

Use of Time

There is no optimum time of the year to approach early settings seeking their cooperation with your studies. However, you should be aware that certain times are more difficult than others for those concerned with year-round care.

This process may be complicated by the fact that, if you are conducting a course of study, the institution itself may choose the time of year when you may do your research. Nevertheless, there are certain factors relating to time that you should consider. Perhaps the most important is to find out is whether the setting actually contains the aspects you wish to research. Do not assume that certain pedagogies or activities are common just because you have been told, or believe, that something is good practice. You may consider that outdoor learning is essential for all children but a particular setting may not! If the setting *does* undertake the type of feature that you wish to research, the next step is to find out when it is included – certain activities may happen only at certain times of the year, or even in certain years (for instance, if settings work on a two-year planning cycle). Remember that it is up to you to fit in with the setting – or change your topic!

Furthermore, you need to consider the impact of the time of year. For instance, the beginning of the year is often concerned with settling in new children. Unless you are studying this process (in which case, it is the only time of the year you may do so) you should consider carefully whether it is an appropriate time for your research.

The final factor that needs thought is time: both how long you will visit on your research visits and the total time for the project. Your visits need, obviously, to take place during the setting's working hours; however, the scheduling of your research may be guided, for example, by the length of sessions and when outside play or lunchtime take place. Another time consideration is how long it will take you to provide feedback to settings after your research visits have been completed. This is the sort of essential information that needs to be gathered from, and given to, settings when arranging access.

Arranging Access to Settings/Permissions

All partners in your research, including the children, need to be fully aware of what you intend to do, how you intend to it and who will know about it. In arranging access to settings and gaining permission you need to be totally transparent about all of these details. There must be no surprises for anyone involved, including those who are researching their own working environment. The better planned you are, the easier it is to tell people what you require and agree arrangements.

Successful negotiation of access will be a crucial factor in your research project. Never underestimate the time and care you need to invest in this part of your project. Think carefully about how and when to contact, meet and talk to possible participants before you start data collection; then everyone may be satisfied they are able to support your research project (this may take several telephone calls, e-mails, or visits). Aim to be flexible and to appreciate the need to fit your research around other activities.

There may be a temptation to assume that certain parts of the research process, such as designing a questionnaire or deciding on interview questions, may be accomplished *after* access has been arranged. However, when planning visits you would not be able to give the child or the setting a true picture of what you hope to do. In addition, there is a risk that you may ask children 'spur of the moment' questions of which you may not have fully considered the impact.

Undertaking Research – Behaviour in Setting/Relationships

Having made the decision (above) about what setting to use, the next step is to consider how to behave in the setting. This will start from the moment you approach the setting through to how you feed back to them after your work is complete, including how you represent them in any written material.

If you know the setting well, your main concern is to signal the change in your role, as discussed above, and how this affects as a result what you may and may not do. It may be that you will have to identify specific periods of time (research time) when your role will change. This will then have to be communicated to others with whom you work. It also applies, and is especially important, for those researching their own respective working environments.

If you do not know the setting, you need to be aware that the impression you make is important. After all, you are asking a setting to let you enter their world as a guest. If you write to ask permission, make sure that the letter clearly explains what you require – with no mistakes in spelling or grammar! If you are phoning or visiting in person, remember that those who work there will be busy people; they put the needs of the children first and yours second. The impression you make may be affected by many factors, such your manner, the way you dress and how much effort you have invested in preparing for the request (whether you have looked at the setting's website, discovered the name of the head teacher/setting leader, and so on).

Once in a setting you will obviously need to meet their professional requirements. In the first instance, you will learn a lot by observing the way adults relate to each other, and whether the children call adults by their first names or surnames. Observe what adults call each other when talking both to children and to each other. Outside the setting, you should remember that your responsibility does not finish when you leave at the end of the day. It would not be ethical to talk about what goes on in the setting, even if you believe people would not know where you are talking about.

In maintaining your *ethical partnerships* with the setting and the participants, you may wish to consider during your planning stages whether or how you will share reflections and findings once your research project has been completed. Consider who you will share feedback with and why. It may be decided and requested by participants that a copy of the dissertation is to be received; otherwise, a summary report or an informal end-of-project meeting/discussion may be appropriate.

Field Notes, Records and Storage of Data

It is necessary when conducting ethical research in early years settings to consider how you are going to record your thoughts and findings and any potential impact these may have on the children in the setting. Much will depend upon the type of research you are conducting and the level of your engagement with the children. If you are adopting a more ethnographic approach, and are trying to understand things 'from the point of view of those involved' (Denscombe, 2007: 63) by sharing in the lives of those being studied, there will be fewer opportunities for recording findings in the traditional written form. If you are observing yet taking no active role in the learning experiences, it will be much easier to keep records. In the latter situation, however, do not be surprised if children come and ask you what you are doing, what you are writing down, and why! It may be best to have an answer ready just in case.

Whatever form your field notes or recordings of observation take they must be accurate and focused on your research questions. Strive for professionalism. You should remember that what you record may be seen by anyone involved, thus should not contain anything that 'labels' or makes adverse comments about the children – or indeed about the adults who work with them. You should feel comfortable that you can say to others anything you have recorded without being worried about their reaction.

Confidentiality absolutely must be honoured. Having made field notes or other records, you next need to ensure that they are stored securely. You will, in gaining permission to do your research there, have given guarantees that data will be securely stored; it is important that this is indeed the case. There may be a temptation to discuss individual children or something they did with others undertaking research. Although this would be appropriate if you were discussing a generic issue, you must ensure that it is not possible to identify a setting or child. This is a particular issue with students on higher education courses: even if the setting is not actually named, other students will know where the work is being undertaken.

Analysing Data

In any research the most important criterion is 'to probe the data in a way that helps to identify the crucial components that can be used to explain the nature of the thing being studied' (Denscombe, 2007: 247). An important ethical consideration is the 'duty of care' you owe to the participants in this process, which means that you need to analyse data objectively and honestly. You are obviously trying to answer your research questions; however, there will be times when you find additional data or even data that contradict your original expectations – you need to be 'open to the unexpected' (Lowe, 2007: 114).

Reporting Findings

Earlier in this chapter, the way in which emotional involvement needs to be considered and acknowledged in choosing a topic were discussed. The same issue should be acknowledged when reporting findings. A fundamental question is whether your own opinions and experiences have affected your interpretation of the evidence. There is an ethical concern to report findings with scientific honesty. Walliman & Buckler point out that 'data should speak for themselves. Your analysis should reveal the message behind the data and not be used to select only the results that are convenient to you' (2008: 41). This is not always easy, especially when the research may be part of assessed course work. It is important to note that markers will see as a strength, not as a weakness, a well-argued and objectively reported realisation that the findings may be contrary to original expectations.

 Group activity 4

You are undertaking research in three early years settings and are asked to report back to your group as part of an undergraduate course. You know that some of your group know the settings you are using and some do not.

How do you ensure that your report maintains the confidentiality you promised, yet gives sufficient detail to support your findings?

 Conclusions and summary

It is essential that students carefully consider how to implement good ethical practices in all aspects of their early years research project. Thoughtful and detailed planning should result in successful outcomes and comfortable working relationships.

Consideration of ethical practice guidelines from the outset will enable students to make a smooth transition from early years practitioner to an early years researcher. This process will provide space for reflection on how to apply the theory and blend this with the practice throughout a research project.

The suggestions made in this chapter are based on shared experiences with early childhood studies students. In essence, it is advised that time invested in all possible details of the planning stages of the project will result in good practice and ethical outcomes.

Key points to remember

- Plan in advance of gaining access to settings and take care to allow sufficient time for this.

- In your planning stage create a checklist highlighting the needs of your project, for example an outdoor play space, children aged 0–2 years, etc.

- Look for settings in your local area and identify a list of those to approach and with whom to discuss your project and partnership ideas.

- Design a *contract for ethical partnerships* to be shared with the setting and participants, outlining the aims of your project and focus of your visits to the setting.

- Select a topic or area of study carefully based on the existing literature on the subject.

- Consider the topic from macro-, meso- and micro-perspectives, taking account of individual needs and the context (within a setting or nationally).

- Consider the wording of your working title carefully.

- Choose an age group based on your understanding of child development – and always check with the setting.

- Plan to make best use of time, checking with settings as necessary.

- Be totally transparent when arranging access to settings.

- When you are working a setting, make sure your role is clear, signalling any changes from any previous role.

- Remember you are entering a setting as a guest and behave accordingly.

- Familiarise yourself with relevant policy and procedures (e.g. child protection).

- Keep field notes carefully and professionally so that you feel comfortable in repeating to someone what you have written without being worried about their reaction.

- Store data securely.

- Analyse data objectively and without preconceived ideas about outcomes.

- Report findings with scientific honesty and consideration for those on whom you are reporting.

Points for reflection and discussion

1. What is the difference between observing an early years setting as a practitioner and doing so as a researcher?
2. You believe from your literature review, and from your own personal experience, that young children learn best in a child-centred, play-based setting, especially if they have access to outdoor learning opportunities. You devise and implement a series of measurements and interviews with teachers. You find that play-based learning has no obvious impact and, in fact, the teachers seem to prefer a more didactic, teacher-led approach. They maintain that children learn more this way. How do you plan to report the findings and how do you reconcile them with your previous reading?
3. Think about the design and content of your *ethical partnership* contracts and consent forms. Are different versions needed for different participants (e.g. practitioners or parents)? Will a child-friendly version be needed for the methods you have selected? How will you record child consent, if needed? For example, the child may select a pseudonym and give consent for observations/learning stories. Young children could use a painted hand-print instead of a signature.

Further reading

Robert-Holmes, G. (2007) *Doing Your Early Years Research Project.* London: Paul Chapman.

References

Allen, G. (2005) 'Research ethics in a culture of risk', in A. Farrell (ed.), *Ethical Research with Children.* Maidenhead: Open University Press.
Campbell, A. & Groundwater-Smith, S. (eds) (2007) *An Ethical Approach to Practitioner Research.* London: Routledge.

Coady, M. (2005) 'Ethics in early childhood research', in G. MacNaughton, S. Rolfe & I. Siraj-Blatchford (eds), *Doing Early Childhood Research: International Perspectives on Theory and Practice*. Maidenhead: Open University Press, pp. 65–72.

Denscombe, M. (1998) *The Good Research Guide: For Small-scale Social Research Projects*. Buckingham: Open University Press.

Farrell, A. (ed.) (2005) *Ethical Research with Children*. Maidenhead: Open University Press.

Groundwater-Smith, S. & Campbell, A. (2007) 'Concluding reflections: new challenges for ethical inquiry in the context of a changing world', in A. Campbell & S. Groundwater-Smith (eds), *An Ethical Approach to Practitioner Research*. London: Routledge, pp. 172–81.

Lowe, M. (2007) *Beginning Research: A Guide for Foundation Degree Students*. London: Routledge.

MacNaughton, G., Rolfe, S. & Siraj-Blatchford, I. (2005) *Doing Early Childhood Research: International Perspectives on Theory and Practice*. Maidenhead: Open University Press.

Robert-Holmes, G. (2007) *Doing Your Early Years Research Project*. London: Paul Chapman.

Walliman, N. & Buckler, S. (2008) *Your Dissertation in Education*. London: Sage.

West, L. (1996) *Beyond Fragments: Adults, Motivation and Higher Education: A Bibliographical Analysis*. Basingstoke: Taylor & Francis.

10

Safeguarding Young Children

Bronagh McKee

Chapter overview

In working towards the new '3Rs' of early years care and education – responsibilities, respect and relationships – this chapter highlights the need to develop pre-service child protection and the safeguarding of education in the undergraduate childcare curriculum. In doing so, practitioners will:

- develop their key 'responsibilities' towards safeguarding children

- 'respect' that children have a right to be protected from all forms of harm and

- understand the importance of forging social 'relationships' so that young children can learn, enjoy and achieve to their full potential.

This chapter draws on international thinking to present a rationale for the development of knowledge of childhood maltreatment among early years professionals and it explores:

- childhood maltreatment as a social problem

- childhood maltreatment as a professional problem and

- childhood maltreatment as a pre-service education problem.

Introduction

The content of the early childhood undergraduate curriculum and the safeguarding practices of the workforce itself may not, for a number of reasons, be divorced from the fundamental question about pre-service child protection preparation. First, the high numbers of children affected by maltreatment and neglect are increasing as professional knowledge and understanding of the topic develops (Munro, 2011). It is therefore quite likely that many childcare students will come into contact with abused and neglected children during their course of study while this social problem continues to exist. Second, global and national thinking about improved safeguarding practices has expanded in recent years to focus on a public health approach to safeguarding, emphasising the importance of early intervention and prevention (Barlow & Calam, 2011). The effectiveness of this model relies heavily on effective communication among professionals (including early years): it is presumed that a newly-qualified workforce will have had, at the very least, basic child protection preparation. Therefore post-qualifying training can focus on more advanced safeguarding topics. Third, legal mandates in certain countries require that those training to work with children receive some element of pre-service child protection preparation (Kirk & Broadhead, 2007). Learning about suitable child protection practices, as well as an improved understanding of the impact of maltreatment on children's learning and development, can lead to more effective responses and support services for children and families and, subsequently, improved outcomes for children.

Recent developments in Northern Ireland – including the Ten-Year Strategy for Children and Young People (OFMDFM, 2006), the cross-departmental statement on Safeguarding Children (OFMDFM, 2009) and local research on developing students' knowledge of the legal and professional child protection requirements of the childcare workforce (McKee & Dillenburger, 2009) – reflect the English strategy Every Child Matters (DfES, 2003) in its aim to improve outcomes for all children. Professional preparation for this unique role in child protection is, however, problematic. Opportunities for pre-service child protection preparation are sporadic and inconsistent leaving many childcare professionals feeling ill equipped to deal with its complexities in practice. Furthermore, little is known about how students feel about the child protection preparation received during their course of study. McIntyre once claimed that, in the realms of education, practitioners:

must accept responsibility for their abused/neglected students for many reasons: legislation mandates it, professionalism demands it, and empathy for children subjected to cruelty and pain morally and ethically necessitates it. (1990: 305)

It is recommended that the reader explore the rest of this chapter in the light of McIntyre's claim that childcare students and practitioners have a legal, professional, moral and ethical responsibility towards young children in their care.

Childhood Maltreatment as a Social Problem

Many families under stress succeed in bringing up their children in a loving and supportive environment. Sources of stress in families may, however, affect the capacity of parents to respond to their child's needs; this in turn can have a direct negative impact on a child's well-being, health and development. While there is a comprehensive discourse about the main causes of childhood maltreatment, there is international recognition that child abuse is prevalent in all societies, driven by 'socio-economic (macro-) and psychobiosocial (individual) factors' (Devaney & Spratt, 2009: 645).

Reflecting social trends in other parts of the UK, children in Northern Ireland have to deal with increasingly complex family and social circumstances. The number of child protection investigations rose by 9 per cent between 2005–6 and 2006–7, with a similar figure of 2,320 investigations between 2007 and 2008. As of 31 March 2008, there were 2,071 children on the child protection register (CPR), representing an increase of 10 per cent on the previous year. Comparing these data with other UK jurisdictions, Northern Ireland had the highest rate of children on the CPR (48 per 10,000 population under 18 years), compared with England (26.6), Scotland (23.3) and Wales (36.4). The number of children on the CPR for multiple types of abuse decreased slightly between 2007 and 2008; however, there has been a marked increase since 2006.

In addition to child protection statistics, an analysis of Police Service Northern Ireland (PSNI) figures regarding crimes against children was commissioned by the NSPCC (Hall, 2007). Of the 31,846 offences recorded during 2006–7, 18 per cent involved children under the age of 18. In addition, 47 per cent of the 1,803 sexual offences recorded were against children under the age of 18. Of this figure, 42 per cent were recorded against children under the age of 12. These figures, as well as those outlined above, starkly demonstrate the ongoing vulnerability of children to sexual and physical abuse in Northern Ireland (McMahon & Keenan, 2008).

Another risk factor associated with childhood maltreatment is domestic abuse. It is estimated that in the UK at least one million children have experienced domestic abuse (Devaney, 2008). In Northern Ireland, one study revealed that almost half of all victims experienced domestic abuse on more than one occasion and over a quarter (27 per cent) were victims on four or more occasions (Carmichael, 2007). The PSNI recorded 23,076 domestic incidents during 2006–7, of which 9,283 were recorded as crimes. Over two-thirds of the recorded crime rate fell within the category of violent crime (PSNI, 2008). Although the figures for children involved in these domestic incidents and crimes did not appear within the Chief Constable's Annual Report, it has been estimated that approximately 11,000 children in Northern Ireland experience domestic abuse on an annual basis (DHSSPS, 2005). Inspections of child protection services in Northern Ireland have been critical of the failure of professionals to respond to the needs of children living in such circumstances, especially since children exposed to domestic abuse show significant social, emotional and cognitive problems (Fusco & Fantuzzo, 2009), may suffer from post-traumatic stress symptoms (Kletter et al., 2009) and are at greater risk of maltreatment (Zolotor et al., 2007).

Children's Rights

Since the adoption of the United Nations Convention on the Rights of the Child (UNCRC) by the UK, it has become widely accepted that professionals have direct and indirect responsibility to protect children and to ensure that their rights are upheld. For the childcare workforce this means that professionals must provide children with the basic life requirements, including water, food, education, health care, shelter and so on. Moreover, children have a right to be protected from all forms of physical or mental violence, sexual or violent exploitation, neglect or negligent treatment, or any form of maltreatment. Participation rights include the rights of children to be consulted on decisions that affect them, the right to freedom of thought, conscience and religion, and the right to freedom of expression (Handley, 2007).

Threaded throughout the UNCRC is the notion of children's holistic well-being. The concept means that well-being is promoted in a safe and supportive environment, where children get the best possible start in life and are provided with opportunities to develop their individual capabilities (Scott & Ward, 2005). A concerted effort has been made to promote, develop and raise awareness of children's rights through the UNCRC; however, over ten years after its adoption by the UK, O'Halloran (2002) found that only 25 per cent of children and 36 per cent of adults had even heard of it. More recently, the results of the 2007 Northern Ireland Young Life and Times (YLT) survey found that 70 per cent of children surveyed had never heard of the UNCRC. Of those who had, 49 per cent did not know their specific rights (ARK, 2007). The recent review of children's rights in Northern Ireland found that the Ten-Year Strategy (OFMDFM, 2006) 'failed to be quite as robust in ensuring the essential overarching authority of the UNCRC' (McMahon & Keenan, 2008: 40). The concluding observations of the Committee on the Rights of the Child (CRC) (2008) highlighted continued concern regarding the lack of awareness-raising about the UNCRC in the UK and Northern Ireland. Specifically, it stated that 'the Committee regrets that the Convention is not part of the curriculum in schools' (CRC, 2008: 5).

Impact on Children: A Developmental Perspective

Because early brain development is influenced by environmental stimuli, there is a clear need for childcare professionals to understand the relationship between childhood maltreatment on the one hand, and academic learning, behaviour and relationships on the other. A chronic state of fear caused by maltreatment can impede the development of critical brain functions, including memory, problem-solving, language and other higher-order thinking (Creeden, 2005). When cognitive development occurs in a sensitive, stimulating environment, one that is loving and nurturing, children are able to understand cause-and-effect relationships, i.e. recognise their own ability to affect what happens to them (van der Kolk, 2005). In contrast, for maltreated children there are no logical cause-and-effect relationships since cognitive development has been occurring in an abusive, inconsistent and unpredictable environment.

It is now well established that academic and social skills are required for children to take the perspective of another person (Nutbrown, 2005). If living in an abusive environment interferes with normal explorative play – the way in which young children learn and develop – the ability to role-play another person's perspective is limited. Additionally, a child's ability to organise academic tasks depends on their ability to organise narrative material (Whitehead, 2003). During childhood, memories and information are encoded episodically as random events rather than as a coherent narrative. Children then develop a sequential semantic memory, usually in an environment marked by consistent, predictable routines and familiar, reliable caregivers. Unfortunately, maltreated children are deprived of such a stable environment thus their move into a more sequential ordering of the world is considerably more difficult.

Childhood maltreatment can also impact negatively on peer relationships. In a study of peer relationships among 400 pre-school-aged children, maltreated children were rated by their peers as being significantly less popular because their behaviour was deemed to be more physically and verbally aggressive, more withdrawn and less pro-social than their non-abused peers (Anthonysamy and Zimmer-Gembeck, 2007). Maltreatment is seen as a longitudinal issue: disengagement from pro-social peers has been known to lead to an increased risk of later behavioural problems (Swenson & Chaffin, 2006). These displays of inappropriate behaviour are, for some children, their only known form of communicating distress and anxiety (Geddes, 2003). Creeden (2005) describes these behaviours as 'survival-in-the-moment', the child's immediate and extreme responses to reminders of abuse, thought to be controlled by pathways in the brain that appraise threat, respond to danger and mobilise the body for fight, flight or freeze.

It is likely that these behaviours are used as a coping strategy for children to avoid reminders of maltreatment and to cope with internal turmoil, including: social withdrawal, aggressiveness, controlling behaviour, hypersensitivity to danger and constantly expressing concern or compulsiveness. Prompted by internal states that are not always understood by the child, and very often not recognised by the professional, abused children can appear demanding, unpredictable and ambivalent. Some professionals in childcare settings struggle to understand the behaviour of abused children and may be quick to reprimand or remove children without looking for the cause of the behaviour (Taylor & Siegfried, 2005).

Perhaps one of the most important roles within the childcare environment is helping maltreated children forge social relationships with peers and significant adults. Because maltreated children struggle with stress and insecure relationships with adults outside the childcare setting, their relationship with professionals and peers can be adversely affected. Maltreated children are so preoccupied with their physical and psychological safety that they become distrustful of others. To gain a sense of control, children can challenge staff, misinterpret non-verbal cues and, in order to mask their feelings of vulnerability, behave aggressively in their relationships (Anthonysamy and Zimmer-Gembeck, 2007). These post-traumatic symptoms, viewed by other children as naughty or inappropriate behaviour, will inevitably disturb a developing relationship with a friend (Perry, 2000).

 Group activity 1

What kind of childcare workforce efforts might improve the behaviour and relationships of maltreated children?

Childhood Maltreatment as a Professional Problem

The lack of professional awareness of child protection is not new. Numerous children have died at the hands of parents and carers. Most, if not all, official enquiries have called for improvements in child protection systems and professional practice; however, a number made specific reference to education. In January 1973, Maria Colwell was beaten to death by her stepfather (DHSS, 1974). Following five years in foster care with her aunt, Maria had been returned to her mother and stepfather, despite her request to remain living with her aunt. Various agencies had been in contact with Maria, yet it was her class teacher who first recognised the early signs of abuse, including physical injuries and severe weight loss indicating neglect. Shortcomings in protecting children came under the spotlight once again by the enquiry into the death of Lauren Wright (Norfolk ACPC, 2002). Lauren died in May 2000 following 17 months of physical abuse. Despite the enquiry's detailing a number of failings, the most significant impact was perceived to be in education. When Lauren's stepmother explained her injuries as accidental, teachers failed to question this response. Lauren's school had at the time of the abuse no teacher either trained or designated in child protection, which constituted a breach of local authority guidelines.

Evidently, schools and childcare settings provide access to the child population, giving unique opportunities to identify and monitor all children, including those experiencing maltreatment and other adversities. The childcare workforce is uniquely placed, as responsible adults outside children's family life, to be able to detect early indicators of abuse. Because of their almost daily contact, the childcare workforce have a positive role in child protection, being able to observe outward signs of maltreatment, changes in behaviour, difficulties with relationships or a failure to develop more generally (Munro, 2011). It is most likely that the professional who may first become alert to a child in need is a childcare practitioner.

Despite their potential to fulfil a crucial role in addressing and preventing maltreatment, and the legal responsibilities regarding child protection in childcare settings, professionals' knowledge about the topic continues to raise concerns in the literature. For example, research conducted by Cerezo and Pons-Salvador (2004) in the Balearic Islands of Spain investigated the impact of child protection training on knowledge development among health, social services and school professionals (including early years). Key findings emphasised that the detection of abuse, following training, tripled from 0.58 to 1.77 per 1,000 children. While the importance of recognising abuse is all too clear, Webster et al. (2005) investigated how and when teachers reported what they had observed in the US. From 11,436 observations analysed, the majority of participants (62.6 per cent) understood as equal the respective importance of recognising and reporting abuse; however, under-reporting was more prevalent (33.2 per cent) than over-reporting (4.2 per cent). Key teacher characteristics identified by under-reporters was their lack of training in and insufficient knowledge of a child's responses to maltreatment.

In the UK, a number of reports identified that while teachers took their child protection role seriously (Baginsky, 2000) they often felt ill-equipped to act. This was due to inconsistent and sporadic pre-service preparation in child protection (Baginsky & Macpherson, 2005; Webb & Vulliamy, 2001). This is problematic since, according to Rossato & Brackenridge (2009), educators are already frequently overstretched once they qualify, making it less likely that they will have time for the required ongoing child protection training.

Childhood Maltreatment as a Pre-service Education Problem

Other writers have explored the self-perceived knowledge of child maltreatment among undergraduate students, as well as the self-perceived adequacy of pre-service education. For example, Kenny (2004) found that only 34 per cent of her sample had received any pre-service child protection education; of these, nearly two-thirds felt that the training was either minimal (43 per cent) or inadequate (23 per cent). A local study found a similarly low percentage of adequate pre-service child protection education among early childhood practitioners (McKee, 2003). Using the early years questionnaire on child protection training and knowledge (EYQCP), 24 per cent of participants had received pre-service child protection education; 64 per cent of the sample reported feeling inadequate in their ability to detect and identify early indicators of abuse; and most felt that pre-service child protection education was either 'poor' or 'non-existent' (McKee, 2003). This lack of familiarity with the early indicators of maltreatment and lack of knowledge of procedures will, understandably, make it extremely difficult for the childcare workforce effectively to report suspected abuse.

In Australia Penter et al. (2005) explored the content of child protection education within a range of undergraduate programmes. Because universities have to manage competing curriculum demands and staff expertise and experience, this provision was similar to that found in the UK – sporadic and inconsistent. There was on some courses very limited specific undergraduate content addressing child protection. Following the review, Penter et al. (2005: 18) called for the inclusion of 'core child protection in undergraduate programmes, particularly for social work, psychology, education and teaching' and a need for 'improved coordination and collaboration between tertiary institutions about child protection training'. McKee & Dillenburger (2009) also found exceptionally low levels of child protection and safeguarding education content in the early childhood studies undergraduate curriculum in Northern Ireland. They agreed with the point made by Sinclair Taylor and Hodgkinson that childcare students are equally vulnerable to disclosure from a child and that:

> [Q]uestions need to be raised about effective preparation for this; after all, the consequences of failing to respond adequately could be grave. (2001: 79)

While some efforts have been made to improve pre-service educators' knowledge of child maltreatment, only limited child protection training continues to be identified in the literature (Walsh & Farrell, 2008). Even in places where basic child protection training was a prerequisite for the licensing of educational staff (Virginia Board of Education & the Virginia Department of Social Services, 2003), a two-hour online course was deemed sufficient to meet training requirements (Virginia Commonwealth University, 2009). Northern Ireland has yet to make any recommendations to mandate pre-service education in child protection and safeguarding; early childhood studies courses do not generally make pre-service child protection training available to students (McKee & Dillenburger, 2009). It is therefore unsurprising that professional knowledge of maltreatment remains lacking. Given the vulnerability of young children, it is essential to address this gap with the undergraduate childcare workforce. Not to do so would be unethical, unprofessional and simply unsafe for young children.

 Group activity 2

Discuss your previous experiences in child protection training and safeguarding education programmes. What are the common features/topics in the content of these programmes? What features/topics have you not yet received? How might these features/topics be integrated into your undergraduate curriculum?

Implications for Practice

There are a number of clear implications for practice. The first relates to the misconception that standard undergraduate topics, for example learning through play, numeracy and literacy development, or the early years curriculum, ensure that the childcare workforce will know how to promote the holistic development of children. They are indeed important elements of early childhood studies, although these topics alone fail to address how child maltreatment and neglect impact on the way children learn, on young children's behaviour or on developing relationships in the early years setting. Failure to include compulsory pre-service child protection and safeguarding education further fails appropriately to prepare early years practitioners for their role in legal, moral and ethical safeguarding.

The second implication relates to the importance of early intervention, which relies heavily on a trauma-sensitive response (Cole et al., 2005). The nature of the response to abuse in children depends on a wide range of factors. One of the most important appears to be childcare professionals' understanding of their role in identifying abuse-related symptoms and, perhaps more significantly, how they are to respond appropriately. Childcare professionals have a major role in the identification, reporting and responding process; they can help prepare children to cope with maltreatment by giving them an understanding of the nature of abuse, teaching children the skills for responding to an emergency, and learning how to support children through the after-affects of maltreatment. An effective and innovative teaching strategy, whereby young children are encouraged to develop concepts of keeping safe, is teaching self-protection through the early years curriculum. Unfortunately, while pre-service preparation for child protection remains inconsistent across the UK (McKee & Dillenburger, 2009; Rossato & Brackenridge, 2009), it is unlikely that preventative education will soon be addressed in an already crowded undergraduate curriculum.

A review by Kenny et al. (2008) reports the increasing number of international safety skills programmes taught by educators; it argues that children as young as three years old can be taught how to protect themselves. The terminology 'self-protection' or 'safety skills programme' is favoured over 'prevention programme', since the latter implies that the child her/himself is responsible for reducing the risk of maltreatment. Conversely, Finkelhor (2007: 643) adds that it would be 'morally reprehensible not to equip them with such skills', if children can be provided with effective strategies to help them to protect themselves. One such programme to include educators, children and parents is the Stay Safe Programme in the Republic of Ireland. Stay Safe covers five key safety skills concepts: feeling safe/unsafe; bullying; touches; secrets and telling; and strangers. Importantly, evaluations of this programme are positive. McIntyre et al. (2000) found that, following children's participation in the programme, there was a significant increase in their reports of concerns, then more effective responses were provided when children disclosed abuse. Regardless of the terminology used, self-protection programmes stress the importance of increasing young children's awareness and knowledge of, and confidence in, disclosing inappropriate behaviour and abuse. There are a number of organisations present in the UK conducting prevention programmes (e.g. Kidscape, or Protective Behaviours UK), yet insufficient attention is paid to these programmes in early years settings. In the context of complying with protection principles laid out by the UNCRC, the key health and welfare standards of Every Child Matters (DfES, 2003) and the safety expectations of the Ten-Year Strategy (OFMDFM, 2006), it appears that the childcare workforce across the UK needs to offer younger children a more detailed and more adequately structured education in self-protection.

Conclusions and summary

The progress of work related to child protection is commendable; considerable effort has been expended during recent years to assess qualified practitioners' knowledge, beliefs and attitudes about child maltreatment. There is, nevertheless, international evidence that the preparation of practitioners in child protection and safeguarding is sporadic and inconsistent. The effectiveness and efficacy of such programmes represents a domain as yet incompletely addressed. Given the importance for children's holistic well-being of their growing up in a safe and supportive environment, receiving opportunities to develop individual capabilities and getting the best possible start in life, the lack of awareness in some professional circles of such issues as child protection and safeguarding is untenable.

The research reported here has raised a number of issues in relation to the pre-service training needs of the childcare workforce with regard to child protection. Some countries have included these training requirements in the compulsory curriculum for teacher licensure and certification and have developed at least some level of compulsory training courses aligned to the needs of students. In essence, the argument of the current chapter is that pre-service childcare professionals and those charged with their professional training and education have stark choices to make if the issue of child protection and safeguarding is to be treated with the seriousness it deserves. The following issues – expressed as a series of questions – are particularly relevant to those in charge of curriculum content and programme design; they should, however, be considered in conjunction with child protection experts, policy-makers and, of course, with students.

Key points to remember

- It is estimated that one in three children suffer abuse.

- Younger children are at greater risk of abuse.

- Child abuse includes physical, sexual and emotional abuse, neglect, domestic abuse and, more recently in the child protection literature, bullying. Collectively, these types of abuse are known as childhood maltreatment and remain a social problem in every society.

- The childcare workforce has access to more children for longer periods of time, therefore they are uniquely placed to identify early indicators of abuse.

- The childcare workforce has a legal, moral and ethical duty to protect young children in their care.

- Many practitioners continue to claim to be ill prepared for their safeguarding role because they receive insufficient grounding in this aspect during their pre-service training.

Points for discussion and reflection

1. How do you feel about education in child protection training and safeguarding? Why do you think this topic is/is not important? How might increased knowledge of maltreatment improve your professional practice?

2. Reflect on your own level of knowledge of childhood maltreatment. How well prepared are you to recognise early indicators of maltreatment and neglect? How well prepared are you to respond appropriately to young children when they disclose abuse? In what ways could your knowledge of the topic be improved in preparation for professional practice?

3. Reflect on the ethical implications if the childcare workforce is not prepared appropriately in child protection and safeguarding. Reflect on your own practice and consider how you might improve your safeguarding strategies, including prevention and early intervention, in the early years setting.

Further reading

Munro, E. (2008) *Effective Child Protection*, 2nd edn. London: Sage.
Walsh, K. & Farrell, A. (2011) 'Locating child protection in pre-service teacher education', *Australian Journal of Teacher Education*, 36(7): Online at: http://ro.ecu.edu.au/ajte/vol36/iss7/3.

Useful websites

The Australian Centre for Child Protection explores, among other topics, the research and training of students and professionals in child protection policy and practice. Available online at: http://www.unisa.edu.au/childprotection/.

The Child Welfare Information Gateway provides comprehensive information on child protection and family support research, training and interventions. Available online at: http://www.childwelfare.gov/.

NSPCC Inform provides a comprehensive reading list on child protection for early years and childcare workers. Available online at: http://www.nspcc.org.uk/Inform/research/reading_lists/child_protection_for_early_years_wda64735.html.

References

Anthonysamy, A. & Zimmer-Gembeck, M.J. (2007) 'Peer status and behaviours of maltreated children and their classmates in the early years of school', *Child Abuse and Neglect: The International Journal*, 31(9): 971–91.

ARK (2007) *Young Life and Times Survey*. Belfast: ARK.

Baginsky, M. (2000) *Child Protection and Education*. Leicester: NSPCC.

Baginsky, M. & Macpherson, P. (2005) 'Training teachers to safeguard children: developing a consistent approach', *Child Abuse Review*, 14: 317–30.

Barlow, J. & Calam, R. (2011) 'A public health approach to safeguarding in the 21st century', *Child Abuse Review*, 20(4): 238–55.

Carmichael, M. (2007) *Experience of Domestic Violence: Findings from the 2005 Northern Ireland Crime Survey*. Belfast: Statistics and Research Branch of the Northern Ireland Office.

Cerezo, M.A. & Pons-Salvador, G. (2004) 'Improving child maltreatment detection systems: a large-scale case study involving health, social services, and school professionals', *Child Abuse and Neglect: The International Journal*, 28(11): 1153–69.

Cole, S.F., Greenwald O'Brien, J., Gadd, G., Rustuccia, J., Wallace, L. & Gregory, M. (2005) *Helping Traumatized Children Learn: Supportive Schools Environments for Children Traumatized by Family Violence*. Boston: Harvard Law School and Task Force on Children Affected by Domestic Violence.

CRC (Committee on the Rights of the Child) (2008) *Consideration of Reports Submitted by State Parties under Article 44 of the Convention: United Kingdom of Great Britain and Northern Ireland*. Geneva: UN.

Creeden, K. (2005) 'Trauma and neurobiology: considerations for the treatment of sexual behaviour problems in children and adolescents', R. Longo & D. Prescott (eds), *Current Perspectives: Working with Sexually Aggressive Youth and Youth with Sexual Behaviour Problems*. Holyoke, MA: NEARI Press.

Devaney, J. (2008) 'Inter-professional working in child protection with families with long-term and complex needs', *Child Abuse Review*, 17(4): 242–61.

Devaney, J. & Spratt, T. (2009) 'Child abuse as a complex and wicked problem: reflecting on policy developments in the United Kingdom in working with children and families with multiple problems', *Children and Youth Services Review*, 31: 635–41.

DfES (2003) *Every Child Matters*. London: HMSO.

DHSS (1974) *Report of the Committee of Inquiry into the Care and Supervision Provided in Relation to Maria Colwell*. London: DHSS.

DHSSPS (2005) *Tackling Violence at Home – A Strategy for Addressing Domestic Violence and Abuse in Northern Ireland*. Belfast: DHSSPS.

Finkelhor, D. (2007) 'Prevention of sexual abuse through educational programs directed toward children', *Pediatrics*, 120(3): 640–5.

Fusco, R.A. & Fantuzzo, J.W. (2009) 'Domestic violence crimes and children: a population-based investigation of direct sensory exposure and the nature of involvement', *Children and Youth Services Review*, 31: 249–56.

Geddes, H. (2003) 'Attachment and the child in school. Part 1', *Emotional and Behavioural Difficulties*, 8(3): 231–42.

Hall, M. (2007) *Child Protection Statistics in Northern Ireland*. Belfast: NSPCC.

Handley, G. (2007) 'Children's rights to participation', T. Waller (ed.), *An Introduction to Early Childhood: A Multidisciplinary Approach*. London: Paul Chapman.

Kenny, M.C. (2004) 'Teachers' attitudes toward and knowledge of child maltreatment', *Child Abuse and Neglect: The International Journal*, 28(12): 1311–19.

Kenny, M.C., Capri, V., Thakkar-Kolar, R.R., Ryan, E.E. & Runyon, M.K. (2008) 'Child sexual abuse: from prevention to self-protection', *Child Abuse Review*, 17: 36–54.

Kirk, G. & Broadhead, P. (2007) *Every Child Matters and Teacher Education: Towards a UCET Position Paper*. London: Universities Council for the Education of Teachers.

Kletter, H., Weems, C.F. & Carrion, V.G. (2009) 'Guilt and posttraumatic stress symptoms in child victims of interpersonal violence', *Clinical Child Psychology and Psychiatry*, 14(1): 71–83.

MacIntyre, D., Carr, A., Lawlor, M. & Flattery, M. (2000) 'Development of the Stay Safe Programme', *Child Abuse Review*, 9(3): 200–16.

McIntyre, T. (1990) 'The teachers' role in cases of suspected abuse', *Education and Urban Society*, 22(3): 300–6.

McKee, B.E. (2003) *Child Protection Training and Early Years Education: Developing the Early Years Questionnaire on Child Protection (EYQCP)*. European Educational Research Association Conference, University of Hamburg, Germany, 18–21 September.

McKee, B.E. & Dillenburger, K. (2009) 'Child abuse and neglect: training needs of student teachers', *International Journal of Educational Research*, 48: 320–30.

McMahon, L. & Keenan, P. (2008) *NICCY Rights Review*. Belfast: NICCY.

Munro, E. (2011) *The Munro Review of Child Protection: Final Report – A Child-Centred System*. Norwich: TSO.

NISRA (2009) *Northern Ireland Statistics*. Belfast: NISRA.

Norfolk ACPC (2002) *Summary Report of the Independent Review into the Death of Lauren Wright*. Norfolk: Health Authority.

Nutbrown, C. (2005) *Threads of Thinking*. London: Paul Chapman.

O'Halloran, K. (2002) 'The rights of the child in Northern Ireland: teenage attitudes and social responsibilities', in A.M. Gray, K. Lloyd, P. Devine, G. Robinson & D. Heenan (eds), *Societal Attitudes in Northern Ireland*. London: Pluto Press.

OFMDFM (2006) *Our Children and Young People – Our Pledge. A Ten-Year Strategy for Children and Young People in Northern Ireland 2006-2016*. Belfast: OFMDFM.

OFMDFM (2009) *Safeguarding Children: A Cross-Departmental Statement on the Protection of Children and Young People by the Northern Ireland Executive*. Belfast: OFMDFM.

Penter, C., Cant, R. & Clare, B. (2005) *Child Protection Training Project Report for the Ministerial Advisory Council on Child Protection*. Australia: Ministerial Advisory Council.

Perry, B.D. (2000) 'Traumatized children: how childhood trauma influences brain development', *Journal of the California Alliance for the Mentally Ill*, 11(1): 48–51.

PSNI (2008) *Chief Constable's Annual Report*. Belfast: PSNI.

Rossato, C. & Brackenridge, C. (2009) 'Child protection training in sport-related degrees and initial teacher training for physical education: an audit', *Child Abuse Review*, 18(2): 81–93.

Scott, J. & Ward, H. (eds) (2005) *Safeguarding and Promoting Well-being of Child, Families and Communities*. London: Jessica Kingsley.

Sinclair Taylor, A. & Hodgkinson, F. (2001) 'Subjecting the initial teacher training curriculum for England and Wales to the test of child protection', *Teacher Development*, 5(1): 75–86.

Swenson, C.C. & Chaffin, M. (2006) 'Beyond psychotherapy: treating abused children by changing their social ecology', *Aggression and Violent Behaviour*, 11: 120–37.

Taylor, S. & Siegfried, C.B. (2005) *Helping Children in the Child Welfare System Heal from Trauma: A Systems Integration Approach*. Durham, NC: National Center for Child Traumatic Stress.

van der Kolk, B.A. (2005) *Childhood Trauma: Our Largest Preventable Public Health Issue*. Paper presented at Massachusetts Legislature – Closing the Achievement Gap: Removing Trauma as a Barrier to Learning, 22 March.

Virginia Board of Education & the Virginia Department of Social Services (2003) 'Child Abuse and Neglect Recognition and Intervention Training Curriculum Guidelines'. Online at: http://www.doe.virginai.gov/VDOE/suptsmemos/2003/inf209a.pdf.

Virginia Commonwealth University (2009) 'Child Abuse and Neglect: Recognising, Reporting, and Responding for Educators'. Online at: http://www.vcu.edu/vista/training/va_teachers.

Walsh, K. & Farrell, A. (2008) 'Identifying and evaluating teachers' knowledge in relation to child abuse and neglect: a qualitative study with Australian early childhood teachers', *Teachers and Teacher Education*, 24: 585–600.

Webb, R. & Vulliamy, G. (2001) 'The primary teacher's role in child protection', *British Educational Research Journal*, 27(1): 60–77.

Webster, S.W., O'Toole, R., O'Toole, A.W. & Lucal, B. (2005) 'Overreporting and underreporting of child abuse: teachers' use of professional discretion', *Child Abuse and Neglect: The International Journal*, 29(11): 1281–96.

Whitehead, M. (2003) *Supporting Language and Literacy Development in the Early Years*. Manchester: Open University Press.

Zolotor, A.J., Theodore, A.D., Coyne-Beasley, T. & Runyan, D.K. (2007) 'Intimate partner violence and child maltreatment: overlapping risk', *Brief Treatment and Crisis Intervention*, 7(4): 305–21.

11

Ethics When Inspecting Early Years Practice

Judi Williamson

Chapter overview

The focus of this chapter is to consider how the inspection and regulation of early years services conforms to ethical practice. It addresses the role of the Office for Standards in Education, Children's Services and Skills (Ofsted), which is identified as the independent body responsible for ensuring that early years settings meet the identified regulatory standards and educational framework of the Early Years Foundation Stage (EYFS) in England.

The chapter aims to help you to develop an understanding of the role of Ofsted, to consider the implications of the role of inspection and regulation of early years settings, critically to consider the relationship between inspection and quality processes leading to improvement and, finally, to review the use of research methods within inspection as an ethical process.

Ofsted and Its Role in the Early Years

The Office for Standards in Education (Ofsted), officially the Office of Her Majesty's Chief Inspector of Schools in England, was set up in September 1992. In April 2007 its name changed to the Office for

Standards in Education, Children's Services and Skills, although the original Ofsted acronym remains. It is the key regulatory body for early years provision in care and education in England and is a non-ministerial government department that functions independently from the Department for Education (DfE).

Ofsted's role has been expanded over successive years; it is now responsible for a range of education and children's services, including the inspection and regulation of registered early years and childcare provision.

Through their inspectorial role, Ofsted is able to collect and collate data and evidence on all aspects of childcare and education in specific reports and surveys (particularly on academic subjects). Ofsted commissions good practice surveys and convenes conferences in order to share identified good practice. Information is published on their website, including inspection reports, best practice publications and research (http://www.ofsted.gov.uk).

Ofsted's role is continually in the public eye. Inspectorial reports provide parents with an assessment of the prospective settings their children may attend; local authority reports identify how effectively services support the duty of care for children and young people; the Training and Development Agency (TDA) has a duty to note Ofsted reporting on their Initial Teacher Training (ITT) when allocating numbers and funding provision. Behind all of these different reports is an agenda of accountability and towards raising standards.

The current inspection arrangements for early years provision were shaped by the Childcare Act, which became law in July 2006. This was seen as pioneering legislation since it was the first Act exclusively designed for early years and childcare. It was linked to the development of key aspects of the Labour government's Ten-Year Childcare Strategy published by the Department for Children, Schools and Families (DCSF) in 2004. The Childcare Act also reformed and simplified early years regulation and inspection arrangements providing for a new integrated education and care quality framework, alongside the new Ofsted Childcare Register.

Inspection and regulation of the early years covers all settings registered on the early years and childcare registers. This is applicable across the multiplicity of early years provision in this country, from childminders through daycare providers to schools' early years classrooms and units.

Is Inspection an Ethical Practice?

Inspection is a tool of government and the process is therefore influenced by its policies which have been developed or are to be reinforced. Inspections of the quality and standards of the registered early years provision are undertaken by Ofsted under sections 49 and 50 of the Childcare Act 2006. Early years provision relates to that made for children from birth to the date of 31 August following their fifth birthday; thus it must demonstrate compliance with the statutory framework for children's learning, development and welfare known as the Early Years Foundation Stage (EYFS).

The role of central government is increasingly evident in the strengthening of inspection systems and thus, by implication, controlling the objectives, targets and plans for early years education and care. Power centralised into a national inspectorate, whose role is to assess and review all aspects of early years education and care with a view thereby to raising its standards and disenfranchising those who fail to meet the minimum standards, runs counter to the policies of other countries, such as Denmark and Finland who have greater freedom though local and regional regulation of the curriculum and through self-evaluation measures (OECD, 2006).

Accountability is inextricably linked to notions of power and control. Whether it is personal or public accountability for services, a judgement is made as to the value or effectiveness of the provision. The notion of judgement implies a link with the legislature and codes of compliance:

> We live in an age of quality. Every product and service must offer quality . . . quality has become reified, treated as it if was (*sic*) an essential attribute of services or products that gives them value, assumed to be natural and neutral. (Moss & Dahlberg, 2008: 1)

Quality, assessed through inspection and checked against given criteria, cannot be seen as neutral; rather, it is overlain with values and assumptions about how that quality may be evidenced. The process has been developed from management theory and constructed to fit the growth of the 'audit society' (Power, 1997).

The work of Moss and Dahlberg (Dahlberg et al., 1999; Moss et al., 2000; Dahlberg & Moss, 2008; Moss & Dahlberg, 2008) has offered a critical review of whether any practice may be said to stand outside ethical considerations. The quality of early years settings becomes a matching exercise against how far the settings conform to a universal, objective and predetermined standard. It becomes a technical process as distinct from an ethical process. It assumes the evaluators (in this case the Ofsted inspectorate) to be rational, detached and objective, thus reinforcing inspection as a technical process.

This interpretation of quality is understood as objective and static in that it identifies and measures the quality of the provision across a particular time and place, focusing on children's shared developmental needs. The opposite end of this continuum is the subjective and dynamic interpretation of quality, which recognises the diversity of ideas about childhood (Dahlberg et al., 1999; Moss et al., 2000; Owen, 2000; Pugh, 2003).

Moss and Dahlberg describe the alternative as the concept of *meaning making*. This approach recognises that the concept of quality has to be seen as more than conforming to predetermined standards: it is instead an understanding and recognition that different interpretations are possible, depending upon the values brought to the process by all concerned in it. Meaning making takes place in relationship with others. Through understanding the values of the setting and its ethos, its relationships with others and its pedagogy are therefore co-constructed. Judgements may still be made from this process, yet become a statement of value rather than a final conclusion (Readings, 1996).

Statements written within inspection reports are attributed with a numerical grade from Outstanding (1) to Inadequate (4). Whether these are recognised as value judgements is debatable; they have an air of conclusion about them and as such carry the weight of degrees of success or failure. To understand how we can make the inspection process work in support of quality improvement is linked largely to how settings apply the grading alongside their self-evaluation measures.

Using the Inspection Process to Foster Improvement

This section will consider how possible it is to utilise the Ofsted process to support the ongoing quality processes that should be evident in early years settings.

The current inspection process of early years provision derives its 'power and control' from recent government Acts, notably the

Children's Act 2004, the Education Act 2005 and the Childcare Act 2006.

Thus one of the key features of the Ofsted inspections of early years now reflects the above by maintaining a 'strong focus on how well the provision helps children to achieve the five outcomes set out in the Children Act 2004' (Ofsted 2011: 10), the Every Child Matters outcomes.

The government also recognised the crucial role of parents, carers and families in improving outcomes for children and young people, as well as the need to provide support for them to do so.

Inspection is not a new concept. What has gathered pace is the notion of public management and accountability: that the outcome of this process is marked by public and official exposure not only of success, but also of failure to meet the predetermined criteria.

The setting of targets and competencies are the direct result of external controls. The power base lies beyond the provision itself and in the hands of the inspectors who make the judgements based on the information they gather, the data they review and the observations they make. The assumption behind this method is that it is through external forces that change and improvements are wrought.

As noted earlier, the aim of inspection is to discover and assess the standards currently in evidence and, furthermore, to identify how those standards may be raised. However, factors that help to improve standards include the ownership of the staff and their responsibility for change – changes that happen through a process of reflection and review, that happen over time and not all at once. Educational research has focused on these elements (Dalin et al., 1994). Many of the findings lead to a more complex system of identifying how to raise standards and support improvement. It may be shown that qualities such as: the personality and leadership style of those in charge of the provision, the ethos of the setting evidenced through its staff and the self-belief and development of those who attend are all seen as elements to take into account. These are, though, seen as constituting too complex a basis for a judgement; also, they are inapplicable in the establishing of targets for all settings. The inspection process therefore becomes one of assessing the systems and structures in place; it focuses mainly on the performance of the staff with each other and with the children. The children themselves and their attainment become a product in this system.

The inspection system for early years provision in England relies on information gathered by one inspector over a period of one day. The visit is made at little or no notice, which is designed to ensure that as far as is feasible the inspection evidence is collected from a typical day. While this is recognised as accepted practice by those in the settings, it could be argued that assuming a right to act in this way emphasises the intrusive nature of the inspection and reinforces the power base.

Regulation or Support?

At the heart of Ofsted's role in regulating and inspecting the early years provision is the protection of children from harm. The inspection process is focused on systems of checking that identify safeguarding policies and procedures. The quality of the provision and the way it is led and managed also contribute to this essential notion and supports the raising of standards.

Inspectors check for minimum standards of compliance. All reports make reference to what must be done in order to secure future improvements. Settings may be identified as Inadequate, in two categories. Category 1 may generate recommendations, yet the focus is on actions under 'notice to improve'. These are time-limited and linked to legal requirements in the Statutory Framework of the EYFS. A further inspection is undertaken within 6–12 months. Category 2 is more serious and will refer to enforcement actions required under the notice to improve. These enforcement actions may take the form of amending the conditions of registration, of cancelling the registration or of seeking the prosecution of the provider.

The judgements above are the culmination of a regulatory process. Ofsted offers no support after this process; instead, it refers the provider to their local authority for support, particularly in cases where Category 2 has been applied.

Where support is offered by Ofsted it is focused nationally through the development of good practice surveys, reports and conferences derived from analysis of the data and evidence generated from inspections. The survey programme is drawn up to influence policy and guidance and to encourage improvement within settings in line with existing regulatory criteria.

Inspection reports are in the public domain and it has been noted (Baldock, 2001) that parents may fail to recognise the difference between recommendations (which appear in all reports, including those judged outstanding) on the one hand, and requirements which must be met on the other. There is an expectation that recommendations made are integrated into the practice and will be reflected in future inspections.

Inspection is a regulatory process; inspectors are not to be seen as consultants. The personnel who inspect early years settings should be experienced within the early years field. However, because of the multiplicity of early years care and education settings, they should not be seen as experts in all areas. Even inspectors with a wide range of previous practice would admit that practice is continually in the process of changing. It is therefore perfectly possible for their experience to become out of date, thus inspectors must be willing to learn from those they inspect.

Are Standards Regulated or Is Quality Measured?

It is clear that Ofsted's remit is the maintenance and improvement of standards (as denoted by their title). The pressure of inspection and regulation is to measure standards rather than to promote the notion of quality. As mentioned above, quality is not a neutral notion: it is value-weighted and therefore complex in its identification.

The regulation of early years practice through compliance with a set of national standards implies that there exists a baseline of consistency expected in all early years settings. It is worth remembering that these standards apply to all those on the early years register, ranging from childminders who work in their own homes, childcare in other domestic and non-domestic premises (group childcare) and early years in schools. The benefit of a national standard means that childcare should therefore be relatively consistent across the country. The advantage to business providers who run a number of nurseries in different areas is that they are able to produce packages of support for all their settings, regardless of the area of the country in which they may be based.

The link between regulation and quality standards is evidenced in the following example. From September 2009 the effectiveness of the safeguarding of children in the leadership and management aspect of the report is informed by the staying safe outcome (part of Every Child Matters) for children. Evidence is drawn from the safeguarding policy and procedures in place (including the procedure to be followed in the event of an allegation being made against a member of staff); the knowledge and skills of the named practitioner; the systems in place for recruiting and checking the suitability of staff; the supervision arrangements for staff awaiting the result of checks; and procedures for handing children over to identified adults.

Having in place such high-level checks on standards is understandable, given the lessons learned from high-profile child abuse cases within childcare settings in recent years. However, it does raise the question as to whether the focus on regulating this aspect within the inspection regime results in a lower profile for other elements in early years settings. Minimum standards in respect of keeping children safe are set high and become increasingly more complex.

It could be argued that there is a correlation between standards and quality. The ability to meet exacting standards, to ensure that policies and procedures are in place and are reviewed regularly, to make certain that risk assessments are comprehensive and that staff undergo regular professional development on safeguarding – all of these demonstrate a commitment to quality in practice.

The development of quality provision contains within it recognition of the importance of flexibility, allowing managers and leaders of teams to focus on those aspects, often generated through their self-evaluation processes. Action planning to deliver or improve quality will obviously identify the aspects which then, to the team, become their priorities. Many settings now grade their development plans Red, Amber or Green (known as the RAG rating) in the light of their agreed priorities, Red being an aspect requiring immediate attention. For example, attention may focus on the review of the setting's outdoor area in the light of changes to resources or routines. This may include attention to the ways in which practitioners inform parents about any changes to the routine and seek their support, or how risk is assessed in the new area, along with evaluations of the equipment to motivate and provide children with challenges. Good early years settings are constantly striving to be innovative and to reflect their ever-changing community.

The notion that quality might permeate an interpretation of the standards by a setting identifies those good quality settings who have the self-confidence to see that the standards framework provides the baseline against which they are constantly able to develop and improve their setting. What must be clear within the setting is how this may be explained satisfactorily in an inspection. It requires also inspectors who are confident in their previous experience in this area and are willing to consider alternative approaches towards the same goal. This consideration reflects the earlier notion (discussed above) regarding contributing to meaning making within the quality agenda.

The Ofsted Inspection and Regulation Process in the Early Years Sector

The final section of this chapter considers certain elements of the inspection process and how it seeks to maintain ethical research practice. The system for inspection in the early years is complicated by the fact that Ofsted is both the regulatory and the inspectorial body. Enough evidence has to be generated within one day to report on the effectiveness of the provision to meet learning and care requirements within a standard reporting framework.

Code of Conduct for Inspectors

The code is clearly identified by Ofsted, which maintains that:

> Inspectors must uphold the highest professional standards in their work, and ensure that everyone they encounter during inspections or regulatory visits is treated fairly and with respect and benefits from the inspection. (Ofsted, 2011: 8)

As part of this code of conduct, inspectors must be able to investigate in an objective and impartial manner, maintain a dialogue with the provider throughout the process, respect the confidentiality of information provided and make judgements, clearly communicated and based on clear evidence. Inspectors have the right of entry to premises registered on the early years and childcare registers and must also take prompt action on any safeguarding or health and safety issues identified.

The methodology used to derive the evidence for the report comes from:

- a review of the self-evaluation form – this is not a mandatory requirement, but can be submitted online by settings or by presenting it to the inspector on the day. If this format has not been used, the inspector will require evidence of an equivalent document in the setting

- observation of activities and routines

- discussions with children, staff and others in the setting – this should include parents

- checking a sample of the setting's policies and procedures, including the safeguarding, equal opportunities and inclusion policies, and checking the Criminal Records Bureau (CRB) disclosures

- tracking children's progress from a representative sample of children.

Review of the Self-Evaluation Form – Building a Picture

As was noted earlier in this chapter, the vast majority of respondents to the consultation on the inspection of the Early Years Foundation Stage identified the view that they would wish to complete a self-evaluation form and submit it to Ofsted. Its content should then inform any inspection of their provision.

Through the use of the most recent self-evaluation form prior to the inspection, inspectors would identify key questions for the manager/leader in the setting.

The self-evaluation should also include the action plans derived from the process and progress on the actions. It could be argued that this may seem a burdensome process for those such as childminders and other small providers; still, the process of reflection, review and evaluation is important as a means of evidencing trends towards improvement. Support for the completion of self-evaluation forms should be available, for instance, from the local authority or from provider networks.

Ofsted have also recognised this need by producing early years self-evaluation form guidance (Ofsted, 2009a). The benefit of the document is that it covers the topic areas considered by inspectors on their visit, thus provides much useful prior information for both provider and inspector.

In the introduction to this document, the importance of self-evaluation for providers is noted:

It will help you to consider how best to create, maintain and improve your setting, so that it meets the highest standard and offers the best experience for young children . . . An up-to-date, accurately completed self-evaluation form gives inspectors an idea of which aspects of your provision you consider work well and which you are seeking to improve. (Ofsted, 2009a: 4)

The use of the self-evaluation form is not mandatory for early years providers. Inspectors would nevertheless expect to see some form of annual self-evaluation process and make a judgement on its content.

Observation as Part of the Inspection Process

Observation forms an essential part of the investigation process in inspections. As with any research process, it is important to identify the difficulties inherent in the method. The observation process is influenced by decisions made on what is to be observed. The observations made are of an artificial situation, that is during an inspection, where the practitioners involved will be trying to show their work and practice in the best possible light. The opportunity is a 'snapshot' in time. While the routine may indicate a typical day, it is influenced by the presence of having in the setting another adult, one who is unknown to the children. The context of the observation has to be easily identified so that the activities and interactions noted by the inspector are accurately reflected.

Discussions with Children, Staff and Others in the Setting – Information Gathering

Parents/Carers

'Parents as partners' is one of the commitments to the EYFS principle of 'Positive relationships'. This includes learning together with parents, involving fathers and male carers, and reflecting on practice in relation to parents and carers. The notion of partnership implies a shared responsibility and joint ownership of the education and care of children.

The guidance on the conduct of inspections in early years settings indicates that 'wherever possible, inspectors should seek the view of parents/carers' (Ofsted, 2011: 22). Consultation with parents/carers may take place prior to or during the inspection – but not after it. Given the short notice period attached to the inspection, it may make reaching a representative sample of parents/carers difficult to achieve. Time must also be set aside if parents indicate they wish to speak to the inspector. Even where children's centres may have parent groups attached to them, the latter are not routinely involved in the inspection process unless the nursery manager chooses to include them.

However, unless parents are knowledgeable about the inspection process and the role of Ofsted, they may regard the opportunity to speak to an inspector with some suspicion. This is why references to keeping children safe, to inclusion and equal opportunities or to the importance of access, for example, to outdoor play may not provide the evidence required if the setting has failed to work with the parents in assisting them to understand the underlying importance of the aspects.

It is more likely that evidence of the working partnerships existing between staff and parents is generated from an examination of documents, part of either the formal or informal feedback to parents. Formal documents would include the system of reporting back to parents on progress, often through parents' evenings when progress is discussed. Informal opportunities are often witnessed through communications between staff and parents at the beginning or end of the day, or through other materials such as daily journals or regular newsletters.

Involving parents in inspections is difficult, although the EYFS framework identifies parents as partners in their child's learning and development. An inspection report focusing the majority of its information on only one of the partners (i.e. the practitioners) does not seem satisfactorily to follow this particular principle within the early years framework.

In *Childcare Groups: A Passion to Be Outstanding* (Ofsted, 2009c), one of the aspects identified by outstanding childcare providers is the quality of their relationship with parents and carers. The advice on how this can be achieved goes on to give examples of how their settings build their relationships with parents. Not identified, though, is the parents' voice in terms of what they consider to constitute an outstanding setting. Similarly, another publication, *Leading to Excellence: A Review of Childcare and Early Education Provision 2005–08 (Third Review of Inspections of Registered Childcare and Early Education)* (Ofsted, 2008b), identifies twenty questions put to early years providers, and for children and local authorities, yet no list of questions for parents. New ways of involving parents in the inspection process need to be found if we are going to interpret adequately the key principle of parents as partners.

Children

Inspectors should talk to children while performing the inspection. They should seek their views on a variety of aspects, as well as observing them in their normal play situations.

The EYFS framework identifies that there should be a high level of child-initiated activity occurring in settings. A high proportion of the professional development opportunities since the inception of the EYFS framework has centred on mechanisms to support and sustain children's interests. Children have greater freedom of choice, with more numerous opportunities to use their initiative and to be creative through this new approach. The framework has echoes of the strong, confident and competent child at the heart of the Reggio Emilia approach (Thornton & Brunton, 2007).

Inspection reports reflect on the behaviour of children, their engagement in activities and the demonstration of their knowledge, understanding and skills. All aspects of the inspection provide evidence towards the way children are cared for and how their learning and development are supported. Reference to children's comments are not made in the report, although inspectors are likely to draw much of their information about what children know and understand by observing and talking to them while they play.

There are difficulties inherent in the short time period of an early years inspection, one being how the inspector is to engage in a meaningful way with the children. This is heightened in the larger settings, which cater for babies, toddlers and pre-schoolers. All age groups are, however, jointly linked by the EYFS; the evidencing of opportunities children have to engage with a variety of resources and activities must be reflected in the final report.

It could be argued that engagement with children in the setting could affect the detached view the inspector is trying to present. The fact that most inspectors are able readily to engage with young children (that is, they have the skills and ability) may be seen as a reason for inspectors indeed not to become engaged with them, as this could affect the objectivity of the situation. The confident child, secure in the situation, may more readily approach the stranger in the setting and establish a dialogue. The curious child will engage with someone they see sitting quietly at the side of the room, particularly if they have a laptop computer. Conversely, the inspector may try to engage the shy or awkward child in conversation. Any reluctance to engage may be misinterpreted, or be related to an external upset that has occurred outside the setting's control.

However, there are positive advantages to engaging with children and trying to discover their understanding of the setting. There are mechanisms allowing practitioners to ascertain from children what they feel about the activities and resources available to them. Discussions using 'smiley' or 'sad' faces could be used by the staff with their key worker group and observed by the inspector. This has the benefit of focusing the children on their known adult and, it is hoped, generating more information than by the inspector alone, because of the knowledge the staff have of the children.

Another approach with the older children could be for staff to ask key children in the rooms to show the inspector around. This has the advantage of reassuring the children that this is an 'acceptable' stranger; it also helps in identifying what areas the children consider important, how independent they can be within the room and how they engage with the resources available.

It is worth remembering that the inspection process will also take the inspector into domestic situations with a childminder. The greater the involvement the inspector has with the normal activities of the day while checking evidence and discussing factors with the childminder, the more valuable will be the information gathering. Even more than in other settings, the inspector must try to blend into this scenario; for example, getting down on her/his hands and knees and engaging with the young children will make them less obtrusive. Other opportunities naturally present themselves, for example mealtimes which encourage social interaction, the explanation of drawings and paintings, and sharing books.

Now more than ever it is expected that young children will be active participants in the shaping of the early years setting and its ethos. Therefore practitioners need to think carefully about how we better utilise opportunities to make them active participants in any inspection process.

Feedback – Testing Conclusions

The inspector's judgements are developed over the period of the inspection process, lasting between a half and a full day. As has been mentioned, this is a 'snapshot' of the provision thus the more readily the answers to the inspector's questions are found the better. There should be ongoing dialogue with the nominated person and the inspector as evidence emerges. It gives the inspector an opportunity to test the conclusions they are forming before they become a matter of record. The opportunity allows providers to find additional evidence, if required, and is an area that may lead to providers' anxiety. In essence, the more clearly evidence is organised and collated by the provider prior to the day or on the day itself, the more organised the leadership and management appear to be. The final feedback session before the inspector leaves should therefore present no surprises and the judgements will have been made. Factual inaccuracies may be challenged, although at that stage no further evidence may be presented.

Feedback should be clear, with judgements backed by evidence. Areas for improvement should be clearly discussed so that the provider understands what needs to be done to remedy them. The discussion is important: it should provide more oral detail than is possible in a final report.

The consultation throughout the day and the reporting in the feedback session support an understanding of the balance of power, which is possible within inspection. The inspector's judgements have to meet the identified standards for regulation.

The Final Report

Following the feedback on the day, the inspector should write the full report immediately. The reports are subject to a national quality assurance process to ensure that, as far as possible, a common standard is maintained. It is important for the providers to understand that the report reflects the judgement made on the particular day of the inspection and that the strengths and recommendations made are incorporated into their amended self-evaluation document.

If settings are inspected and graded as Satisfactory or above, it is unlikely that they will be inspected again within three years, unless many changes occur in personnel or in practice. The setting has ample time to reflect upon and review its practice towards shaping or maintaining improvements in standards. It is, therefore, essential that the report received by the setting after the inspection supports and aids their evaluation process. The provider must be able clearly to identify from the report what is being said. It will identify those aspects the inspector has found to be strengths, and will also detail recommendations for improvements. In implementing them, there is a temptation to focus on those areas requiring development; it is, though, important to note the strengths, too, and identify how these will be maintained.

Conclusions and summary

The purpose of this chapter has been to investigate the ethics of a universal inspection framework which is centrally regulated and controlled. The role of Ofsted is to act as the regulatory and inspectorial body for the policy and practice laid down by national government. Through the structure of its inspection process and reporting, it is evident that inspection provides a measure of assessment at the objective/static end of the quality continuum. Dahlberg & Moss (2005) clearly articulate that quality measured in this way becomes a technical measure to ensure conformity to the norm, calibrated against standards and regulating practice. This then shapes early years practice.

Within the context of the process, there is a clear code of conduct for the inspectors, which identifies their need for objectivity, impartiality, clarity of judgement and confidentiality. The report is developed from analysis of the setting's self-assessment process and through the interplay of key research methods on the day of the visit. There is an emphasis on dialogue with those being inspected, although the resulting report is the responsibility of the inspector with the authority to make the final judgement.

A centralised scheme such as this may be seen as identifying minimum standards; also, it constitutes a starting point from which to move the quality standard beyond these requirements and to include more of the views of the stakeholders (the children, parents/carers, the community, who have different values and goals for the children, and the setting). Notions of quality practice are not achieved through simple compliance with these standards. Rather, improvement becomes more subjective and dynamic, through an ethos of reflective practice.

Key points to remember

- The authority for inspection and regulation of early years services resides with the Office for Standards in Education, Children's Services and Skills (Ofsted) through powers conferred by government and through the Childcare Act 2006.

- All settings which provide care and education for children from birth to the date 31 August following their fifth birthday must be registered with Ofsted and are inspected and regulated for compliance with the Statutory Framework of the Early Years Foundation Stage.

- Safeguarding policies and procedures that reduce the risk of harm to children are given the highest priority in inspection and regulation.

- An ethical code of conduct for inspection exists and adherence to it is expected of both inspectors and providers.

- Quality improvement must be embedded in any early years setting through a clear self-evaluation process, supported by inspection and regulation.

- Quality, assessed through inspection and checked against given criteria, cannot be viewed as neutral; it is overlain with values and assumptions about how that quality maybe evidenced.

Points for discussion and reflection

1. How do inspection and regulation support quality improvement?
2. Every child deserves to be in an outstanding setting. Investigate how the grade of Outstanding is achieved, by reviewing some examples from recent Ofsted early years reports.
3. What is the setting like from a child's viewpoint? How can we involve children in the evaluation of their setting? Does the self-evaluation process enhance quality practice?

Further reading

Department for Children, Schools and Families (DCSF) (2009) *Improving Quality and Raising Standards in the Early Years. A Directory of Resources for Local Authorities*, 2nd edn. Nottingham: DCSF.

Moss, P. & Dahlberg, G. (2008) 'Beyond quality in early childhood education and care – languages of evaluation', *New Zealand Journal of Teachers' Work*, 5(1): 3–12.

Useful websites

Ofsted: http://www.ofsted.gov.uk
Department for Education: http://www.dfe.gov.uk

References

Anning, A. & Edwards, A. (2006) *Promoting Children's Learning from Birth to Five: Developing the New Early Years Professional.* Maidenhead: Open University Press.
Baldock, P. (2001) *Regulating Early Years Services.* London: David Fulton.
Dahlberg, G. & Moss, P. (2005) *Ethics and Politics in Early Childhood Education.* Abingdon: Routledge Falmer.
Dahlberg, G. & Moss, P. (2008) 'Beyond quality in early childhood education and care', *CESifo DICE Report*, 6(2): 21–6.
Dahlberg, G., Moss, P. & Pence, A. (1999) *Beyond Quality in Early Childhood Education and Care. Postmodern Perspectives.* London: Falmer Press.
Dalin, P., Ayono, T., Brazen, A., Dibaba, B., Jahan, M., Miles, M. & Rojas, C. (1994) *How Schools Improve an International Report.* London: Cassell.
Moss, P. & Dahlberg, G. (2008) 'Beyond quality in early childhood education and care – languages of evaluation', *New Zealand Journal of Teacher's Work*, 5(1): 3–12.
Moss, P., Dahlberg, G. & Pence, A. (2000) 'Getting beyond the problem with quality', *European Early Childhood Education Research Journal*, 8(2): 103–20.
Office for Standards in Education, Children's Services and Skills (Ofsted) (2008a) *Outcome of the Consultation on Inspection Provision in the Early Years Foundation Stage from September 2008*, Reference No. 080022. London: Ofsted.
Office for Standards in Education, Children's Services and Skills (Ofsted) (2008b) *Leading to Excellence: A Review of Childcare and Early Education Provision 2005–08. Third Review of Inspections of Registered Childcare and Early Education.* London: Ofsted.
Office for Standards in Education, Children's Services and Skills (Ofsted) (2009a) *Early Years Self Evaluation Form Guidance*, Reference No. 080103. London: Ofsted.
Office for Standards in Education, Children's Services and Skills (Ofsted) (2009b) *Are You Ready for Your Inspection?*, Reference No. 090130. London: Ofsted.
Office for Standards in Education, Children's Services and Skills (Ofsted) (2009c) *Childcare Groups: A Passion to Be Outstanding*, Reference No. 090108, 28 August. London: Ofsted.
Office for Standards in Education, Children's Services and Skills (Ofsted) (2011) *Conducting Early Years Inspections*, Reference No. 080164. London: Ofsted.
Organisation for Economic Cooperation and development (OECD) (2006) *Education at a Glance 2006.* OECD Publishing. Available online at: http://www.oecd.org.
Owen, S. (2000) 'Assessing quality in childminding', *Children and Society*, 14(2): 147–53.
Power, M. (1997) 'From risk society to audit society', *Soziale systeme*, 3(1): 3–21.

Pugh, G. (2003) 'Early childhood services: evolution or revolution?', *Children and Society*, 17: 184–94.

Pugh, G. & Duffy, B. (2006) *Contemporary Issues in the Early Years: Working Collaboratively for Children*. London: Sage.

Readings, B. (1996) *The University in Ruins*. Cambridge, MA: Harvard University Press.

Tanner, J., Welsh, E. & Lewis, E. (2006) 'The quality-defining process in early years services: a case study', *Children and Society*, 20: 4–16.

Thornton, L. & Brunton, P. (2007) *Bringing the Reggio Approach to Your Early Years Practice*. London: Routledge.

12

Ethical Leadership in Early Years Settings

Trevor Male

Chapter overview

The chapter begins by determining the difference between leadership and management then explores the relationship of leaders and followers in educational settings. Effective leaders, it is concluded, are those whose influence is more important than merely the formal authority their post commands. Leadership in early years settings faces an ethical challenge: a balance needs to be struck between satisfying the needs of the community the organisation seeks to serve and the demands of funding agencies. Leaders in early years settings need clarity of vision particularly in regard to core purposes. Once established, those become the driving force and template for decision-making. The task of the formal leader becomes to fulfil the need to build leadership capacity with other staff in order to deliver that vision to the highest level. The chapter concludes by illustrating the way in which the formal leader has to become a 'second-order practitioner', in which situation agreed objectives are achieved with and through others.

Introduction

The concept of leadership is often used as a means of describing the behaviour of those with formal responsibility within a system, organisation or institution. This confuses 'authority', which refers to the way in which some people are seen as having the right to direct others, with 'leadership', where the person in charge persuades others to take certain actions. There is therefore a difference between formal and informal authority: the most successful leaders have the ability to inspire others rather than rely on the power of their formal position to enforce people's actions. Leaders are those who are 'trusted, respected for their expertise, or followed because of their ability to persuade' (Doyle & Smith, 2001). Leadership, it may be concluded, has an added dimension with regard to the way in which individuals behave toward one another. Bass (1981), for example, regards leadership as a social interaction where one person influences others to a greater degree than s/he is influenced by them. Leaders, he concludes, have followers. In Bass's words, the leader is the one who 'modifies the motivation of competencies or motivation of others in the group'.

Such aims may, however, also be achieved through management techniques, thus it is important to recognise that a difference exists between leadership and management. The two concepts are frequently run together in conversations and publications to the point where a reader could be forgiven for thinking that they were in fact one word 'leadershipandmanagement'. Management is probably best described as the delivery of policies or services determined by others. Leadership attributes in such situations correspond to the enhancement of performance by others for whom the lead person has responsibility, a set of behaviours corresponding to a model of 'expect and inspect' (Sergiovanni, 1992) and one that fits a model of 'managerial leadership'. In settings where a choice of actions is possible or desired, leaders have also to establish the direction of their organisation. In distinguishing between the two concepts Covey (1992) suggests that management is a bottom-line focus where actions are taken to accomplish certain ends, whereas leadership addresses the top line by determining the ends that are to be accomplished, a definition he sums up as:

> Management is efficiency in climbing the ladder of success; leadership determines whether the ladder is leaning against the right wall. (Covey, 1992: 101)

Leadership may, consequently, be conceived as a process greater than the delivery of predetermined policies or actions; it requires more skills and attributes than the modification of competencies and motivation. With this in mind, leadership includes the determination of purpose, aims and objectives.

Leadership in social systems, such as schools, colleges and early years settings, has the dual responsibility to deliver the services required by the funding agency while providing for difference and diversity evident at the local level. Formal leaders in these organisations often face conflict between system requirements and local needs, and this may lead to moral dilemmas. Successful leadership in this context is, as I have argued previously, 'the reconciliation of personal, organizational and systemic needs and aspirations . . . into an effective gestalt of activity' (Male, 2006: 1). What, then, does this mean for leaders and aspirant leaders in social systems?

Purpose and Ethics

For an organisation or institution to provide an effective service there must be clarity of vision, particularly in regard to core purpose. In exploring the ethical issues relating to educational leadership Bottery (1992: 10–12) concludes there are competing purposes, all of which are usually to be found in each and every institution. Schools, he suggests, could exist for the purposes of *cultural transmission* or *social reconstruction*, to support the *Gross National Product* (GNP) or simply to be *child-centred* in nature. *Cultural transmission* he describes as the way in which cultural heritage is reflected in organisational value systems appropriate to the continuation of that society and consequently transmitted to passive learners. *Social reconstruction* he sees as dealing with pressing issues that need to be resolved where learners are actively engaged in defining resolutions through interactions with others. The support of the *GNP* he considers to have the key aim of furthering the economic well-being of that society, while a *child-centred* approach focuses on individual experience and interests, with learners being 'active, involved, unique constructors of their own reality'. In this mode he sees 'the process of exploration and discovery . . . as being vastly more important than the end-product'. Through recognising that provision for young people contains competing value systems, Bottery effectively requires formal leaders to explore how these may be identified and dealt with or accommodated within the working relationships in the organisation.

Such a need to accommodate any differences immediately raises the spectre of moral dilemmas. It must be asked whether a leader in early years settings sustains a provision that matches the aspirations of the funding agency, or does s/he follow a different path – one that may conflict with those aspirations yet still be ethically sound? Sadly, there is no simple answer, no straightforward process to apply to this conundrum, although the process begins with the establishment of a core operational ethos (see Figure 12.1). The term 'ethos' is not to be confused with ethics; in this instance, 'ethos' refers to 'the way we do things around here'. The ethical issue is to determine whether the subsequent chosen courses of action are morally and philosophically acceptable.

© Male (2007)

Figure 12.1   The establishment of a core operational ethos

It is not the intention to start a debate here about the difference between morality and notions of goodness, so all that will be done at this point is to remind the reader that morality is socially derived and what is sometimes acceptable to one society is not always universally acceptable. The key to successful and effective leadership in social systems is to establish a value set that corresponds to the society served. Values define standards of 'goodness, quality or excellence that undergird behaviour and decision-making' (Deal & Peterson, 1999). It is important, therefore, that you as early years practitioners seek to establish a value set that is meaningful to you and appropriate not only for the funding agency, but also for your service users and the local community. You will also need to be prepared constantly to evaluate and review this value set to take account of changing circumstances.

The resulting value set then becomes the basis for establishing principles to underpin subsequent actions and should be reflected as the core ethos of the organisation. From that value set will flow both an agreed priority in terms of purpose and a framework for decision-making within the organisation.

The Challenges to Early Years Settings

Support for young children in England is considered the joint responsibility of parents and the state, with evidence of increased intervention and support by government over the last few years, especially after 2003 with the publication of Every Child Matters and 2008 when the Early Years Foundation stage became statutory for the early years sector in England. Public funding has been provided to ensure young children are given better opportunities to be healthy and safe, to enjoy and achieve, to be able make a positive contribution to society and to achieve economic well-being, these being the five principles of policy published under the title of Every Child Matters (ECM) and enshrined in the Children Act of 2004. Provision for young children is thus jointly provided through care and education, with parents supported through a combination of child minding, playgroups, children's centres and nursery schools, with some of these organisations seeking to match all of these aspirations.

The principal challenges perceived appear to fall into two categories; however, it must be borne in mind that there will be local challenges which must be taken into account. Challenge number 1 is to determine what type of provision is to be offered, and Challenge number 2 is to create and sustain the organisation that can deliver this provision.

Challenge 1: Determining Purpose and Vision

Government policy towards early childhood settings is ambitious in that it seeks to support the principles of both care and education, having invested heavily in financial support mechanisms for parents of young children and through the publication of a range of educational guidance. A principal mechanism in government strategy has been the establishment of children's centres, based on the concept that providing integrated education, care, family support and health services is a key factor in determining good outcomes for children and their parents.

The end result is confusing, though, with mixed messages being transmitted – to the point where early years providers are unsure of their core purpose. Close examination of the five principles of the ECM agenda, for example, shows a range of purposes that include social care (health and safety), child-centred education (enjoy and achieve), cultural transmission (positive contribution to society) and wealth-creation (economic well-being), with the last of these elements seeming dominant in the Green Paper *Meeting the Childcare Challenge* which underpinned the Children Act of 2004. The Secretaries of State for Education and Social Security extolled those virtues of childcare they considered would make 'our economy grow stronger [through giving] people the childcare they need so they will be able to take up jobs'. Along with this statement, however, we witness a focus on the education of young children through the Early Years Foundation Stage curriculum, which requires providers 'to use the EYFS to ensure that whatever setting parents choose, they can be confident that their child will receive a quality experience that supports their development and learning'. The resulting confusion of purpose is further compounded by a lack of clarity over the focus of such education provision with one government minister Margaret Hodge – at the time Under-Secretary of State for Employment and Equal Opportunities – suggesting the foundation stage 'is about developing key learning skills . . . that will prepare young children for Key Stage 1 of the national curriculum' (QCA/DfEE, 2000: 3).

The conclusions that may be drawn from such policy statements are that early years settings release parents from the burden of childcare and function as 'waiting rooms' for school. In other words, the core purpose of such provision is to provide childcare and to prepare passive learners who will be acclimatised to school requirements and routines by the time they enter compulsory education (usually during the year in which they become five). Such objectives conflict strongly with ambitions for early years education, as these are child-centred and reconstructive in nature, aiming to produce active learners who are 'constructors of their own reality' (see Bottery, 1992). Indeed, there is a mass of evidence from research into early childhood development illustrating the importance of such learning environments and, in particular, the use of play as a core ingredient (e.g. House of Commons, 2001; BERA, 2003; DfES, 2004).

Challenge 2: Creating the Organisation to Deliver the Core Vision

Proceeding from the assumption that the formal leaders in the early years setting have determined their own core values, the first step to successful leadership of that organisation is to establish how widely such values may be shared and converted into principles for action. It is critical that personal values either become shared values to which other organisational members are able to subscribe or that personal values are amended and adapted to match the prevailing social climate. For formal leaders this can be a painful experience: treasured aspirations may quickly become diluted in the harsh reality of everyday life, sometimes to the point where the original intentions seem to have been lost. It is critical to ensure shared ownership of core organisational values and, therefore, the process of reviewing personal values must be undertaken. Some of the least effective leaders are those who fail to compromise or demonstrate awareness of any agenda other than their own; such individuals may cause a situation where there is little or no real commitment from members to the success of the organisation. To understand such a scenario, early years practitioners need to be aware of the difference between commitment and enrolment.

The terms 'commitment' and 'enrolment' are offered as methods of understanding the relationship of members to the values and aims of the organisation. A committed person wants those values and aims to be achieved and will do whatever is necessary to make them a reality, whereas someone who is enrolled will do whatever is to be done only within the 'spirit of the law' (Senge, 1990: 219–20). Enrolled people will exhibit levels of compliance ranging from 'genuine' through 'formal' to 'grudging'. There are also degrees of non-compliance, some passive and some active, which may sometimes be noticed either within a subsection of the organisation or from individuals. The genuinely compliant are able to perceive the benefit of the vision without owning it, although they will do everything expected of them – and more – within the 'letter of the law'. Those who are formally compliant see, on the whole, the benefits of the vision, but nevertheless do only what is expected of them. The grudgingly compliant fail to see the benefit of the vision yet do not want to lose their jobs; consequently, they do enough of what is expected because they have to, while letting it be known that they are not wholeheartedly 'on board'.

For the successful implementation of core values it is necessary to achieve an ideal balance of commitment coupled with genuine and formal compliance in order to establish an appropriate ethos within the organisation. The balance may be achieved through a few key individuals, while needing to be such that 'the way we do things round here' remains the core principle for action by all members of the organisation. In other words, there are enough staff who are committed and positively engaged to outweigh the passive contributors and non-conformists and thus counter any potentially negative views and behaviours. The achievement of that balance may require you, therefore, to review your personal values in an attempt to align them with other key stakeholders and the Zeitgeist or 'spirit of the times' (Hodgkinson, 1991: 68). Once achieved, however, the shared values underpin the principles for action that guide decision-making in the organisation.

Building Leadership Capacity

In any organisational setting, success that focuses on the well-being and development of young people cannot be based on the principle of singular leadership. It is hardly possible for one individual to identify and respond to the range of challenges emanating from a social system such as those found in early years settings. Leadership responsibility needs therefore to be shared and individuals empowered to take decisions corresponding to the shared value system that has been described above as a prerequisite for success. As may be deduced from Figure 12.1 a senior leadership team needs to be created; it will facilitate and guide the practitioners within the organisation, who in turn need to be empowered to take individual decisions at the point of delivery (operational leadership).

The word 'team' does not, however, automatically assume that a group of people will behave as a team merely because they are labelled as such. Teams have special qualities distinguishing them from staff who are grouped according to the structure of the organisation or system in which they are employed. Teams have a common purpose, a specific set of aims and, most importantly, a set of behaviours that binds them together in their quest to achieve their objectives. For them to engage fully as a member of a team, individuals have to be prepared to support mutual objectives rather than only their own desires. In other words a good team member is prepared to undertake a task on behalf of the group with no guarantee of personal reward.

Mutual responsibility and accountability set a team apart from other similar groupings of people. Teams and team building could be further discussed at length, yet early years practitioners should bear in mind that teams work for the benefit of all.

Leadership in Early Years Settings

With a successfully formed set of shared values and a senior leadership team in place, most organisations are well prepared to support decision-making at the operational level. This brings us back to the core issue of this chapter: the creation of an early years setting that meets the development needs of the young children it seeks to support. The delivery of that provision is ultimately entirely in the hands of those who are in direct contact with the children, i.e. the first-order practitioners. Formal leaders and members of senior leadership teams are actually second-order practitioners whose job consists of achieving the aims and objectives of the organisation with and through other people. The key issue now, therefore, is to provide the first-order practitioners with the framework they need to aid decision-making in their practice.

Each practitioner will need to know what their fundamental priority is when the demands of practice present them with conflicting opportunities. The tools needed in determining their priority are found in the principles for action that are derived from the framework of values. In turn, the values need to be simplified into simple codes of practice such as, for example, engendering respect by being respectful. In this example, the job of the formal leader and all second-order practitioners is for them to have determined the ethical code on which practitioners will draw. If the prime needs of the young child, for example, are basic human ones such as safety, warmth and food, the practitioner must be empowered to take operational decisions that determine the best way of satisfying those needs. If, on the other hand, the provision for the young children is a higher-order need, such as learning how to be constructors of their own realities, the practitioner must have support to provide learning opportunities relevant to that need. In the latter situation there may well be a need to provide an opportunity for play rather than for formal learning. The key issue is that the practitioners have the right to respond to the prevailing context, providing they do not contravene the ethical code established for the organisation.

The Role of the Formal Leader

The formal leader in any educational organisation is the person accountable to the funding agency and the social system they serve. Their key roles are to define the organisational mission, manage the educational programme and promote the core ethos (adapted from Hallinger & Heck, 1998). In order successfully to undertake this task they need to be 'designers, stewards and teachers' (Senge, 1990: 340). As designers they are responsible for the generation and determination of the core purpose of the organisation; for those in early years settings they will thus be responsible for exploring personal values and reconciling these with the reality of the environment in which they live and work. As stewards they are the keepers of the flame, the ones whose personal behaviour reflects the core ethos of their organisation and who are able to influence others to sustain the shared and agreed values underpinning action within their setting. As teachers they seek to achieve the delivery of that ethos with and through other people and to become second-order practitioners.

Those formal leaders who encourage leadership behaviour throughout their setting have to place trust in their first-order practitioners that the latter will make decisions in keeping with the core values and ethos as determined and agreed. Collective leadership of this nature carries a degree of risk; it therefore requires the formal leader (who retains overall accountability) to introduce measures of control in order to prevent potential disaster. On the one hand, there must be sufficient flexibility of practice to allow for mistakes, as without these there would be no learning; on the other, those mistakes must not be catastrophic. Formal leaders must determine, therefore, whether they are able to deal with the consequences of mistakes before allowing a risk to exist. Two simple maxims for a leader apply here: to your first-order practitioners you can say 'make as many mistakes as you like, but do not keep making the same mistake' while to yourself you say 'what is the worst thing that can happen here and, if that occurs, how able would I be to live with the consequences?' If a leader is able to abide by the consequences of a mistake then take the risk; if not, do not allow the risk to exist in the first place.

Conclusions and summary

Ethical leadership in early years settings is about determining the range of provision a practitioner desires, establishing core values for the organisation, and sustaining those values in practice with and through other people. Placing responsibilities in the hands of others (and thus becoming a second-order practitioner) does not absolve a leader of accountability; therefore, a degree of control is still needed in order to prevent the occurrence of unnecessary risks. Delivering a high-quality learning environment in early years settings requires the formal leader to develop the framework for effective decision-making by all members in support of their provision of young children's learning. Ethical leadership, therefore, is ultimately based on the formal leader being organisational designer, steward and teacher.

Key points to remember

- Successful early years settings are those where there is clarity of vision and core purpose.

- Formal leaders are unable to achieve the objectives of the organisation on their own thus need to become 'second-order practitioners'.

- Building the leadership capacity of the staff is the fundamental priority for the establishment of effective and appropriate provision.

Points for discussion and reflection

1. Consider the core values and how you will be able to sustain these in your work context.
2. How do you perceive the balance between the needs of the community served by your setting and the demands of the funding agency?
3. Consider the opportunities for or barriers to building leadership capacity in the organisation in which you work. Reflect on how you feel about being a second-order practitioner.

Further reading

Aubrey, C. (2011) *Leading and Managing in the Early Years*, 2nd edn. London: Sage.

Miller, L. & Cable, C. (2010) *Professionalization, Leadership and Management in Early Years*. London: Sage.

Moyles, J. (2006) *Effective Leadership and Management in the Early Years*. Maidenhead: Open University Press.

References

Bass, B. (ed.) (1981) *Stodgill's Handbook of Leadership*. New York: Free Press.

Bottery, M. (1992) *The Ethics of Educational Management*. London: Cassell.

British Education Research Association (BERA) (2003) *Early Years Research: Pedagogy, Curriculum and Adult Roles, Training and Professionalism*. Warwick: BERA.

Covey, S. (1992) *The Seven Habits of Highly Effective People*. London: Simon & Schuster.

Deal, T. & Peterson, K. (1999) *Shaping School Culture: The Heart of Leadership*. San Francisco: Jossey-Bass.

Department for Education and Skills (DfES) (2004) *The Effective Provision of Pre-School Education (EPPE) Project: Final Report: A Longitudinal Study Funded by the DfES 1997–2004*. Annesley: DfES Publications.

Doyle, M.E. & Smith, M.K. (2001) 'Classical leadership', in *The Encyclopedia of Informal Education*. Online at: http://www.infed.org/leadership/traditional_leadership.htm (accessed January 2010).

Hallinger, P. & Heck, R. (1998) 'Exploring the principal's contribution to school effectiveness: 1980–1995', *School Effectiveness and School Improvement*, 9(2): 57–91.

Hodgkinson, C. (1991) *Educational Leadership: The Moral Art*. Albany, NY: SUNY.

House of Commons (2001) *Select Committee Report*: Early Years Education.

Male, T. (2006) *Being an Effective Headteacher*. London: Paul Chapman.

QCA/DfEE (2000) *Curriculum Guidance for the Foundation Stage*. London: QCA.

Senge, P. (1990) *The Fifth Discipline: The Art and Practice of the Learning Organization*. New York: Doubleday.

Sergiovanni, T. (1992) *Moral Leadership: Getting to the Heart of School Improvement*. San Francisco: Jossey-Bass.

Index

Added to a page number 'f' denotes a figure and 't' denotes a table.